W9-AKC-762

The Teaching For Social Justice Series

William Ayers
Series Editor

Therese Quinn
Associate Series Editor

Editorial Board: Hal Adams, Barbara Bowman, Lisa Delpit, Michelle Fine,
Maxine Greene, Caroline Heller, Annette Henry, Asa Hilliard, Rashid Khalidi,
Gloria Ladson-Billings, Charles Payne, Mark Perry, Luis Rodriguez,
Jonathan Silin, William Watkins

A Simple Justice: The Challenge of Small Schools
WILLIAM AYERS, MICHAEL KLONSKY, AND GABRIELLE H. LYON, EDITORS

Holler If You Hear Me: The Education of a Teacher and His Students
GREGORY MICHIE

A Simple Justice

THE CHALLENGE OF SMALL SCHOOLS

Edited by

*William Ayers, Michael Klonsky,
and Gabrielle H. Lyon*

Teachers College, Columbia University
New York and London

Published by Teachers College Press, 1234 Amsterdam Avenue, New York, N.Y. 10027

Copyright © 2000 by Teachers College, Columbia University

All rights reserved. No part of this publication may be reproduced or transmitted in any form or by any means, electronic or mechanical, including photocopy, or any information storage and retrieval system, without permission from the publisher.

Library of Congress Cataloging-in-Publication Data

A simple justice : the challenge of small schools / edited by William Ayers, Michael Klonsky, and Gabrielle H. Lyon.
    p.   cm. — (The teaching for social justice series)
  Includes bibliographical references and index.
  ISBN 0-8077-3963-4 (alk. paper) — ISBN 0-8077-3962-6 (pbk. : alk. paper)
    1. Educational equalization—United States.   2. Small schools—United States.
  3. Social justice—Study and teaching—United States.   I. Ayers, William, 1944– .
  II. Klonsky, Michael.   III. Lyon, Gabrielle H.   VI. Series.

  LC213.2.S56 2000
  371—dc21   00-022913

ISBN 0-8077-3962-6 (paper)
ISBN 0-8077-3963-4 (cloth)

Printed on acid-free paper
Manufactured in the United States of America
07   06   05   04   03   02   01   00   1   2   3   4   5   6   7   8

Contents

Series Foreword

Teaching for Social Justice might be thought of as a kind of popular education—of, by, and for the people—something that lies at the heart of education in a democracy, education toward a more vital, more muscular democratic society. It can propel us toward action, away from complacency, reminding us of the powerful commitment, persistence, bravery, and triumphs of our justice-seeking forebears—women and men who sought to build a world that worked for us all. Abolitionists, suffragettes, labor organizers, civil rights activists: Without the sweat and blood of countless individuals fighting countless fights, liberty would today be slighter, poorer, weaker—the American flag wrapped around an empty shell—a democracy of form and symbol over substance.

Rousseau argues in regard to justice that equality "must not be understood to mean that degrees of power and wealth should be exactly the same," but only that with respect to power, equality renders it "incapable of all violence" and only exerted in the interest of a freely developed and participatory law, and that with respect to wealth, "no citizen should be so opulent that he can buy another, and none so poor that he is constrained to sell himself." The quest for equality and social justice, over many centuries is worked out in the open spaces of that proclamation, in the concrete struggles of human beings constructing and contesting all kinds of potential meanings within that ideal. Nothing is settled, surely, once and for all, but a different order of question presents itself: Who should be included? What do we owe one another? What is fair and unfair?

This series gathers under one roof examples of popular education being practiced today as well as clear and new thinking concerning issues of democracy, social justice, and educational activism. Many contributions will be grounded in practice and will, we hope, focus on the complexities built into popular education: difficulties, set-backs, successes, steps forward—work that reminds us of what Bernice Johnson Reagon calls "the sweetness of struggle." We seek as well, developing theoretical work that might push us all forward as we labor to grasp anew the meaning of democracy in changing times, the demands of justice, the imperatives of social change. We want to encourage new voices and new ideas, and in all cases to contribute to a serious, grounded, thoughtful exchange about the enduring questions in education: Education for what? Education for whom? Education toward what kind of social order?

For every human being life is, in part, an experience of suffering and loss and pain—there is always a tragic dimension to our brief time within the light. But our living experience also embraces other inescapable facts: One, that we are all in this together, of course, passengers and crew on spaceship Earth, adrift concurrently on our little life-raft; two, much (but not all) of what we suffer in life is the evil we visit upon one another, that is, unjustified suffering, unnatural loss, unnecessary pain—the kinds of things that ought to be avoidable, that we might even imagine eliminating altogether.

Encountering these facts thrusts us into the realm of human agency and choice, the battle field of social action, and change, where we come face to face with some stubborn questions: Can we, perhaps, stop the suffering? Can we alleviate at least some pain? Can we repair any of the loss? We lurch, then, toward deeper considerations: Can society be changed at all? It is remotely possible—not inevitable, certainly, perhaps not even very likely—for people to come together freely, to imagine a more just and peaceful social order, to join hands and organize, to struggle for better, and to win?

If society cannot be changed under any circumstances, if there is nothing to be done, not even small and humble gestures toward something better, well, that about ends all conversation. Our sense of agency shrinks, our choices diminish. What more is there to say? It is sufficient simply to wander weeping in the streets, or to find a nearby bridge from which to leap, or to retreat into narcissism, concluding that human life is nothing more than a brutish, vicious thrashing fight and that if I am to be spared—please, God—many others will have to be sacrificed, and I will agree to look on with indifference, or with most a superficial nod toward compassion.

But if a fairer, more sane, and just social order is both desirable and possible, that is, if some of us can join one another to imagine and build a participatory movement for justice, a public space for the enactment of democratic dreams, our field opens slightly. There would still be much to be done, for nothing would be entirely settled. We would still need, for example, to find ways to stir ourselves and our neighbors from passivity, cynicism, and despair; to reach beyond the superficial barriers that wall us off from one another; to resist the flattening effects of consumerism and the blinding, mystifying power of the familiar social evils—racism, sexism, and homophobia, for example; to shake off the anesthetizing impact of most classrooms, most research, and of the authoritative, official voices that dominate the airwaves, the media, and so much of the space of what we think of as common sense; to release our imaginations and act on behalf of what the known demands, linking our conduit firmly to our consciousness. We would be moving, then, without guarantees, but with purpose and with hope.

Education is, of course, an arena of struggle as well as hope—struggle because it stirs in us the need to reconsider everything we have wrought, to look at the world anew, to question what we have created, to wonder what is worthwhile for human beings to know and experience, to justify or criticize or bombard or maintain or build up or overthrow everything before us—and hope gesturing toward the future, toward the impending, toward the coming of the new. Education is where we gather to question whether and how we might engage and enlarge and change our lives, and it is, then, where we confront our dreams and fight out notions of the good life, where we try to comprehend, apprehend, or possibly even change the world. Education is contested space, a natural site of conflict—sometimes restrained, other times in full eruption—over questions of justice.

The work, of course, is never done. Democracy is dynamic, a community always in the making. Teaching for social justice continues the difficult task of constructing and reinvigorating a public. It broadens the table, so that more may sit together. Clearly, we have along, long way to go. And we begin.

William Ayers, Series Editor
Therese Quinn, Associate Series Editor

CHAPTER 1

Simple Justice

THINKING ABOUT TEACHING AND LEARNING, EQUITY, AND THE FIGHT FOR SMALL SCHOOLS

William Ayers

EDUCATION IS ALWAYS AND EVERYWHERE about opening doors, opening minds, opening possibilities. Education is about opening your eyes and seeing for yourself the world as it really is in all its complexity, and then finding the tools and the strength to participate fully, even to change some of what you find. That this educational ideal is regularly undermined is not really a surprise—too many schools, after all, are all about sorting and punishing, grading and ranking and certifying. Education is unconditional—it asks nothing in return. Some schools demand obedience and conformity as a precondition to attendance. Education is surprising and unruly and disorderly, while the first and fundamental law of big, factory-like schools is to follow orders. Education frees the mind and resists anything that might bureaucratize the brain. An educator unleashes the unpredictable, while too many teachers are encouraged to start with an unhealthy obsession with classroom management and linear lesson plans.

Working in large schools—where the fundamental truths and demands and possibilities of education are obscure and diminished and opaque, and where the powerful ethical core of our efforts is systematically defaced and erased—requires a reengagement with the larger purposes and deepest meanings of education at its best. When the drumbeat of our daily lives in schools is all about controlling the crowd, moving the mob, conveying disembodied bits of information to inert things propped at desks before us,

A Simple Justice: The Challenge of Small Schools. Copyright © 2000 by Teachers College, Columbia University. All rights reserved. ISBN 0-8077-3962-6 (pbk.), ISBN 0-8077-3963-4 (cloth). Prior to photocopying items for classroom use, please contact the Copyright Clearance Center, Customer Service, 222 Rosewood Dr., Danvers, MA 01923, USA, tel. (508) 750-8400.

students can easily become the enemy, the obstacle. The need, then, to remind ourselves of the meaning of teaching at its best becomes intense, and the desire to fight for ourselves and our students becomes imperative; there is, after all, no basis for education in a democracy outside of a faith in the enduring capacity for growth in ordinary people and a faith that ordinary people—unpredictable, unmanageable, unlikely to fit into any neatly prescribed slots in our increasingly bureaucratized and regimented society—can, if they choose, change the world.

Seeing the student, seeing the world—this is the beginning: To assume a deep capacity in students, an intelligence (sometimes obscure, sometimes buried) as well as a wide range of hopes, dreams, and aspirations; to acknowledge, as well, obstacles to understand and overcome, deficiencies to repair, injustices to correct. With this as a base, the teacher creates an environment for learning that has multiple entry points for learning and various pathways to success. That environment must be abundant with opportunities to practice justice; to display, foster, embody, expect, demand, nurture, allow, model, and enact inquiry toward moral action. A classroom organized in this way follows a particular rhythm: Questions focus on issues or problems (What do we need or want to know? Why is it important? How will we find out?) and on action (Given what we know now, what are we going to do about it?).

A primary challenge to teachers is to see students as three-dimensional creatures—people much like themselves—with hopes, dreams, aspirations, skills, and capacities; with bodies, minds, hearts, and spirits; with experiences, histories, a past, a pathway, and a future; with a family, a community, a language, and a culture. This knotty, complicated challenge requires patience, curiosity, wonder, awe, and humility. It demands sustained focus, intelligent judgment, inquiry, and investigation. It requires teachers to be wide-awake, since every judgment is contingent, every view partial, every conclusion tentative. The student is dynamic, alive, in motion. Nothing is settled, once and for all. No perspective is every perspective, no summary can be authoritative. The student grows and changes—yesterday's need is forgotten, today's claims are all-encompassing and brand-new. This, then, is an intellectual task of serious, massive proportion.

This task involves, as well, an ethical stance, an implied moral contract. The good teacher communicates a deep regard for students' lives, a regard infused with unblinking attention, respect, even awe. An engaged teacher begins with a belief that each student is unique, each the one and only who will ever trod the earth, each worthy of a certain reverence. Regard extends, importantly, to an insistence that students have access to the tools with which to negotiate and transform the world. Love for students just as they are—without any drive or advance toward a future—is false love, enervating and disabling. The teacher must, in good faith, convince students to reach out, to reinvent, to seize an education fit for the fullest lives they might hope for.

As difficult as these challenges are, they are made tougher and more intense because teachers typically work in institutions of scripted and predictable power, command and control, where the toxic habit of labeling kids by their deficits is the commonsense and the commonplace, where the mechanistic model of interchangeable parts is triumphant, and where hierarchy and one's predetermined place in it are large, encompassing lessons. These schools are burdened by deeply ingrained practices that perpetuate injustice. In many big schools, simply herding the pack through the cafeteria without incident can seem an accomplishment, a victory. There are simply too many kids and too little time. The language of schools becomes, then, almost exclusively a language of sorting, a language of reduction, a language lacking spark, dynamism, or imagination. It is an authoritative and often authoritarian language. TAG, LD, BD, EMH, whatever these point to—even when glimpsing a chunk of reality—are reductive and overdetermined in schools. The children become opaque and then invisible, the teacher muffled and then muted. The thoughtful teacher, the caring and fully engaged teacher in this situation, must fight to look beneath and beyond the labels. The ethical teacher must resist.

With eyes wide open and riveted on learners, a further challenge to honest and righteous teachers is to stay wide-awake to the world, to the concentric circles of context in which we live and work. Teachers must know and care about some aspect of our shared life—our calling, after all, is to shepherd and enable the callings of others. Teachers, then, invite students to become somehow more capable, more thoughtful and powerful in their choices, more engaged in a culture and a civilization, able to participate, to embrace, and, yes, to change all that is before them. How do we warrant that invitation? How do we understand this culture and civilization?

Teachers must always choose—they must choose how to see the students before them, how, as well, to see the world, what to embrace and what to reject, whether to support or resist this or that directive. In big schools where the insistent illusion that everything already has been settled is heavily promoted, teachers experience a constricted sense of choice, diminished imaginative space, a feeling of powerlessness regarding the basic questions of teaching and the larger purposes of education. But in these places, too, teachers must find ways to resist, to choose for the children, for the future.

Education, clearly, is political in this sense. Schools are necessarily a work in progress, always a conversation unfinished. Yet in a time when the universe of political discourse is receding, disappearing, teachers need to wonder how to continue to speak the unhearable. How can the unspoken be heard? How does self-censorship perpetuate the silence? The tension between aspiration and possibility is acute, and the question of what is to be done a daily challenge.

Here is where we can powerfully engage the question of small schools and the struggle to rescue education from its entanglements and its burdens. Bigness in schools was and is deliberate, originally a policy response to the stated needs of the captains of industry, the builders of factories. Big schools tend to be mechanistic and managerial, hierarchical and bureaucratic. Everyone does the same tasks in the same way, like miniaturized factory workers or little soldiers. While all kids are different, in big schools those differences usually make no difference; youngsters and their teachers are treated as if they are interchangeable, even expendable. Big, comprehensive, competitive schools worked for some and failed for many others. Too many students, alienated from schools, disconnected from education.

Teaching and learning are fundamentally relational, but large schools most often are structured in ways that make real relationship impossible, eclipsing students' lives and reducing teachers to clerks or assembly-line workers. The business metaphor and the factory model, then, fill up much of the public space; we are bombarded with images of "clients" and "products" and "goods and services" and "efficiency" and "the bottom line." Teaching is dangerously diminished in the "schools as businesses" model—the ethical and intellectual dimensions are destroyed in pursuit of something sleek and gleaming and modern.

In reality the business metaphor and the factory model are proven mistakes based on false promises, failures even in their own terms—dropout rates, suicides, and instances of violence all are higher in big schools. By contrast, small schools hold on to kids longer and have significantly higher rates of success, particularly for African American, Latino, and immigrant youngsters and for students from high-poverty neighborhoods.

Why is this so?

When asked, students who drop out tell us again and again that the main reason they left school is that no adult cared if they stayed. An easy response from school people is, "Oh, those damn parents." But the kids said "no adult," and no one includes us. In fact, large, impersonal structures make it terribly difficult to let most students know whether we care if they stay or not. It's hard even to know their names as they stride past us in 50-minute blurs, 30 kids to a class, 150 kids a day. It's impossible to care much, to embrace them fully, to demand much from them. It's impossible to have much of a relationship. The kids become, then, the crowd, the herd, and much of our teaching bends toward a single goal: to manage the mob. This is the structuring of unethical behavior, the structuring of indifference, the opposite of a calling to the moral dimension. Or, so the dropouts tell us. And what of those who stay? For many it is different (but nonetheless serious) forms of disconnection, alienation, hopelessness, and despair.

Small schools is a restructuring strategy aimed pointedly at this disconnection. Just as bigness was a deliberate policy, smallness is an intentional answer and antidote, a gesture toward the personal, the particular, the integrated, the supportive. Small schools is a counter-metaphor, perhaps, a more hopeful emblem. It points, first, toward students at the center of the educational enterprise. In small schools every student must be known well by some caring adult, and every student must have a realistic possibility of belonging to a community of learners. There is in students a sense of visibility, of significance, of the hope to negotiate here the tricky terrain of identity. The message to children and youth is clear: You are a valuable and valued person here; without you this entire enterprise would flounder and fail.

Small schools is, as well, an emblem for teaching as intellectual and ethical work, and for teachers at the center of classroom practice. Teachers, then, collectively are responsible for the content and the conduct of their work—for curriculum, pedagogy, assessment—and, more, for the school lives of a specific group of students. Teachers are not mindless bureaucrats, soulless clerks, obedient and conforming quislings. They are, rather, people of courage and initiative, inventors and creators, thinkers and doers. Teachers can be engaged, present, available. And, importantly, they are accountable to the community for their actions and their outcomes. Small schools are places for visible teachers, and perhaps they are places to build a cohort of crusading teachers as well.

Small schools is, finally, an emblem for parents and communities as the center of the school's life. Parents are not annoying outsiders to be tolerated, nor phony "partners" in a patronizing nod toward fairness. In small schools parents must be gift and asset, and often decision-makers regarding broad policy and direction.

Small schools must strive to be sites of education, arenas of learning, protected spaces for an intimate encounter with minds and hearts. There must be freedom to teach, freedom to learn. There are rigorous standards and demands, but whereas standards in big schools are typically generated from afar and imposed from above, standard-setting in small schools is part of the real work of teachers, students, and parents. Standards, then, are not imprisoned in the cliché, "What every educated person should know and experience," nor corrupted by the single-minded focus on sorting winners from losers. Standards can become dynamic, alive, both challenging and nurturing, and, most important, can raise the question of why some kids are privileged to know and experience, while others are being denied access to that knowledge and those experiences. The world presses in. How do some tests and approaches keep some kids out? How does authoritative knowledge deny some kids' experiences? How do some schools and class-rooms suppress curiosity and desire?

All of this is to resist reducing the small schools movement to a defini-tional conceit, an administrative convenience, or an organizational scheme. Small schools cannot become simply a mechanistic policy option—this opens the door to elitist small schools, to racist small schools, to anything at all. But if justice driven, small schools can point to the kind of schooling worthy of all children—of poor kids and city kids, for exam-ple. Smallness, then, is an emblematic characteristic of worthiness in schools.

There is the danger that we will become complacent, satisfied with an anemic version of what could be. There is a danger as well that through overuse and misuse our language will undermine our larger purposes, will become clichéd and ridiculous. It is crucial then that we fight to be sure that the solution is not swallowed by the problem. We must embrace and organize every potential ally.

The question of whether a good urban school can be built has been answered all over the country with a resounding yes. The questions facing us today are more daunting: Can a system of successful schools be built that are accessible to all children? Can big, failing urban schools be trans-formed into vital sites of decency and learning with today's teachers and children and families? Can we overcome the structures of failure that pre-dictably impact poor children disproportionately? This is what our work must be about. This is the work of this collection.

Our larger goals must be oriented toward the creation of a system that provides a decent, adequate education to all children. There exists now a patchwork of successful schools and a shambles of failing ones. When mapped against socioeconomic status, school success correlates directly with advantage and disadvantage, with race and class. It is largely the wide-spread collective anger over school failure linked to endemic racism, privi-lege, and oppression that continues to fuel school reform and the small schools movement. Fighting for change in this critical public arena links to other justice struggles in society, even as it is an immediate effort on behalf of the lives of disadvantaged children here and now.

In this volume we gather activists, scholars, practitioners, and theorists to reexamine small schools and to locate the struggle in a context of justice. We review how and why small schools work for youngsters, provide thick descriptions of small schools strategy in action, and draw together theory and practice as we point to what is to be done if the promise of social justice is to be realized. We begin with insights about building small schools grounded in recent practice; we then offer portraits of schools in motion; finally we draw lessons from the hard, uneven work of building small schools.

If we take as our goal the education of all children—or even a gesture in that direction—our system is a failure. It is an unjust system. Our impulse to change must build, then, an opposition to this injustice. Some school people say in effect, "If the administration would let me, I'd be a risk-taking teacher." In reality, if the system permitted the boldest and best things teachers are capable of, it wouldn't be a risk to do them. We learn to become freedom-loving, risk-taking teachers by practicing action toward justice. The fight itself—the struggle to create small schools—must be justice work, the fight for inclusion, for example, the struggle for success for all, and the resistance to continuing elitist arrangements. Thus, the first thing we learn (and that our students witness) is to be fighters for fairness, teachers crusading on behalf of children's lives.

We can bring, of course, knowledge, experience, and thoughtfulness to our efforts to change schools. We can know, for example, the importance of attacking structures of failure and simultaneously the need to disrupt the cultures and standards and expectations of failure. We can work to build capacity at all levels in order to be successful in recultured and restructured schools. If the danger in large schools is the development of the pathology of the prison—the culture of passivity, complaint, and failure—the danger in small schools is the pathology of the cult with its unhealthy obsession on like-mindedness and the correct line. We can do better.

We must bring our commitments to fairness, equity, and justice—our fundamental commitments—with us into our efforts to promote change. School change is an instance of social change, and it is no less complex or demanding than any other. Every change effort occurs in context, and every context bristles with constraints that must be engaged in pursuit of something better, something fairer. Our commitments should include a faith in the ability of ordinary people to shape the solutions to their problems, the importance of rethinking each step as we go, and a willingness to embrace partial measures, small changes, that gesture toward justice.

It is important in our work that we tell no lies and claim no easy victories. There is no easy solution, no one right way to oppose injustice, to mobilize for a better way. We must remain skeptics and agnostics, even as we stir ourselves to act on behalf of what the known demands of us. We can, then, resist becoming credulous in the face of official, authoritative knowledge, and resist as well the debilitating tendency toward cynicism about the possibility of people to act and change their lives. We can doubt, even as we act. We can engage, even as we wonder. We can get moving.

Our Country Is Rich, Our People Are Poor

EDUCATION, JUSTICE, AND THE POLITICS OF STRUCTURAL ADJUSTMENT

William H. Watkins

THE WORLD IS CHANGING more rapidly than any of us ever could have imagined. Humankind is on the verge of a breakthrough of monumental proportions. We have harnessed nature as never before. Food now can be grown overnight. Homes can be constructed in hours. The mysteries of long dreaded diseases are rapidly being unlocked. Computer chips, fiber optics, robotics, and other advanced technologies are creating a push-button world. Ten years of uninterrupted growth, a booming stock market, and massive corporate profit-taking have exceeded all expectations. The United States is undeniably the center of the world's commercial wealth.

Today's sociopolitical and economic environment is characterized by a wide range of structural adjustments including shifting fortunes, realignments, and displacements. Power and wealth are concentrated in the hands of a very few. Less than 1% of the population now controls more than half of the country's wealth. The top 5% of our population controls nearly 80% of the wealth. In the political arena, Republicans and Democrats no longer quarrel over ideological issues as both support the politics of big wealth. Millions of the dispossessed have moved from relative to absolute poverty. In New York City, billionaires live across from Central Park while others sleep in that park possessing only a shopping cart and green garbage

A Simple Justice: The Challenge of Small Schools. Copyright © 2000 by Teachers College, Columbia University. All rights reserved. ISBN 0-8077-3962-6 (pbk.), ISBN 0-8077-3963-4 (cloth). Prior to photocopying items for classroom use, please contact the Copyright Clearance Center, Customer Service, 222 Rosewood Dr., Danvers, MA 01923, USA, tel. (508) 750-8400.

bag. The $7-per-hour job greets our nation's high school graduates. The fast-growing "punishment industry" now houses and/or supervises over 5 million "clients."

Society is being reengineered before our very eyes. Democracy has given way to *kleptocracy* as those at the top steal the wealth collectively created by all of us. The notion of aiding the less fortunate is disappearing. Public aid, public housing and low-cost medical care all are endangered. The IBM Corporation recently announced that it no longer supports the concept of pension. Can other companies be far behind?

We enter the new millennium with great uncertainty. Alongside increased possibilities for progressive change, equity, opportunity, and harmony many troubling things are evident. Authoritarianism, intolerance, and force increasingly order our society. We are at a historical crossroads. Issues of justice are being subsumed by greed and power. Which way are we going to go? The juxtaposition of massive wealth to abject poverty is glaring and irreconcilable.

Nowhere are the issues more troubling than in the intellectual life of the country. Ideas and ideology are crucial in any society. The brokers of culture and makers of myths are busily spinning tales of "deficit theories," genetic intelligence, and national chauvinism. Sophistry is presented as legitimate knowledge. One recent "study" concluded that the abortion policies of yesteryear are responsible for the decline in crime today.

In the new millennium a handful of giant telecommunications companies will monopolize *all* forms of public communications including news, movies, television, the Internet, and so forth. We are likely to witness the continued narrowing and partisan constriction of the knowledge base. We know that knowledge is socially and politically constructed. We also know that knowledge selection is inextricably connected to power. The question for educators is what role schools will play in this unfolding drama.

Like other social institutions, schools are contested arenas. Within and around their walls is a battle over ideas. Will schools be a part of the constellation of authoritarian partisan forces shaping society in their interests, or will schools be a part of the democratic impulse, which inevitably will oppose such naked power?

As currently organized, public schools are very problematic. It must be reaffirmed that schools are instruments and agencies of the state. They have become large and bureaucratic because they have been shaped by the political state and the corporate order. They have become alienating because racism and class privilege are both the official and unofficial policies of the state. They transmit "official knowledge." They have become instruments of ideation and socialization. They justify inequity and the existing social order. They legitimize the culture of difference. They too have become part of the centralization of power, wealth and ideas in our society. Schools have become complicit in the stupefication of the masses.

William Ayers has written about ethical teaching and teachers. No one could possibly disagree that the bureaucratic organization of schools can stifle even the most well-intentioned, most caring teachers. Throughout our society, we find those assigned to serve the people, especially the poor, placed in positions where they cannot really be effective. The message is clear. The upper classes will be serviced, the dispossessed will not. We continue with the absurd contradiction articulated by W. E. B. DuBois more than fifty years ago—"Our country is rich, but our people are poor."

We are left with the inescapable conclusion that schools have been turned against many students. As Ayers points out, too many schools are stultifying rather than stimulating. They are becoming rigid with scripted lessons and test overkill; they are losing their humanizing mission as beacons of hope, warmth, and social amelioration.

Thus we must raise political questions about the future of our schools. We already know what we the people want. We the people want schools and schooling that capture the imaginations of our children. We want our children to grow, care, love, respect, appreciate, and express themselves. We want schools that wage war on ignorance, bias, and privilege.

The essential question is accessibility: Who is going to have access to schooling? Who is going to benefit from the school experience? Most important, how can the schools be changed?

Ordinary people can and must change both schools and society. We have reached a point in history where the interests of the poor and dispossessed *cannot* be reconciled to the interests of big wealth and power. Two separate and clearly identifiable agendas are in place. Interests vested in wealth and power desire maintenance, efficiency, and social control. Above all else, they demand order. For them, schools must be redefined and adjusted to better execute those objectives.

The poor and propertyless of all colors, in contrast, want a total reorganization of both schooling and society. We want an end to tracking, ability grouping, and the kind of bureaucratization that fosters alienation and neglect. In short, we want equality in both funding and opportunity. We want justice for all, not just for some.

Public sentiment to democratize schools is widespread. The movement for smaller classes and schools is objectively linked to a larger movement for change and social justice. It flows from the same sentiment that demands equalized funding and an end to the demonization of our children.

As we move into the new millennium let us not be tricked by high-sounding phrases of accountability, back-to-basics, and the maintenance of discipline. Both school and society must change to meet the needs of all people for decent housing, medical care, guaranteed employment, safety and the opportunity to learn and participate—to be fully free human beings.

A Gesture Toward Justice

SMALL SCHOOLS AND THE PROMISE
OF EQUAL EDUCATION

Sonia Nieto

LATELY I HAVE BEEN VERY TROUBLED by the corporate mindset that seems to have taken hold of education. As William Ayers so rightly asserts, the idea of "schools as business" has been the archetype for our public schools for the past century. This idea is more entrenched than ever, with the discourse of schooling increasingly relying on terms such as "consumers," "clients," "accountability," and "products." The joy and excitement of learning are distant memories when terms such as these are used to describe what takes place in schools. There is little humanity in these images.

Small schools can be an antidote to an educational system that has lost its soul as it has become more bureaucratic and impersonal. If teaching and learning above all are about the relationships constructed by teachers and learners—and I believe they are—then small schools hold out the promise of equality in education because they can promote the demanding but affirming personal relationships essential for high levels of student learning. These relationships cannot take place when students are anonymous and teachers are disrespected. In a study of Puerto Rican high school dropouts that I did several years ago with my colleague Manuel Frau-Ramos (1993), the numbers were scandalous: 68% of Puerto Rican youths in one town had dropped out of high school before graduating. Even more distressing were the comments a number of young people made when we

A Simple Justice: The Challenge of Small Schools. Copyright © 2000 by Teachers College, Columbia University. All rights reserved. ISBN 0-8077-3962-6 (pbk.), ISBN 0-8077-3963-4 (cloth). Prior to photocopying items for classroom use, please contact the Copyright Clearance Center, Customer Service, 222 Rosewood Dr., Danvers, MA 01923, USA, tel. (508) 750-8400.

spoke with them: "I felt alone," said one. "I was an outsider," said another (p. 160). But even one of the young people who had graduated, when asked to make recommendations to the school department geared toward helping Puerto Rican students stay in school said, *"Hacer algo para que los boricuas no se sientan aparte* [Do something so that the Puerto Ricans do not feel separate]" (p. 161).

Ayers aptly asserts that teaching must be "a gesture toward justice." His eloquent comments on the possibilities for social justice created by the small schools movement reinforce what all good teachers know: Real learning can take place only in a socially just environment that recognizes the talents and hopes of all students. Anything that can help bring this idea closer to reality is welcome indeed. As such, the small schools movement is a reminder that education is about larger purposes than inputs, outputs, and standards as measured only by tests.

Small schools can free up minds to think big. They can give both teachers and students the space to dream. They can provide an atmosphere where teachers do not need to feel afraid and students are not simply a name on a page. They epitomize a learning climate based on trust and confidence. The fact that these are the kinds of environments demanded by wealthy parents for their own children is ample proof that small schools are generally more effective and successful than large ones. But, absent other significant changes, having small schools will not necessarily guarantee that what takes place in them will be any more creative or transformative than what takes place in large schools. As Ayers himself says, although small schools represent tremendous hope, they are not the solution to the complex and vexing problems of education today. These problems are especially obvious in urban public schools, which the public has for all intents and purposes abandoned. Making urban public schools smaller will not in itself ensure that students will learn more effectively, that the curriculum will become more substantial, or that tired teachers will become inspired and caring. As such, we shouldn't idealize what small schools can do.

Major problems facing urban public schools include lack of resources (Kozol, 1991), inadequate preparation of teachers (Darling-Hammond, 1998), policies and practices that discourage engagement with learning (Nieto, 1999), and racism and other biases that reflect deeply seated structural inequalities in society (Lipman, 1998). Small schools by themselves can do little to change these conditions. If we only move the administrators and teachers from large schools to smaller ones, without providing needed resources and further education and other types of support, we will simply end up with small schools that replicate big ones. For example, small schools are not necessarily antiracist. A great deal depends on the teachers in those schools, on their knowledge and awareness, and on the ease with which they handle issues of difference. In a telling study documenting the first year of a New York City public school, Kathe Jervis (1996) found that most teachers conspicuously avoided issues of race and difference, despite their expressed commitment to structures that supported equity and respected diversity. She concluded,

> One lesson that could be taken from this selective account is that even in the "best" schools, where faculty try hard to pay attention to individuals, Whites' blindness to race clouds their ability to notice what children are really saying about themselves and their identities. (p. 573)

Small schools are a visible example of current school-reform efforts that include restructuring and teacher empowerment. These schools hold tremendous potential in part because they challenge assumptions about the transformative power of teacher involvement in the management of schools and teachers' relationships with each other as professionals. But, as Pauline Lipman (1998) found in her study of a junior high school undergoing extensive restructuring, school-reform efforts unaccompanied by a fundamental change in teachers' ideologies simply may reinforce beliefs that are destructive to students. In her study, most teachers continued to view the problems of their African American students as situated primarily in pathologically deficient families; they rarely considered deficiencies within the school itself as contributing to students' academic failure. Not surprisingly, in both of the research studies cited, it was only the small number of African American teachers who struggled to introduce issues of race and racism in staff conversations. But because their viewpoints were largely dismissed, these teachers soon completely disengaged from the restructuring effort.

I give these examples not to discredit the small schools movement—a movement that I believe has great potential for positively affecting the learning of students who have been largely forsaken by society—but because small schools must not be viewed as the remedy for the many intolerable problems facing large schools. In the long run, it may well be that the by-products of small schools are more significant than small schools themselves. That is, by creating environments where customary structures are challenged, where caring relationships are allowed to flourish, and where conversations that are taboo in larger schools can take place, small schools open the door to new possibilities. But even if small schools open the door, the rest is up to educators and our society. Above all, what is needed is a redefintion of teaching and learning so that it becomes what Mildred Dickeman (1973) many years ago called "a subversive activity," an activity that is daring and courageous and that helps students dream. This is the kind of teacher envisioned by Angel Nieto—my husband and companion of many years and a poet as well as a gifted and courageous teacher—in his poem, "Ser Maestro/To Be a Teacher" (Nieto, 2000), part of which reads,

Ser maestro es ...	To be a teacher means ...
Hacer reglas y romperlas,	To make rules and to break them,
no confiar en lo obvio	to mistrust the obvious
descartar lo cómodo	to reject the comfortable
escapar de la rutina.	to escape routine.
Contestar y preguntar,	To answer and to ask,
siempre preguntar.	always to ask,
No hacer caso al qué dirán.	not paying attention to what people might say.
Dormir poco y soñar mucho,	To sleep a little and dream a lot,
soñar dormido, despierto soñar,	to dream asleep, and dream awake,
siempre soñar y	always to dream and
lo imposible buscar.	reach for the impossible
Aprender, compartir, enseñar.	To learn, to share, to teach
y aprender una vez más.	and to learn again.
Descrubir, formar, lograr	To discover, to shape, to achieve
y luego volver a empezar.	and to then start all over again.

REFERENCES

Darling-Hammond, L. (1998). Teachers and teaching: Testing policy hypotheses from a National Commission report. *Educational Research, 27*(1), 5–15.

Dickenman, M. (1973). Teaching cultural pluralism. In J. A. Banks (Ed.), *Teaching ethnic studies: Concepts and strategies* (43rd yearbook, pp. 4–25). Washington, DC: National Council for the Social Studies.

Frau-Ramos, M., & Nieto, S. (1993). "I was an outsider": An exploratory study of dropping out among Puerto Rican youths in Holyoke, Massachusetts. In R. Rivera & S. Nieto (Eds.), *The education of Latino students in Massachusetts: Issues, research, and policy implications* (pp. 147–169). Boston: The Gaston Institute for Latino Community Development and Public Policy.

Jervis, K. (1996). "How come there are no brothers on that list?": Hearing the hard questions all children ask. *Harvard Educational Review, 66*(3), 546–576.

Kozol, J. (1991). *Savage inequalities: Children in America's schools.* New York: Crown.

Lipman, P. (1998). *Race, class, and power in school restructuring.* Albany: State University of New York Press.

Nieto, S. (1999). *The light in their eyes: Creating multicultural learning communities.* New York: Teachers College Press.

Nieto, S. (2000). *Affirming diversity: The sociopolitical context of multicultural education* (3rd rev. ed.) New York: Longman.

PART I

Grounded Insights

Michael Klonsky

MALL SCHOOLS should not be offered or taken as a fad nor as the latest in a string of reforms, off-the-shelf packages, or once-a-month professional-development seminars. One could argue, in fact, as Deborah Meier often has done, that small schools are the most traditional of reforms in the sense that they are rooted in the rural, turn-of-the-century, one-room schoolhouse, where school and community were tied together by an invisible umbilical cord. Meier, who is not a sentimentalist, expresses a great sense of loss of community or public space, in her chapter, "The Crisis of Relationships," as the last vestiges of small-town democracy are swallowed in the drive for bigness. She sees the current small-schools movement as the single best reform alternative to vouchers and other attacks on public space.

Other chapters in this section offer grounded insights on the roots of small schools and strategies for their implementation. In my own chapter, "Remembering Port Huron," I try to forge a link from the values of activism and participatory democracy to critical notions of education found in the radical movements of the 1960s. In much of the post-Reagan literature, that decade has come to represent years of educational chaos, a loss of standards, and relativism. However, as the perceived crisis in public education—and urban education in particular—has deepened, many of the ideas experimented with 30 years ago are now being grabbed as alternatives. In the aftermath of the shootings at Columbine High School in Littleton, Colorado, and other cases of suburban school violence, small schools finally are being looked at as a serious alternative to metal detectors, intensified security, and militarized schools. One could even argue that the current trends of *school restructuring, external partnerships* (partners called "organizers" or, pejoratively, "outside agitators" 30 years ago), or *systemic change* all borrow from radical and reforms movements of that time.

Small schools—with many of the characteristics taken from John Dewey's utopian vision (see William Schubert's "John Dewey as a Philosophical Basis for Small Schools"), the alternative schools movement of the 1960s–70s, the Mississippi Freedom Schools (as described in Charles Payne's chapter, "Education for Activism: Mississippi's Freedom Schools in the 1960s,") and small schools in Barbados (as described in Pedro Noguera's "Where Race and Class Are Not an Excuse")—have achieved impressive results. These results, documented in the chapter by Alfred Hess on Chicago's dramatic reform effort, "Who Leads Small Schools? Teacher Leadership in the Midst of Democratic Governance," have come not in a few marginal experiments but largely as attempts to radically reconceptualize schooling in the heart of struggling urban school systems including New York, Philadelphia, Chicago, Boston, and Oakland. However, utopian ideals and concepts are doomed to the margins of the system, as Deweyans discovered long ago. Of course, Dewey, the father of American pragmatism, could have told us that great educational ideas are worthwhile only to the degree that they can be implemented. The small-schools movement has tried to adapt itself to the current issues of standards-based instruction and accountability without losing its democratic soul— without becoming just another reform package to be taken off the shelf and sold to school districts with the promise of automatic test score increases.

Education Week writer Lynn Olson (1999) suggests that groups trying to package whole-school reform should practice truth-in-advertising, with a warning label that reads: "Works if implemented. Implementation variable." She cautions that as we come to embrace the concept of school-wide change, the degree to which the school community is willing to carry out the ideas and practices of a particular reform model as envisioned by its designers has emerged as the "weak link." The link is so weak that it is threatening the Federal government's promising Comprehensive School Reform Demonstration Program that began with a pot of $150 million for schools to adopt whole-school reform designs with the support of external partners. The partners were rated on the basis of "empirical data" gleaned by educational research labs. These data were then given to schools and districts to help them choose a package that would offer them the best chance of success. About half implemented their programs and half did not.

Hearing this bit of news was one of those "duh!" moments for many teachers. Despite all the empirically based assurances of success, even the best school-improvement programs and packages won't work unless teachers, parents, students, and school leaders put them into practice. Big, anonymous schools, where teaching is practiced in isolation and kids are invisible, will turn even the most promising package into just another nibbling reform effort.

Small-schools restructuring only recently has been considered by legislators and policy-makers as a viable alternative. While ready-to-use packages may not fit Dewey's democratic aims, they certainly are easier for the public to understand. They also are a lot easier for evaluators to measure and compare for effect. Yet indications are that in schools and districts where small-schools restructuring is going on, student achievement is on the rise. In his assessment of Chicago's small-schools experiment, Hess documents the gains made by small schools and their continuing struggle against marginalization, whether self-inflicted or systemic.

Small-schools restructuring focuses directly on transforming the relationships and the culture that exist within a school. The two key ingredients must be: (a) teachers working together in a professional community, and (b) staying together with a group of students long enough to get to know them well. The specific curricular or instructional approach will vary from school to school (often within the same building). This is not to say, however, that curriculum and instruction are not central issues for small-school educators. They are. Schubert shows how teachers can be brought into the curriculum process in its conceptual and implementation stages. Susan Klonsky ("Art, with Algebra, Guards the Gate") shows how curriculum can be liberated in small schools, from the cages of standardization and isolation of subject matter. But, she asks, who will have access to the new curriculum if schools continue to function as sorting mechanisms and gatekeepers? This may well be the civil-rights issue of the new century.

A decade ago, the focus of Chicago's small-schools movement, described by Hess, was on starting new autonomous schools. The success of many of these start-ups—including many small charter and pilot schools—stood as an image of what is possible. They began to attract many excellent teachers to inner-city neighborhood schools based on the opportunities they offered for collaboration and freedom. The definition of success was based largely on their unique qualities, including their focus. Small schools were good because they were different, whereas traditional large schools were considered good because of their sameness.

By 1995, the landscape of urban school reform was shifting. The conservative "accountability" movement, with its focus on high-stakes testing, brought with it new opportunities for external partnerships and intervention in failing schools. There was a noticeable increase in the flow of federal and state dollars aimed at school improvement and whole-school change. But this highly political trend offered only a menu of prepackaged goods to districts hungry for outside help. The hopefully well-intentioned resources were grabbed up by administrators who, under great pressure to "do something," used whatever money was available to bring the best package to their school or district. The problem, of course, was "implementation."

Small schools offer an alternative strategy for whole-school change as well as for new start-ups. The process of small-school restructuring is one that encourages teacher collaboration and high levels of autonomy. It offers a chance for new relationships and an escape from the factory (bureaucratic, worker-supervisor) relationships that are a holdover from the factory era.

The questions facing the small-schools movement then become:

- Can small schools become part of a strategy for systemic or whole-school change?
- Can they do it without losing their unique qualities and commitment to social justice?
- Can they be a vehicle for turning around failing high schools?
- Can they help to get schools "off the list"?
- Can they have more than a marginal impact on the majority of schools in a district?

If implementation is the key link, small schools have a good chance of success.

REFERENCE

Olsen, L. (1999, April 14). Following the Plan. *Education Week.* (Online: http://www.edweek.org/ew/1999/31implem.h18)

CHAPTER 2

Remembering Port Huron

Michael Klonsky

If we appear to seek the unattainable, as it has been said, then let it be known that we do so to avoid the unimaginable.

From the 1962 Port Huron Statement,
manifesto of SDS

PORT HURON, Mich. (May 18, 1999)—A third of the desks sat empty Monday at Holland Woods Middle School because students and their parents were afraid of what evils might prowl the school grounds after a bomb was found and four boys were accused of planning a Colorado-style school massacre here.

The New York Times

PORT HURON, once a metaphor for social change, is now one more name on a list of communities scarred by violence. Small schools have a lot to offer as a strategy for dealing with threats of school violence. The alternative seems to be a new brand of religious/techno/militarizing of the schools, of transferring responsibility for students from teachers to security guards or the church. Instead of the "tragedy" of Littleton, Colorado, becoming a springboard for building greater community and democracy in schools, as many of us had hoped, it has become the signal for school-funding streams to be diverted into security measures, a strengthening of conservative/religious values, indoctrination, and the further disempowerment of teachers.

Immediately following the April 1999 school shootings in Colorado, the issue of school size temporarily jumped onto the front burner as a means of social control and maintenance of the status quo. Even though

A Simple Justice: The Challenge of Small Schools. Copyright © 2000 by Teachers College, Columbia University. All rights reserved. ISBN 0-8077-3962-6 (pbk.), ISBN 0-8077-3963-4 (cloth). Prior to photocopying items for classroom use, please contact the Copyright Clearance Center, Customer Service, 222 Rosewood Dr., Danvers, MA 01923, USA, tel. (508) 750-8400.

Columbine High School in Littleton was moderately sized by today's standards, with about 1,800 students and a senior class of 440, it was plenty big enough to foster the sense of anomie that pervades many secondary schools today. Students often got lost at Columbine. However, the shootings also sprang from the well of racist, neo-Nazi ideology that had plenty of room to flourish in an environment where guns were readily available and little personal connection existed between teachers and students. Even though the Trench Coat Mafia to which the killers belonged was heavily influenced by fascist ideology (the shootings coincided with Hitler's birthday) and even though the incident was part of a nationwide wave of violence on the part of white supremacist and neo-Nazi organizations, the killings were played off as the work of two isolated, troubled kids. Social cliques, movie violence, video games, black clothing, and nearly every other symbol of nonconformity were attacked by nervous administrators and politicians. Few policies have been made concerning Nazi paraphernalia, membership in racist organizations, or gun ownership. After a summer of fortifying Columbine with more metal detectors, surveillance cameras, and undercover security while giving the community a heavy dose of old-fashioned religion, swastikas were found carved on lockers the day school reopened in the fall of 1999.

The Port Huron Statement, which helped usher in the student revolt of the 1960s, declared ". . . there is an alternative to the present, that something can be done to change circumstances in the school, the workplaces, the bureaucracies, the government." Thirty-five years later, many are wondering if school reform is really possible (see Sarason, 1990). While the information age has witnessed the collapse of many bureaucratic institutions, our large factory-like schools and school systems have remained remarkably intact.

The Port Huron story in the *Times* presented a link between small schools and social justice. The 1962 manifesto of the Students for a Democratic Society celebrated participatory democracy and created a framework for student activists to oppose the war in Vietnam and march against racial injustice. Port Huron, an industrial town on the Canadian border, offered the promise of America's heartland. Alexis de Tocqueville visited Port Huron in 1831 and found many of the images of democracy he was looking for. Little could he have imagined that it would be the latest addition to a list of names including Littleton, Colorado, Jonesboro, Arkansas, and Conyers, Georgia, places where anger, estrangement, and alienation of youths would lead not to participatory democracy but to "the unimaginable"—murderous assaults by teenagers on their schoolmates and teachers. In nearly every case, the shootings took place in large schools attended primarily by White, middle-class students. The noted AfricanAmerican psychiatrist Carl Bell called these predesigned mass murder/suicides part of a "White, male entitlement disorder." Others, far less conscious of issues of race and power or of the history of patterned mass-murder–suicide, simply wrote the killings off as a modern "tragedy."

The word *tragedy* comes from the Greeks and was used in literature to describe the relationship of man and the gods, or greater forces of destiny. Tragedy represents forces that regular people seem powerless to control. To question or challenge authority sets oneself up for a fall. The tragic issue, the defeat of the individual, leads to the realization that human presumption to determine one's destiny is necessarily ruinous. The heyday of Greek tragedy was 2,500 years ago, but the thought that students, parents, teachers, and community members actually can take control of many of the things that affect their lives is still ephemeral. It is a simple idea that Tocqueville spotted in the U.S. heartland 170 years ago and one that made the Port Huron Statement so powerful.

The collapse and departure of much of Port Huron's industry since the SDS statement also was written off by many as a tragedy. People in rust belt towns as well as in changing urban communities generally talked about schools "going down" as a metaphor for changing racial and class demographics. As with the word *tragedy*, the implication was that "shit happens." The widespread use of the word *tragedy* in explaining school bombings and shootings mystifies events over which ordinary people should have influence. Can we say that mass murders in schools by neo-Nazi cliques are the inevitable by-products of the modern age? Can't educators really get to know kids to the degree that the seeds of violent, antisocial behavior can be detected well in advance and dissipated?

There is a growing body of research and experience pointing to smaller schools and school restructuring as a vehicle for making education more powerful for students and teachers, for enabling them to take control of the institutions that affect their lives. Small schools, while not a panacea, may offer a more powerful antidote to school violence than does militarization.

Small schools are designed with the following ideas in mind:

- Teachers work together collaboratively in a professional community.
- Students are known by teachers and teachers known by students.
- A group of teachers remains with a cohort of students for several years.
- Schools have a focus or a clear sense of purpose.
- Several schools can exist within one building. Schools are not seen as brick and mortar; rather they are considered to be learning communities.

The modern small-schools movement arose largely as a response to the urban crisis of the late 1960s that was marked by the failure of school desegregation and the Black revolt. Since the movement began, it has taken root primarily in urban settings as part of a larger school-reform effort for comprehensive improvement in decaying systems. Districts in middle-class suburbs largely have turned up their noses at the prospect of restructuring, preferring to conserve conventional, highly tracked school structures that have served them well since the early days of suburbia. To engage in restructuring would be an admission that things were not all rosy in places like Littleton. Such an admission would not make sense in places where "good schools" translate into high real-estate prices and attractive neighborhoods for professionals and mid-level managers with school-age or soon-to-be children. But the events in Littleton, Conyers, and Port Huron may change some attitudes about what good schooling means.

Although suburbia is dotted with large, shopping-mall high schools, suburban education generally is done on a smaller scale than in urban centers. Both schools and classes tend to be larger in urban areas than in nonurban areas, even though the needs of the children are often greater. The Quality Counts Study (1998) showed high school students in the 74 big-city districts 25% more likely than the average U.S. teenager to attend a school with more than 900 students. According to the study: "Many of these giant schools resemble vast warehouses where students float anonymously through what passes for an education. Where they can skip school and no one will notice. Where the first sight to greet them when they walk through the door each morning is a metal detector or a police officer checking for weapons" (p. 18).

There are 11 million young people going to school in urban districts, where they are less likely to graduate and more likely to fail on standardized tests. They tend to go not only to larger schools but also to schools with higher truancy rates, less involvement from parents, more violence, unlicensed teachers, and decrepit physical conditions.

While the latest and most publicized wave of violence took place in mainly white suburban schools, the real militarization of education is taking place in large urban schools attended primarily by poor students of color. A study by the National Center for Education Statistics (NCES; Heaviside, Rowand, Williams, & Farris, 1998) polled over 1,200 school principals nationally and found that students who attend large schools or who are poor and minority are more likely to encounter random metal detector searches than other students. The NCES study also confirmed that the use of police or security officers takes place at a higher rate in large schools and in schools with high minority enrollments.

When violent episodes broke out in Littleton, Port Huron, and other districts, they dominated the national media scene for months in a way that student deaths in the inner city never have. *Time* magazine ran a cover special report on school violence with an article on the need for smaller schools. Hillary Rodham Clinton, campaigning in New York with her finger on the pulse of middle-class voters, said that one of the saddest comments after the Littleton massacre was made by the principal of Columbine High School, when he claimed never to have heard of the Trench Coat Mafia. "Well how could he?" asked the First Lady. "Those were just a small group of kids in a very large institution. . . . Right now most of our schools are no longer communities, and too many kids are passing through them anonymously. . . . So we are going to have to change the way we think about, how we build and construct and organize our schools" (Pandolfi, 1999).

Hillary shouldn't be so surprised. The current administration is gearing up to spend hundreds of billions on new schools without any constraints on school size. Since World War II, in fact, the number of schools has decreased by more than 70% while the average size has increased fivefold. High schools with student populations of 2,000 to 5,000 are not uncommon. The new Belmont Learning Center High School in Los Angeles is being built for 5,000 students at a cost of more than $225 million before overruns.

In nearly all of the violent outbreaks, the responsible adults in the school building have offered the tragedy rationale, taken no responsibility, and insisted that they had no idea that "anything like this was going on" in their school. One educator who emerged as a hero from the series of school shootings was Cecil Brinkley, the assistant principal in Conyers, Georgia, where a student wounded fellow students and then threatened to commit suicide. In an interview on NBC's *Today* show, Brinkley described how he followed the student outside toward the football field and asked him to hand over the handgun, which at that point was pointed at Brinkley:

> I stepped back a couple of steps and I turned to him again and I said, "Give me the gun," and I said again, "Give me the gun." I saw him lower the barrel of the gun and I kept getting closer and closer to him. Then I held out my hands and he laid the gun in my hands. Then he gave me a real big bear hug and he said, "I'm scared, I'm scared."

When Brinkley was asked what happened next, he replied: "I asked him, 'What's your name?'" The student was invisible until he acted violently. Brinkley's heroism stood out against the backdrop of a system of large, factory-model schools where kids often are anonymous, even to the well-meaning, the skilled, and even the heroic. It seems highly improbable that such a disconnection between educator and student could exist in small schools.

During the 1998–99 school year, 47 Chicago public school students were shot to death. Five students were from one southside high school. The dead students were all AfricanAmerican or Latino. Not one death made the front page of the local papers. There were no national voices of indignation. The deaths were written off as "gang-related."[1] There were no speeches calling for small schools or for putting any responsibility on educators. No one in the school stepped forward to claim any of the dead. In fact, the schools' first response was, and often is, to deny any connection to their students, whether they were the victims or the victimizers. A top school administrator went so far as to tell the grief-stricken audience, following the fifth shooting: "Thank God, he wasn't killed inside the school." In another case, educators told the media that the dead student only recently had transferred to the school and therefore couldn't really be called "their student."

Evidence is beginning to mount that, even in their early, least-developed stages, small schools and schools-within-a-school can have a great impact on school violence. A case in point is another Chicago high school, located in the southside AfricanAmerican community of Englewood. Paul Robeson High School was placed on academic probation by the board and then reconstituted in 1996–97. It was plagued by violence and poor student achievement until the principal led a restructuring effort to create six small academies. Police records show that in the years 1995–96, there were 105 arrests inside the school: 26 were for assault or battery and 13 were for possession of weapons. When restructuring began the next year, things got even worse, with 156 arrests: 14 for mob action, 16 for weapons possession, and 25 for violent assaults.

The first year after restructuring (1997–98), the small schools within Robeson were far from perfect. Problems in scheduling did not allow a cohort of teachers to stay with the same kids throughout the year. Although there were few changes in instructional methods that first year, the rudimentary qualities of a learning community began to appear. Teachers and students began greeting each other in the hallways. Teacher teams began meeting across departmental lines. There was and still is a long way to go in the change process, but in 1998 the number of arrests dropped by two thirds. The number of violent-assault arrests went down to six, and dropped to two the following year. Many cases of misbehavior, traditionally resulting in outside suspension and arrests, now are being handled by teachers within each small school.

Not all teachers are happy with the "extra burden" of having to deal with antisocial behavior, however. Some even argued that the reduction in arrests was caused by a lack of a "zero tolerance" policy. The results, though, are still promising. It should come as no surprise that a year later, math and reading scores at the school more than doubled.

This is not to say that small schools alone are a panacea for the problems of school violence or low test scores. These early data only offer hope. Decreases in violent behavior and increases in attendance have been noted early in most of the small-school restructuring projects I have been involved with. As the small schools develop and as teachers can spend more time with students and with each other, comprehensive school improvement can take place. Something can be done to counter the culture of tragedy.

The large, anonymous high schools and junior highs that formed the backdrop for the violence of 1999 did not evolve naturally from the small, one-room schoolhouses and community schools that preceded them. In large part, they were the result of things that people did or failed to do, of battles and arguments. Their formation had to do much more with the politics of the Cold War, for example, than it did with isolated educational values and policy.

The current wave of violence occurs exactly 40 years after James B. Conant's (1959) famous study of the American high school. In the Conant Report, issued 2 years after the Russian launching of Sputnik, the scientist and former Harvard president called for the consolidation of small-town schools and the creation of the comprehensive high school, replete with intensive tracking and sorting systems for kids and a hoped-for teacher-proof curriculum. In the decades that followed, the number of school districts nationally decreased from 40,000 to 16,000, and many small high schools were closed in the name of efficiency and cost effectiveness.

In most states, principals have been rewarded with pay incentives in proportion to the size of their schools. Until October 1999, when Secretary of Education Richard W. Riley began promoting small schools as an alternative to militarizing schools, school size was never high on the Department of Education's research agenda. This lack of interest existed despite ample evidence, statistical and anecdotal, to support small schools as safe schools and their particular benefits for children of color and those from low-income families.

There were hopeful signs after Littleton that some small-schools initiatives would be forthcoming from the DOE or from state legislatures. Democratic Senator Jeff Bingamon of New Mexico drafted a bill to promote small schools and smaller learning communities under Title X of the

Elementary and Secondary Education Act of 1995. The bill would award grants to local educational agencies to develop small-schools strategies.

After dozens of post-Littleton speeches by politicians, the mood in Congress and in state legislatures swung back to the right. Posting the Ten Commandments on classroom walls, banning violent movies and television programs, and militarizing schools are ideas conservatives hope will play on the fears of the middle class. Gov. George W. Bush of Texas is running his 2000 presidential campaign on a platform advocating more religion in schools, more freedom for teachers to punish unruly students, and more aggressive prosecution of children who carry guns. In Georgia, following the Conyers shootings, the *Christian Science Monitor* reported that Georgia State School Superintendent Linda Schrenko asked for legislation to "go back to small-size schools" (Chaddock, 1999). Telling of the times, Schrenko also proposed authorization for principals to carry Mace, pepper spray, or stun guns. A Jewish student in Mississippi was suspended from school for wearing the Star of David around his neck, an obvious gang symbol to the ever-alert administrators.

The decade following the Port Huron Statement was a period of rapid change. There were countercultural communities that attracted disaffected youth like magnets. There was a vibrant movement for social justice, centered on the war and the Black freedom struggle. Both the counterculture and the movement had their reflections in education, especially in the alternative schools and the freedom schools in the South. The SDS letterhead stationery depicted a schoolhouse, drawn without the benefit of the stock computer graphic you see today in every reform group's logo. Students, marching in lockstep, entered through the front door of the schoolhouse. As I recall, dour looks were etched on the faces of the students as guardlike teachers directed them though the school entrance. The joyous part of the letterhead depicted these same students exiting the rear door with smiling faces, carrying picket signs for peace and social justice.

That decade saw the real emergence of the alternative school. More than 11,000 such schools were created nationwide, attracting many of those the mainstream had failed. Education alternatives have existed about as long as has the mainstream. Some have been highly effective, others horrible, but a preponderance of the research shows the alternatives capturing many more of the features essential for student success: focus, organizational climate, culture, downscaling, personalization, worker commitment and satisfaction, visionary leadership, and shared decision-making. These advantages have been known to educators since the Eight-Year Study compared students in the 1930s matriculating from the alternative schools with those from traditional schools. The Eight-Year Study, which Schubert (1986) called "the most extensive curriculum research project" in the first half of the 20th century (p. 263), showed that students from restructured high schools (mostly small) and schools using alternative curricula fared as well or better in college than those coming from traditional schools. In fact, students from schools that had made the most fundamental changes achieved higher standing than students of equal ability with whom they were compared (Aikin, 1942). Students in those experimental schools were generally superior to students from traditional schools in creativity, the ability to make independent decisions, and the ability to work well with others. Despite their successes, most of these schools eventually abandoned their programs. Why? The war put a damper on programs that were out of step with the new standards, much as Sputnik would do some 30 years later. Schools and districts could not resist the pull toward the big and traditional. Will the latest outbreak of violence produce another trend toward standardization?

Small schools run counter to the dangerous conservative response to school violence. While increased security measures at schools understandably meet with approval from many parents and, to some degree, students, the emphasis on security will prove to be ineffective unless it is combined with school restructuring and democratic education. The spirit of the 1962 Port Huron Statement and the precepts of participatory democracy and social justice remain viable as a lens through which to examine school change.

NOTE

1. The Trench Coat Mafia was never referred to as a "gang" in the national media. Violent groups of white, neo-Nazi teenagers were referred to in the media and by school administrators as "cliques" without distinction from cliques of athletes or "nerds."

REFERENCES

Aikin, W. (1942). *The story of the Eight-Year Study* (pp. 110–115). New York: Harper & Brothers.

Chaddock, G. R. (1999, May 24). Act of valor may help Georgia town to heal. *Christian Science Monitor.* Available: http://www.csmonitor.com/infoarchive/ infoarchive.shtml

Conant, J. B. (1959). *The American high school today.* New York: McGraw-Hill.

Heaviside, S., Rowand, C., Williams, C., & Farris, E. (1998). *Violence and discipline problems in U.S. public schools: 1996–97.* Washington, DC: National Center for Education Statistics.

Pandolfi, A. (1999, May 10). First Lady criticizes large schools. Associated Press wire.

Quality Counts '98. (1998, Jan. 8). The urban challenge: Public education in the 50 states. Study in collaboration with the Pew Charitable Trusts. *Education Week* *XVIII*(16). (Online: http://www.edweek.org/sreports/qc98/)

Sarason, S. (1990). *The predictable failure of educational reform.* San Francisco: Jossey-Bass

Schubert, W. H. (1986). *Curriculum: Perspective, paradigm, and possibility.* New York: Macmillan.

CHAPTER 3

The Crisis of Relationships

Deborah Meier

THERE ARE A HOST OF IRREFUTABLE REASONS why small schools are the easiest, most economical, and wisest single school-reform idea around. This is not to say that they will always be highly successful, but then no single idea for school reform will. However, if I had to put my bet on one, and only one, this is where I'd start. I know it in my gut, but I must also consider why. Of course, in part my choice is influenced by the simple fact that I cannot imagine wanting to work with or lead anything else. I have my own problems about institutional life, anonymity, and wanting to know everything. These three qualities lead me to smallness. Besides, I can't remember too many names—I need lots of repetitive contact to get straight who's who. Finally, I happen to have never attended a really large school. Even the first public school I taught in—Chicago's Beulah Shoesmith School—was very much on the small side. I didn't know any better.

This time, my personal predilections happen to be right. An even greater crisis than declining academic achievement—about which there is no little real evidence—is a decline in the quality and quantity of long-term and stable personal relationships. The impact of this decline is far-reaching—probably least of all on some narrowly defined measure of "academic achievement." Its impact on the building of a democratic society, where people take responsibility for themselves and others and feel a stake not only in today but also in what will happen tomorrow, is incalculable. So if it is true that what we face is a crisis of relationships, that's important stuff. And its consequences "academically" are serious, but not in the ways in which we usually measure them—test scores.

A Simple Justice: The Challenge of Small Schools. Copyright © 2000 by Teachers College, Columbia University. All rights reserved. ISBN 0-8077-3962-6 (pbk.), ISBN 0-8077-3963-4 (cloth). Prior to photocopying items for classroom use, please contact the Copyright Clearance Center, Customer Service, 222 Rosewood Dr., Danvers, MA 01923, USA, tel. (508) 750-8400.

The glue that holds responsible relationships with other people together has largely disappeared. We do not belong to anywhere near as many stable communities—workplaces, hometowns, neighborhoods, or extended families—as we once did. People often felt as though these stable communities would drive them crazy, and many went to great lengths to flee them. But they were there through most of our growing-up years— just there. Even when rejected, they were important. Through them, we knew lots of people unlike ourselves—old and young. Our families were embedded in the same relationships with others—the same shopkeepers and librarians, the same sisters and brothers in the church or union, and the same teachers that our siblings had. Most of us left school before finishing high school (that only changed during World War II) and began our work lives surrounded by experts in our trade. Adolescent life—with its attendant risk-taking—existed, but briefly and without much fanfare. Teenagers didn't have a lot of money, were expected to carry their share of the workload, and were soon required to enter the same adult world as their families.

All this changed after World War II and then changed even more dramatically as we entered the age of computers and high technology, although it has taken time to see the impact. In 1930 there were 200,000 school districts with a 1.5 million citizens sitting on local school boards. The schools they supervised were close to home and very small. Today, with twice as many citizens, there are fewer than 20,000 school districts, a few hundred thousand citizens serve on boards, and most supervise large, highly dispersed schools and districts. Public schools have lost their *publics*.

Just as mobility affected communities, increasing school and district sizes have had an impact on the cohesion of school life. This was only one of many symptomatic changes that helped isolate the young from the adult world, and vice versa. Are we perhaps the only civilization in history that has organized itself so that the closer one gets to being a grown-up, the less contact one has with grown-ups?

By the time youngsters reach their late teens they know barely any adults outside of their families well, and they see relatively little of even these. In their jobs their time is largely spent not as apprentices to more skilled employees, but in the company of teams of peers—in businesses like The Gap or McDonald's. The April 1999 killings in Littleton, Colorado, put a spotlight on the way adolescents naturally seek a sense of community. Except for the jocks and the nerds they belong to small schools-within-schools, which include no adults at all and rarely another person who is not exactly the same age or grade. They are at best only bureaucratically responsible to others, and few of these are the adults whom they can "let down," who count on them, or who matter in a personal way. One of the most efficient and natural ways of learning is by imagining oneself in the role of an esteemed expert, yet today's students have few opportunities for such learning. They are hobbled in an apprentice-less world. Even their peer settings are largely only for entertainment, and thus are limited in the lessons they can teach. This is not a community of peers in which membership confers responsibilities. Students belong to virtually no such communities. They know, in short, precious little of what it means to be a member, not a consumer or customer. Everything is a calculated trade-off. There is nothing larger and more significant than one's own agenda.

Of course this is an exaggeration. Like good science fiction it rings true, yet it exaggerates. But, in fact, if we were to invent institutions for the young to produce what I have described above, the place we would devise is the typical U.S. school, above all the typical junior or senior high school. And we have done it on purpose. We said big is good, small is bad. This wasn't a happenstance or a by-product.

At a time when so many other community-building institutions were falling apart for reasons beyond our control, we invented the post–World War II high school, and then later we copied it for junior high schools and even elementary schools. We stacked the deck against communities that wanted to preserve their own small neighborhood schools. We viewed them as throwbacks, old-fashioned, anachronisms. In the 1960s we did it at times for a just cause—integration—even though the big schools we built were often racially segregated by academic tracks. But in fact we did it everywhere with or without cause. Or the cause was bigness itself—more. More kids meant more specialists and, in many schools, more modern equipment and fancy gyms, pools, labs, and libraries. In my own local community in Columbia County, New York, we just did it again—eliminating the last vestiges of "smallness" with one huge new school to replace four existing ones. In this case the argument was painful and simple: It was the only way to get the needed monies from the state. By now folks had heard that it wasn't good education.

We have created a mythology that fuels bigness. Big schools have bigger and better teams, huge dances, large parking lots; anonymity becomes a virtue, not a vice. In a big school you can create your own sub-school. You can ignore the larger ethos for your own kind. Teachers matter less, because often no individual teacher appears more than once in a child's 4-year career in high school. By the time my son graduated from his high school of 3,000 students, he did not know a single teacher well enough to ask for a personal letter of reference. Nor did I.

Democracy itself is imperiled by this crisis in our relationships with others. Democracy is not simply a juridical system of checks and balances, voters' rights, and the like. It is built on a foundation of naive trust. Whoever the body politic may be—and in the history of this word it has not usually meant everyone by a long shot—they are to be trusted and counted on, their word is good. They are "us," writ large. That's the given. They are our brothers' keepers, and now our sisters' keepers, too. Democracy rests on inexact acts of judgment made by our peers—not reliance on ultimate wisdom, truth, or expertise. No one knows whether the same verdict would be arrived at by a different jury on a different day. We put our lives into the hands of our peers. We do not always elect people who are smarter than those we did not elect, and history does not suggest that they always make wise decisions—even if they were the popular choice. In part, we trust because the alternatives are even less trustworthy! But partly we trust because we have experienced trust—it seems reasonable, and it seems feasible. Ordinary people, like ourselves, seem capable of caring, of acts of both altruism and evil, and of lots of to-be-expected self-interest. What a good education in a democratic society means, and has always meant, is learning how to read one's community, how to best judge when trust is and is not called for, and what to trust people with and what to keep private. As the "us" has become both more universal and less like us, it has become more complicated. This is a good reason for sticking with public schools, with their greater potential for universality. But it is also a good reason to be sure that the schools we create can be built around such trust. And big schools can't. It may be that fewer citizens vote these days not because they are more ignorant than they once were about the Big Questions, but because they no longer believe they can do anything about the little questions that vex them most. They used to be able to look the guy they voted for in the eye, and he (probably not she) was often in a position to fix it up, before we got rid of human-sized local politics. Trust in the larger picture depends first on trust in the small ones. Schools are one place where we can restore the proper scale, and do it when kids are still impressionable and where the lessons learned might stick. And we might draw some adults into it while we're at it.

We are in a period of politics and school reform in which trust is at a low ebb. We are trying vainly to invent substitutes for it—data that will automatically trigger sanctions or rewards without the intervention of a single human heart or mind. There are none that do the job. If there were, we would have substituted them for democracy itself long ago. Heaven knows, we've tried. This would not even be a good way to run a judicial system, or to test drivers or cooks (something about human beings makes them hard to measure once and for all), and above all it's a terrible way to train future citizens to be members of democratic communities. There is no way such means will serve such ends. The sooner we accept this simple dilemma, the less time and money we will waste searching for fool's gold. And that includes our favorite substitute—test scores. If my son were in high school in Massachusetts these days he could breathe a sigh of relief. From now on the universities have promised to attend to nothing else but test scores—and eliminate the need to look at letters of recommendation or grade point averages or extracurricular life. They have noticed that the latter are fraught with the risk of subjectivity. That could be the death knell for the very idea of democracy—a society by definition ruled by the collective will of private subjectivities. Why not just give a test?

Besides anonymity and distrust, bigness leads the way to ever-increasing bureaucratization—and loss of local power. We already have too great a concentration of power in too few hands. Anything that helps disperse that power over matters of importance is to the good, and anything that threatens to remove still more power from local hands must be resisted. Resistance is the key to the preservation of democracy—while we figure out other ways, besides schools, to restore some semblance of balance. A balance of power is a key to democratic life, and we are close to losing it.

Finally, large schools lead the way to vouchers and marketplace fantasies. Ironically, the thing people believe they can get from vouchers is the chance to send their children to smaller, safer, and more personal schools. They want schools that stand for something, where they and their children are known, and that will respond to them quickly when necessary. In the name of economy and efficiency we are holding on to big schools while undermining the fiscal basis for all schools. Once we go the whole voucher way, especially using tax money to help for-profit schools to make money, the very raison d'être for public funding of other people's children begins to erode.

Finally, the data are convincing that—even on matters of serious academic work, learning to be lifelong learners, coping with college and real-life work, and closing the achievement gap between rich and poor or black and white—small schools work. They produce the kind of responsible and thoughtful bonds among students and between generations that help pull the young into the world of responsible adulthood.

CHAPTER 4

Who Leads Small Schools?

TEACHER LEADERSHIP IN THE MIDST OF DEMOCRATIC GOVERNANCE

G. Alfred Hess, Jr.

THE CHICAGO PUBLIC SCHOOLS were mandated to implement school-based management through the establishment of Local School Councils as a result of the Chicago School Reform Act of 1988 (P.A. 85-1418). These Local School Councils (LSCs) were comprised of six parents, two community representatives, two teachers, and the principal; in high schools, a student was also elected to the LSC. Thus, for a decade, schools in Chicago have been formally governed under a theory of democratic localism (Bryk, Easton, Kerbow, Rollow, & Sebring, 1998) that gives disproportionate voting strength to lay members of LSCs.

The small-schools movement emerged in Chicago several years after the reform act was adopted by the state legislature. Although in theory small schools could exist under any form of school governance, the generative literature on small schools has emphasized teacher leadership (see Meier, 1995). Small schools are frequently portrayed as having a small, cohesive group of teachers who can easily interact around a common faculty table and discuss all of the children in the school and their specific strengths and needs. Notice that the definition of a small school is rooted in the adult community, not the students. Such faculties may operate democratically, but the vision of teacher-led schools is contradictory to the vision of parent- and community-led schools. Not surprisingly, the small-schools movement in Chicago has struggled continuously with defining the appropriate leadership roles of teachers, principals, parents, and community members.

A Simple Justice: The Challenge of Small Schools. Copyright © 2000 by Teachers College, Columbia University. All rights reserved. ISBN 0-8077-3962-6 (pbk.), ISBN 0-8077-3963-4 (cloth). Prior to photocopying items for classroom use, please contact the Copyright Clearance Center, Customer Service, 222 Rosewood Dr., Danvers, MA 01923, USA, tel. (508) 750-8400.

Ironically, advocates for both the Chicago School Reform Act and the small-schools movement were motivated by the same deep commitment to changing the context of education for poor minority students who had fared poorly in the city's schools for years. During the 1980s, the Chicago Public Schools was a large, centralized school system, dominated by an extensive bureaucracy employing more than 4,000 non–school-based staff and organized into large schools. Whereas the average elementary school in Illinois outside of Chicago enrolled just under 350 students, the average city elementary school was nearly twice that size. The average district outside of Chicago in 1988 enrolled just 1,385 students in about four schools of about 350 students, while Chicago enrolled more than 410,000 students in 542 schools (an average of 756 students per school) and operated 36 high schools and 10 elementary schools with more students than the average district. The average *high school* in Chicago in 1994 enrolled 1,568 students, several hundred more students than in the average school *district* in Illinois excluding Chicago (Hess, 1991).

The city school system was doing a horrible job of preparing Chicago's youth for full and meaningful adult roles. In 1985, two of every five entering high school freshmen ended up dropping out (Hess & Lauber, 1985), and only one of the remaining three graduated reading at the national norms (Designs for Change, 1985). In 1989–90, the baseline year of the school-reform implementation effort, only 30.6% of 9th- and 11th-grade students read at the national norms (a figure that slipped to 20.5% by 1996) and fewer than a quarter of elementary students (23.5%) did so (Chicago Public Schools, Office of Accountability).

The advocates for both school-based management and small schools (some actors advocated both) were committed to trying to change this dismal record of failure with the city's low-income minority students. Thus, the scene was set for competing reform strategies, both of which had similar goals.

PRIOR EVIDENCE ON EFFECTS AND DISTRIBUTION OF SMALL SCHOOLS

My own research into the failings of the Chicago Public Schools led me into advocacy for both school-based management reforms and the creation of small schools. I began studying the Chicago Public Schools in 1980 as the school system was working to create a desegregation plan. This was a tumultuous time in education in Chicago. In December 1979, the school system had been unable to meet its payroll, leading to a holiday season strike by employees. With the system virtually bankrupt, a bailout scheme was devised by city leaders, particularly from the business community, state legislators, and the governor meeting in the Governor's Mansion over the New Year's holiday. A School Finance Authority (SFA) was created with the ability to borrow funds as bridge financing until the school system could return to fiscal stability. The SFA was given authority to monitor the system's finances, to require annually balanced budgets, and to prevent the schools from opening unless there was a balanced budget. The SFA's own finances were underwritten by assuming about 15% of the school district's property-tax revenue, thus further reducing the financially crippled district's resource base. The former members of the Board of Education were removed from office and a new, minority-dominated Board (a first in this city) was appointed with five Black, three Hispanic, and three White members.

Although restoring the district's fiscal stability was the new Board's primary focus, its minority majority moved quickly, during the waning days of the Carter administration, to settle a 4-year-old legal battle over desegregation with the U.S. Department of Justice. Desegregation had been the nation's primary vehicle for school reform during the 1960s and 1970s, an era that was just coming to a close as Chicago finally joined it.

The theory behind desegregation as a reform strategy was that the education of minority students was impaired because fewer resources were expended on the schools they attended, and that this underfunding would cease if minority students were attending schools with Whites. To be sure, the key testimony in the 1954 Supreme Court case that overturned legal segregation of the races in schools, *Brown v. Topeka Board of Education*, turned on the argument of social scientists that separateness created a stigma of inferiority such that "separate" could never be "equal" (the key component of the 1898 *Plessey v. Ferguson* decision that *Brown* overturned). However, the desegregation reform strategy had more to do with giving minority students access to equal resources. Thus, the initial desegregation plans had to do with closing all-Black schools and integrating their students into existing all-White schools. This strategy for mixing students seemed to "work" in many communities in the South, where Blacks and Whites lived in the same communities and within easy walking distance of the same schools, although some African American scholars suggest that desegregation actually lowered the level of academic achievement of Black students by reducing the impact of African American teachers for these students (Foster, 1993; Ladson-Billings, 1994). Desegregation became more difficult in Southern cities, where the residential patterns were more segregated over larger distances, necessitating extensive busing. In Northern cities, the distances were even greater, and the backlash against busing became quite violent.

Chicago, because of the political clout of the Richard J. Daley machine, which claimed credit for electing John Kennedy president in 1960, was able to avoid desegregating its schools during the 1960s and 1970s (see Hess, 1984, for a fuller account of this history). By 1980, only 18% of Chicago's students were White. In the city's high schools, 77.3% of White students attended the 16 schools that were still majority White. Only 832 White students were enrolled in the 47 high schools with fewer than 15% White students. Fewer than 10% of the city's Black and Hispanic students attended majority White high schools. Among the elementary schools, 121 of 549 were majority White, enrolling two thirds of all White students in the city (67.5%), while 93% of Black students and 58% of Hispanic students attended schools with fewer than 15% White students (Hess & Warden, 1987). Ten elementary schools had more than 90% White students. Thus, while White enrollments had shrunk so that White students were a small minority of the total enrollment, they still mostly attended schools dominated by White enrollments and with largely White faculties. In 1978, under court order, faculties were desegregated across the city, causing great personal disruption and frequently leading to acrimonious racial groupings in faculties across the city, a pattern still evident in many schools 20 years later.

In 1980, the majority of White schools were better funded (largely because of having more senior faculty members who were higher on the systemwide pay scale), were generally smaller in size, and had higher levels of student achievement. The Desegregation Consent Decree obligated the school system to change that by eliminating the "all-White" schools. By 1986, we were able to report, "The Chicago Board of Education has successfully desegregated its predominantly White schools" (Hess & Warden, 1987, p. ii). At that time, 34% of White students attended majority White schools, down from 67.5% in 1980. The number of "integrated" high schools (schools with at least 30% White or Minority students) had risen from 14 to 21, while the number of integrated elementary schools had increased from 84 to 124. This desegregation was accomplished by massive voluntary busing (costing about $40 million annually) to magnet schools and to receiving schools outside the minority residential areas.

Although White students were now more integrated into minority schools, there were so few of them that most minority students were unaffected by this massive desegregation plan. Only 5.9% more minority high school students attended schools with as many as 30% White students and only 2.1% more minority elementary students attended such schools. A total of 11,472 additional minority students, out of 368,161 in the system, benefited from desegregation in the sense of attending schools with larger numbers of White students. The vast majority of minority students continued to attend racially isolated or predominantly minority schools where student achievement was low and financial resources continued to be less than in the integrated schools and significantly less than in the newly expanded number of magnet schools. As a reform strategy, desegregation did more for White students than it did for minority students. However, many White families seemed not to appreciate this benefit, as White enrollments continued to slip to about 11% of the student enrollment by 1988.

Although desegregation was the first arena I studied, and one that I revisited periodically (Easton & Hess, 1990; Hess, 1984; Hess & Warden, 1987), I spent most of the 1980s focused on two other issues: (a) the financing of the city schools and the distribution of those resources among schools across the city, and (b) studies of the dropout problem. The finance studies showed that the roots of the 1980 bankruptcy were not in higher expenditures but in reduced state support of public schools (Hess & Greer, 1984). However, they also showed that the school system distributed funds inequitably among the schools, giving the schools with 90–99% low-income students $355 less per pupil than those schools with low-income enrollments under 30% (Hess, 1995). The schools with fewer low-income students were also smaller.

But it was in the studies of dropping out that I really discovered the advantages of small schools. While I was the executive director of the Chicago Panel on School Policy (1983–96), we conducted five studies of the dropout problem. The first (Hess & Lauber, 1985) simply calculated a longitudinal cohort dropout rate for the school system as a whole and for each individual high school for the classes of 1982, 1983, and 1984. The longitudinal cohort calculation tracked all the entering freshmen from entry to departure from a Chicago school, calculating the number who graduated, transferred out of the system, or dropped out; 43% of the entering freshmen who did not transfer eventually dropped out. High school size did not seem to be a factor in determining dropout rates. The second study sought to determine why some high schools were more successful in graduating their students than were others with similar enrollments. It was a matched-pairs ethnographic study of eight high schools that demonstrated that how schools operated did make a difference (Hess, Kaplan, Liffman, Prindle, & Wells, 1986). This research was an important underpinning for the school-based management reform advocacy, showing that there were things within the control of schools that could be changed. However, it also showed there were systemwide practices that put city students at a disadvantage compared with students in the suburbs: shorter class periods and a more extensive use of study halls, for some of which students were not expected to come to school.

It was when we tried to assess the impact of elementary schools on high school dropout rates that we discovered the benefits of small schools. In 1987, we traced the students from our original study who were in the class of 1982 back to the elementary schools from which they had graduated, calculating an eventual dropout rate for each one (Hess & Greer, 1987). We found that 20% of the elementary schools provided their students with an adequate education, and their students mostly graduated from high school (graduation rates above 75%). Ten percent of the schools did very poorly, with the median reading score of graduating eighth graders at less than a third-grade level, and nearly two thirds of these students (64.5%) eventually dropped out. The middle 70% of schools plodded along, with between a third and a little over half of their students dropping out before completing high school. By contrast, the top 10% of the schools graduated the average student reading at levels within three months of the national norm, and 86% of the students from these schools eventually graduated from high school. On average, these schools had only two thirds as many eighth graders as did the average Chicago elementary school; schools in the second decile had graduation rates of 76% had only three quarters as many eighth graders. Thus, the schools with the lowest dropout rates were smaller schools, generally.

However, these schools also enrolled very few low-income students, few with limited English proficiency, and few minorities. Only 11% of the students in the schools in the two deciles with the highest graduation rates came from low-income families (compared with 41% of all of these eighth graders), and fewer than 200 out of 3,853 students in these schools were limited in English proficiency. Some 63% of the students in these schools were White, representing 43% of all White students in the eighth grade that year.

In 1978, Chicago had three types of schools graduating eighth graders (students who would become the high school class of 1982). There were kindergarten through eighth grade schools, middle schools (with various configurations from fifth through eighth to only seventh and eighth grades), and what we called de facto middle schools (K–8 schools that received large numbers of students from other schools for the last few years of elementary school). The worst performing of these groups of schools were the middle schools, which had an aggregate dropout rate of 45.2%, compared with 38.9% for all K–8 schools. Many of these middle schools had been built as part of a ghetto containment strategy during the 1960s and 1970s, positioned just inside the edge of the ghetto to avoid transferring Black students into underpopulated, predominantly White schools just across the residential racial dividing line. Not surprisingly, only 8% of the eighth graders in these middle schools were White, compared with

34.5% in all K–8 elementary schools. Correspondingly, 56.6% of the middle school students came from low-income families, compared with only 31.3% of K–8. Only 28% of the teachers in these middle schools had 12 or more years' experience, compared with 35% in the K–8 schools. Not surprisingly, 57% of the students graduating from middle schools entered high school with below-normal reading scores, the single most powerful predictor of eventual dropping out, whereas only 39% of K–8 students were at that level.

Thus, the best performing elementary schools tended to be smaller schools, but they also tended to enroll the least disadvantaged students. It is not surprising that they had the highest achievement outcomes, given the students they were enrolling. The issue of which students attended small schools would persist into the mid-1990s, leaving some uncertainty about the actual academic effects of small schools. The size differences among Chicago schools were not coincidental. They represented the results of a set of student assignment policies that provided school advantages to students who already were more advantaged than the average Chicago student.

THE REFORM YEARS

During the first few years after the enactment of the Chicago school reform legislation, most of the reform activists were focused on providing assistance to fledgling Local School Councils and the many new principals who were selected during the first 2 years of principal evaluations. LSC training in how to conduct meetings, how to understand school budgets, how to read standardized test scores, and how to evaluate principals consumed most of the reform advocacy groups and dominated the attention of foundations seeking to support the reform effort with grants to these groups.

Some reformers were also engaged in designing ways to document the effects of the reform. My organization, the Chicago Panel on School Policy, designed a 5-year longitudinal study of the implementation of the governance reforms in 14 representative Chicago schools (10 elementary and 4 high schools). The results of this research were released in nearly annual reports, culminating in a final report in 1996 (Hess, 1996). At the same time, the Chicago Panel contracted with Professor Anthony Bryk and the Center for School Improvement at the University of Chicago to study changes in student achievement so that we might identify those city schools that were improving; we intended to conduct a qualitative retrospective study to determine what had led to that improvement. In this way we hoped both to study the contemporary dynamics of schools implementing the reforms, only a few of which would likely be in the most successful group, and to look backward at the most successful to see what they had done differently from those with less success. Unfortunately, studying changes in student achievement proved far more difficult than any of us expected, and the study grew in scope and duration, finally appearing in 1998 (Bryk et al., 1998), 3 years after the close of the initial reform implementation period.

As reform implementation was starting, Maxey Bacchus, the director of the Chicago Public Schools Research Department, asked Bryk to develop a coalition of research groups that could help the school system discharge its legally mandated responsibility to monitor the implementation of the reforms. Bryk convened several meetings of groups of nonprofit and university researchers, developing the entity that was to become the Consortium on Chicago School Research. The Chicago Panel was one of the founding members of the Consortium, and Panel research staff worked closely with other researchers on many of the Consortium's initial research projects. One of those projects again underlined the value of small schools.

A survey of teachers, conducted in 1994, produced evidence that small schools were more congenial sites for school-based management to be an effective reform strategy (Sebring et al., 1995). The report of this survey showed that teachers were more positive about the reforms at the end of the initial implementation period than they had been when surveyed 3 years previously. It showed the importance of good school leadership and the diminishment of conflictual relationships at the city's elementary schools. It described the heightened sense of professional community that had emerged in many elementary schools and highlighted the much greater difficulty in developing program coherence or radical change in the city's high schools (as noted above, the level of reading achievement dropped significantly during the initial reform period in the high schools, even while it was improving in the elementary schools across the city). The report noted that program coherence was easier to accomplish in smaller schools and was not as prevalent in larger schools.

As the researchers sought to analyze their findings, they identified "cooperative adult effort toward school improvement" to be a key indicator of schools that were moving forward under reform. This indicator was composed of responses to a number of different questions on the survey instrument. A key finding of the report reflected which schools were more likely to manifest this "cooperative adult effort":

> Small elementary schools—where enrollment is less than 350 students—
> have consistently more positive reports on most measures of school leadership, parental involvement, and professional community and orientation.

In comparing the 30 highest- and 30 lowest-rated schools on a composite indicator of cooperative adult effort toward school improvement, there are six times as many small schools in the top group as in the bottom group (Sebring et al., 1995).

The researchers also found that integrated schools were highest on adult cooperation, whereas more negative reports came from predominantly African American schools. The highest-rated schools also had slightly more advantaged student populations, but the differences were not described as large. Schools with lower student mobility also were more likely to manifest cooperative adult effort. Thus, 8 years after the Panel's elementary-level dropout study had been released, there appeared to have been some closing of the gap between the most segregated schools and the most White-dominated schools, reflecting, perhaps, both the effects of desegregating the formerly majority White schools and improvements under reform in the racially isolated schools. The constant in both reports was the beneficial effects of small school size.

Although most reform advocacy groups focused on school-level training, and some returned to their traditional focus on research, there were some advocates and some teachers who focused on creating small, cohesive learning communities. Frequently, these small-schools initiators were emulating New York City, where small schools had been developing since 1974 (Fliegel, 1989). John Falco, an administrator in New York's District 4, came to speak at the University of Illinois at Chicago. Not long after, Debbie Meier, lead teacher at one of District 4's most well-known schools, Central Park East, spoke to a roomful of would-be imitators. But others in Chicago had already begun forming their own small schools.

The principal of Dumas Elementary, Sylvia Peters, one of the earliest principals to wholeheartedly embrace the school-based management reforms, recruited a group of like-minded teachers to revamp the educational approach at her inner-city, poverty-impacted, all-Black school and to expand its offerings in the fine arts. However, when Peters left Dumas to join a national school-reform group, the new principal was not sympathetic to their approach, and the like-minded group decided to try to start its own school. With the help of members of the business and foundation community, they started Foundations School in the building of Price Elementary, after failing to find a home in one of the city's museums. With about six teachers and 100 students, the school was established, an inquiry-based curriculum developed, and classroom and faculty practices established. However, it was not long before conflict arose between the two schools sharing a building but operating under completely different philosophies, time schedules, and orientations. Foundations moved to a nearby high school with quite a bit of underused space. Within a few years, though, the faculty was again looking for a new space. Other small schools were also developing, some with groups of teachers, others with as few as two.

By 1994, with the support of a new superintendent hired away from the New York City schools, the Board of Education announced an initiative in support of developing more small schools across the city. Outside support was coming from folks at the University of Illinois at Chicago (who had organized themselves as the Small Schools Workshop), from Leadership for Quality Education (an outgrowth of the business community's school-reform effort), and Business and Professional People in the Public Interest (BPI, a public-interest law firm that had previously focused on issues in public housing). In 1995, the latter two groups created the Small Schools Coalition to provide staff support to the burgeoning movement. The groups recruited representatives from other reform advocacy groups to serve on the coalition's policy advisory committee.

One of the first activities of the policy committee, on which I was privileged to serve, was to develop a statement of principles about small schools in Chicago. Although the research of the Chicago Panel and the Consortium on Chicago School Research had identified benefits that derived simply from a small number of students in a school, the Coalition sought a more circumscribed definition that included like-minded teachers, autonomy, an agreed-upon curricular focus, and inclusiveness. The first draft of these principles focused on the teacher leadership of small schools; for example, the statement included the following characteristics: "Like-minded Teachers. Small school faculties are cohesive, self-selected and share an educational philosophy." Although the introduction of the statement indicated that "The Coalition views small schools as enabled by, not in tension with, Chicago school reform," advocates of the 1988 school-based management reforms quickly pointed out the contradictions of such statements with the already legally mandated reform effort. Under the 1988 reform act, teachers are not "self-selected," they are selected by principals who are, in turn, selected by the Local School Councils (LSCs). Further, it is LSCs who determine the curricular focus of schools, not the faculty by itself. Thus, in the second draft of the principles, produced a week later, this characteristic was restated: "Like-minded Teachers and Families. Small school faculties are cohesive, self-selected and share an educational philosophy. Families and students then choose small schools whose goal they also share and they participate together in that school's growth and development" (March 22, 1998, draft). This revision broadened the focus beyond just teachers, but still did not deal with how teachers became part of the group. Nor did it deal with the relationships of the teachers to LSCs. The introduction of the statement of principles indicated that the goal of small-school development was to create "a personalized learning community that gives students a sense of purpose and belonging and teachers and parents a sense of authorship and ownership."

WHO CONTROLS? TEACHER-LED OR COMMUNITY-LED SCHOOLS?

Small schools that had been established under the conventional guidelines of the Chicago Public Schools were governed under the provisions of the 1988 reform act. A number gained independent status as a result of the act's requirements that each school have a principal and an LSC. Generally, these newly autonomous units had operated as branches of larger, nearby schools, with the principal of the larger school also serving that function for the branch, although the branch might have a head teacher who provided day-to-day leadership while also being responsible for his or her own class. These "smaller schools" had all the attributes of the average Chicago public school: they were governed under the 1988 Chicago School Reform Act with Local School Councils, principals, and teachers selected by principals on the basis of merit; they just had fewer students.

By contrast, the Small Schools Coalition mostly dismissed these schools as being not worthy of attention because they were not designed on the basis of an ideology of smallness. Thus, the term *small schools* became associated almost entirely with "schools within schools." When given the chance to create independent small schools (which would then be subject to the 1988 governance requirements), teacher leaders in the schools that combined to create the Cregier Multiplex in 1996 chose instead to create a fictive "Cregier School" with a principal and an LSC (though they received permission to structure the LSC somewhat uniquely under rules originally promulgated a decade earlier to deal with nontraditional special-purpose schools). Other schools were linked in a nongeographical "scatterplex" under a loosely presiding principal. Thus, there was an inherent conflict in organizational policy between (a) a school run by teachers, eschewing the educational necessity of a principal with administratively different status in favor of a more democratic faculty decision-making process, and (b) schools governed by LSCs and run by principals who had the right to make independent day-to-day decisions regardless of teacher input.

In 1995, the Illinois legislature amended the 1988 reform act to place ultimate responsibility for the school system in the hands of the mayor of Chicago. The systemwide governance structure was simplified, with a smaller governing Reform Board of Trustees directly appointed, without City Council review, by the mayor. Similarly, the school system's top five managers were directly appointed by the mayor, and the title of the system's leader was changed from General Superintendent to Chief Executive Officer. This more corporate administrative governance structure was designed to facilitate rescuing the school system from its chronic fiscal difficulties and included a streamlining of financial controls and decision-making such that the leadership of the school system had more control over the system's finances than had any previous Board of Education. When the city's budget director was appointed Chief Executive Officer, no one was surprised to find the system's fiscal difficulties solved in a matter of months.

The amendments also included a set of accountability provisions, originally proposed by the prior school system administration and its advisor, the University of Chicago's Anthony Bryk. A semiautonomous Academic Accountability Council was created to make recommendations on educational sanctions and remediation efforts. Provisions for central administration intervention into low-performing and failing schools were greatly expanded, and the ability of employee unions to resist or protect their members through grievance proceedings was reduced. In the hands of the new Chief Executive Officer, Paul Vallas, these provisions were used aggressively to focus schools on student outcomes. This focus on student outcomes was to have serious repercussions for teacher leaders in the small-schools movement.

In addition to the ideology of smallness noted above, many small-schools advocates also looked to more constructivist, inquiry-based forms of instruction. These advocates were interested in fostering student learning that they believed would not be easily captured by most standardized tests, particularly not by the tests used in the Chicago Public Schools. Thus, they resisted the emphasis on standardized testing. In an earlier victory, opponents of standardized testing had convinced the school system that variations in development were so great among students in kindergarten through second grade that schools were permitted to stop using standardized tests prior to third grade. But resistance to standardized testing in general was frowned upon by the new district leadership team, which was anxious to closely monitor schools with low student-performance levels.

Interestingly, it was Argie Johnson, superintendent from 1994 to 1995, who had introduced the idea that the school system should pay closer attention to the city's lowest-performing schools. She contended that these schools needed the most assistance from the school district and laid out a plan to identify the schools in the lowest third of the performance spectrum and provide them with extra help. Surprisingly, a number of the 1988 school-reform activists resisted this effort to identify underperforming schools on the basis of student achievement. Despite the primacy given to achieving national norms in student performance at every school in the system in the 1988 reform act, these activists preferred instead to distinguish schools on the basis of more nebulous "process" criteria of progress.

Although Johnson's efforts to focus support on the most needy schools never got off the ground, her successors implemented the idea with a vengeance. During the fall of 1996, 109 schools were placed on probation because fewer than 15% of their students could read at or above the national norms. The state also announced an academic watch list, which was dominated by Chicago schools. Small schools that resisted being measured by standardized test scores were given a sharp warning. In a celebration of grants given to support the initiation of some 45 new "small schools," the Chief Education Officer made it clear that these schools would have to show steady improvement of student achievement if they wanted to continue to exist.

Leaders of some existing small schools protested that standardized tests did not match the goals set by the school faculties. However, because they did not move aggressively to develop other outcome measures by which they would be willing to be held accountable, their protests sounded suspiciously like prereform teacher complaints that they should not be held accountable for the learning of their students. When several of the more established small schools continued to show little improvement in the proportion of their students reading at or above the national norms, the small-schools movement began to lose favor with the district leadership. For example, the small school Foundations dropped from having 20% of its student body at or above the norms in 1995 to 16.8% in 1996, dangerously close to the level for which schools were put on probation later that year. Fortunately for Foundations, the percentage at the norms rose to 24.7 in 1997 and 28.2 in 1998. This 11.4% improvement from 1996 was greater than the citywide improvement of 5.6% and worked to ease some of the pressure on small schools.

However, in the high schools, student achievement had plummeted between 1990 and 1996, with the percentage of 9th- and 11th-graders reading at or above the national norms falling from 30.6% to 20.5%. Several high schools, such as Chicago Vocational (CVS) and DuSable, had moved to create small schools that would encompass all of their students. In others, such as Harper, several small schools had been created that incorporated about a third of the school's enrollment. Both DuSable and Harper were placed on probation, and CVS escaped only after extensive intervention by reform activists. At the end of the 1996–97 school year, both DuSable and Harper were reconstituted (all staff positions were vacated, and although existing staff were allowed to reapply for their jobs, they were not guaranteed of being rehired). Small schools were "put on hold" at DuSable, and the plan to expand to small schools schoolwide at Harper was abandoned. Because the small-schools strategy dealt only indirectly with the quality of instruction provided in those schools, it was not seen by administrators in the district's central office as a powerful intervention strategy for boosting student achievement. In response, small-schools advocates began to develop "teacher talks" and other tactics to address the quality of teacher performance in the schools they were assisting.

WHERE ARE WE NOW?

At the end of 1998, small schools still retained the support of a group of fierce adherents and the ambiguous support of central office administrators seeking to help schools across the city improve. On the one hand, administrators have been disappointed by student achievement changes in many small schools. Logistical and personnel difficulties in a number of small schools have contributed to more negative opinions among some administrators. However, generally better student performance in small schools within larger schools has been encouraging, although such results have been continually subject to the counterclaim that these schools simply "creamed" the better performing students into their midst. On the other hand, despite ambiguity about the ultimate value of the existing small schools, support was provided for the establishment of others and the school system embraced the General Assembly's enabling legislation by creating 15 charter schools in the city (the only jurisdiction in Illinois to fully embrace the notion of charter schools).

Small schools seem to have found a niche in the Chicago school system. However, it appears that this niche is a marginal one—a place for innovative teachers to attempt something different in school design and operations. At one point, as a task force was putting together a design for high schools that would call for radical restructuring focused on developing enhanced personalism and greater academic press, it was proposed that all large high schools would be broken up into small schools, with six or eight in a building. But that proposal was rejected by the administration and by the Reform Board of Trustees. Thus, the small-schools strategy remains a marginal one, with advocates seeking to parlay individual instances of success into wider support and expanded numbers. That the efforts continue is encouraging. That these efforts ultimately will prove successful in bringing about the extensive use of small schools to improve student learning is less assured.

REFERENCES

Bryk, A. S., Easton, J. Q., Kerbow, D., Rollow, S., & Sebring, P. B. (1998). *Charting Chicago school reform: Democratic localism as a lever for change.* Boulder, CO: Westview Press.

Chicago Panel. (1988). Illegal use of state Chapter I funds. Paper distributed by the Chicago Panel on Public School Policy and Finance.

Designs for Change. (1985). *The bottom line: Chicago's failing schools and how to save them.* Chicago: Designs for Change.

Easton, J. Q., & Hess, G. A., Jr. (1990). *The changing racial enrollment patterns in Chicago's schools.* Chicago: Chicago Panel on Public School Policy and Finance.

Fliegel, S. (1989). Parental choice in East Harlem schools. In Joe Nathan (Ed.), *Public schools by choice* (pp. 95–112). Minneapolis: Institute for Learning and Teaching.

Foster, M. (1993). Savage inequalities: Where have we come from? Where are we going? *Educational Theory, 43*(1), 23–32.

Hess, G. A., Jr. (1984). Renegotiating a multicultural society: Participation in desegregation planning in Chicago. *The Journal of Negro Education, 53*(2), 132–146.

Hess, G. A., Jr. (1991). *School restructuring Chicago style.* Thousand Oaks, CA: Corwin.

Hess, G. A., Jr. (1995). *Restructuring urban schools: A Chicago perspective.* New York: Teachers College Press.

Hess, G. A., Jr. (Ed.). (1996). *Implementing reform: Stories of stability and change in 14 schools.* Chicago: Chicago Panel on School Policy.

Hess, G. A., Jr., & Greer, J. L. (1984). *Revenue shortfalls at the Chicago Board of Education.* Chicago: Chicago Panel on Public School Finance.

Hess, G. A., Jr., & Greer, J. L. (1987). *Bending the twig: The elementary years and dropout rates in the Chicago public schools.* Chicago: Chicago Panel on Public School Policy and Finance.

Hess, G. A., Jr., Kaplan, B., Liffman, P., Prindle, C., & Wells, E. (1986). *"Where's Room 185?" How schools can reduce their dropout problem.* Chicago: Chicago Panel on Public School Policy and Finance.

Hess, G. A., Jr., & Lauber, D. (1985). *Dropouts from the Chicago public schools.* Chicago: Chicago Panel on Public School Policy and Finance.

Hess, G. A., Jr., & Warden, C. (1987). *Who benefits from desegregation?* Chicago: Chicago Panel on Public School Policy and Finance.

Ladson-Billings, G. (1994). *The dreamkeepers.* San Francisco: Jossey-Bass.

Meier, D. (1995). *The power of their ideas: Lessons for America from a small school in Harlem.* Boston: Beacon Press.

Sebring, P. B., Bryk, A. S., Easton, J. Q., Luppescu, S., Thum, Y. M., Lopez, W. A., & Smith, B. (1995). *Charting reform: Chicago teachers take stock.* Chicago: Consortium on Chicago School Research.

CHAPTER 5

John Dewey
as a Philosophical Basis
for Small Schools

William H. Schubert

REQUENTLY, I AM ASKED TO CONSULT on ways to help teachers and administrators to revise and improve their curriculum. To stimulate the interests of these individuals and help them embrace the project of curriculum improvement, I have developed a repertoire of strategies, often beginning with what might be called educational entertainment.

Ever since I mustered the courage to role-play as a prehistoric man with sixth graders during my elementary-school teaching days, I have enjoyed conjuring up characters to challenge others to consider a wider range of ideas and dispositions. For example, I recall coteaching a unit on world religions, and as a culminating activity, we role-played as a man and woman talking about religion, while our students were challenged to determine what religion we represented. When controversies arose in class, even about something so mundane as why we have to learn to divide fractions, I often would role-play as an advocate of one position after another to illustrate a diversity of possible viewpoints on the topic. As I became a teacher of curriculum studies, I began to develop several personae to represent different tendencies I found to recur in curriculum history (e.g., Schubert & Lopez, 1980; Schubert, 1986). For 2 decades these "guest speakers" (the *social behaviorist, intellectual traditionalist, experientialist, critical reconstructionist*, and others) have been frequent visitors to my classes and consultancies.

A Simple Justice: The Challenge of Small Schools. Copyright © 2000 by Teachers College, Columbia University. All rights reserved. ISBN 0-8077-3962-6 (pbk.), ISBN 0-8077-3963-4 (cloth). Prior to photocopying items for classroom use, please contact the Copyright Clearance Center, Customer Service, 222 Rosewood Dr., Danvers, MA 01923, USA, tel. (508) 750-8400.

BRINGING JOHN DEWEY TO SMALL SCHOOLS

Several years of interaction with teachers in Chicago and across the United States have taught me that many of the teachers who want to try small schools have become frustrated with the large, impersonal schools in which they have worked. They are quick to concede that smaller groups would help them improve what they can provide for students. They also want to break down the isolation of teachers from one another and from students, and enable them to meet in small groups. They hope that smaller units of people will bring more worthwhile educational experiences. However, most of those who try to design small schools find that this jump from a smaller structural arrangement of teachers and students to greater meaning and worth in their pursuits is far from automatic.

It is precisely to the transformation necessary to bridge this gap that much of the work of the Small Schools Workshop in Chicago has devoted time and effort. Moreover, it is here, too, where members of this group invited me to enter the scene. They knew that I taught that the basis of educational reform lay in addressing fundamental curriculum questions, that is, questions of worth: What is worth knowing, experiencing, needing, being, becoming, overcoming, contributing, and sharing? How does one pursue and realize these considerations of worth? How does one help others (policy-makers, educators, parents, students, and others) to pursue such questions? Who benefits from that which is alleged to be worthwhile, and who doesn't? Who decides what is worthwhile, and who should decide?

Beginning in 1996, I brought in my "guest speakers" to many of these schools (as illustrated in the format of a play, dialogue, or multilogue; Schubert, 1996, 1997). Sometimes I would "bring" Dewey (e.g., Schubert, 1987). These "speakers" seemed to help teachers release their imaginations (see Maxine Greene, 1995) and consider new possibilities for themselves and their students as well as different kinds of public spaces in which they might interact in an effort to discover new educational possibilities. As my "speakers" (who bore a striking resemblance to me) made their presentations, these builders of small schools (teachers, administrators, and sometimes parents and students) would engage with them in dialogue, question ideas, clarify ideals, and begin to reflect on possibilities for the experiences they hoped to provide through small schools.

At least during our encounters, these designers of small schools could step apart from their daily pressures to consider new possibilities. Even as their lives were surrounded by the difficult and complicated demands of the state, the school district, standardized test-makers, publishers of instructional materials, national agendas, and more, they seemed to relish the time to reflect. Often, the teachers would want to know more about some of the neo-Progressive notions that seemed intriguing but alien to the realities they experienced. Thus, in 1996, at a Summer Institute developed by the Small Schools Workshop for teachers from many small schools, I was asked to "bring" John Dewey, who this time would return to Earth to share ideas with small-schools teachers who wanted to build progressive alternatives. I was not certain I was up to the task.

CONVEYING DEWEYAN PERSPECTIVE

The Institute took place at a wooded camp on a beautiful lake in Wisconsin. In a rustic conference hall, lights were flicked, emblematic of a seance, and I proceeded to relate who I (as Dewey) was. I made it clear that I was not the admiral, the explorer, the presidential candidate, the library decimal system creator, or the Disney duck. Instead, I was John Dewey: the philosopher, educator, activist, parent, and public intellectual. Background for this was derived from Dykhuizen (1973), Nathanson (1951), Ryan (1995), Westbrook (1991), and others, as well as from Dewey's many writings.

In the context of Dewey's life, I tried to share some of his key ideas— not only ideas drawn from his books on education but also those that infused his larger public philosophy. I was invited back in the summers of 1997, 1998, and 1999, and the appearance of Dewey at the Summer Institute has become something of a tradition—an opportunity to interact with Dewey. Still, I worry that I may not be responding to teachers' queries as Dewey would have. Nevertheless, I try my best, because the interest is high and the teachers may not all want to (or have time to) pursue Dewey's work on their own.

Over the years I have tried different approaches to conveying the messages of Dewey through role-playing. Sometimes, Dewey would symbolically relate some of his key beliefs to events that occurred during the year of his birth, 1859. In that year Darwin published his *Origin of the Species*, which relates to Dewey's emphasis on growth, change, and breaking with the dominant paradigm; surely, Dewey's work did that. Or, maybe, with Deweyan protégé L. Thomas Hopkins (e.g., 1937, 1941, 1954), the Darwinian influence can be seen in learning envisioned as a biological process that moves (as in the growth of cells) from expansion to differentiation to integration—continuously respiraling through the inherently natural process of development and maturation. Too, in 1859, Horace Mann died. Symbolic here is Dewey's commitment to carry on the project of universal education and his quest to determine what that might entail in a democratic society. To enable democracy in an unequal society, however, requires that protest and activism occur, as symbolized by John Brown's Raid, which also took place in 1859.

Usually, I remind the audience that Dewey—who lived from before the Civil War to the Korean War—had ample opportunity to claim warranted assertability for his admonition that we should learn from experience and respond to inequities. From his wandering in forests near Burlington, Vermont, with siblings and neighbor children to his exposure to New England town meetings, emergent industrialization, and one-parent family status while his father was in the Civil War, I try to draw a portrait of a child learning from experience. From his work as a high school teacher in the boom town of Oil City, Pennsylvania, I try to show his concerns as a teacher and his quest for intellectual pursuits as he worked on articles to submit to William Torrey Harris, editor of the *Journal of Speculative Philosophy*, and returned to the natural settings near the University of Vermont to walk and speculate with H. A. P. Torrey, his philosophy professor of earlier undergraduate days. All this was a basis for Dewey's entering doctoral studies at Johns Hopkins University and beginning his distinguished career in philosophy. To show the expanse of his philosophy I bring many of his books and match some of them with his contributions to the perennial categories of philosophy: metaphysics (e.g., *Experience and Nature*, 1925), epistemology (e.g., *Knowing and the Known*, with Bentley, 1949), axiology (e.g., *Democracy and Education*, 1916), ethics (*Ethics*, with Tufts, 1932), logic (*Logic: The Theory of Inquiry*, 1938b), aesthetics (e.g., *Art as Experience*, 1934a), politics (e.g., *The Public and Its Problems*, 1927), and theology (e.g., *A Common Faith*, 1934b). Interestingly, each of these works overlaps into each of the other areas, demonstrating the need for continuous reconstruction in philosophy to address all of the enduring questions about life's mysteries.

I like to emphasize the integration of Dewey as philosopher and Dewey as activist. For instance, I do this by having Dewey recount personal activities such as the following: Dewey's support of freedom of speech through the opening of his home to Maxim Gorky when, in 1906, Gorky was shunned by U.S. hotels for bringing a mistress on his lecture tour; similarly, Dewey's later (early 1940s) defense of Bertrand Russell's right to deliver lectures in the United States on his radical ideas about marriage and morals, even though Dewey did not agree with Russell on these matters; Dewey's involvement in Jane Addams's Hull House in Chicago, 1892–1904, raising his consciousness of the plight of the poor and the need for social justice; Dewey's participation in efforts to found the NAACP and probable association with W. E. B. DuBois in that effort; Dewey's staunch support of women's suffrage (1911–19), even once absent-mindedly carrying a sign that said, "Men can vote, why can't I?" Moreover, Dewey's activism also included efforts in 1916 to help found the American Civil Liberties Union; his work to support collective action by helping to found the original teachers union in New York City in 1916, later becoming a charter member of the American Federation of Teachers and the first president of the American Association of University Professors in 1915; his presidency of the Peoples Lobby and chairmanship of the League for Independent Political Action in 1929; his role as a member of the 1937 Commission of Inquiry into the Charges against Leon Trotsky, then exiled in Mexico; and furthering his stature as a public intellectual through his many commentaries in such publications as the *New Republic* and *The New York Times*. Connected with all of this is, of course, Dewey's array of lecture tours and consultations in Europe, China, Russia, Japan, Turkey, Mexico, and more.

I frequently have Dewey point out, too, that it may make sense to note how the titles of his books can be seen as symbols of his career-long crusade against dualistic (either–or) thinking. His book titles often consist of two key words linked by the conjunction *and*. If we simply convert the word *and* to *is* in our mind's eye, we can get a glimpse of the synthesis he tried to convey in some of his major works. For instance, we then see that democracy *is* education (from *Democracy and Education*, 1916), the school *is* society (from *The School and Society*, 1899), the child *is* the curriculum (from *The Child and Curriculum*, 1902), experience *is* education (from *Experience and Education*, 1938a), experience *is* nature (from *Experience and Nature*, 1925), liberalism *is* social action (from *Liberalism and Social Action*, 1935), human nature *is* conduct (from *Human Nature and Conduct*, 1922), philosophy *is* civilization (from *Philosophy and Civilization*, 1931a), the public *is* its problems (from *The Public and Its Problems*, 1927), freedom *is* culture (from *Freedom and Culture*, 1939), and knowing *is* the known (from *Knowing and the Known*, with Arthur Bentley, 1949).

On matters of education and schooling, I have Dewey relate that in 1894 he agreed to come to the University of Chicago from his philosophy professorship at the University of Michigan only because Chicago agreed with his unusual and imaginative request to create a department that integrated philosophy, psychology, and pedagogy and would further facilitate his desire to have a laboratory school. He usually needs to clarify, as he did in *The School and Society* (1899) and *The Child and the Curriculum* (1902), that his concept of a lab school was far from a teacher-training school or a mere demonstration school. Instead, it would be a testing ground for philosophical, psychological, and related ideas—a place to explore possibilities in human inquiry, culture, and democracy. He relates his notion of progressive organization of subject matter through which teachers enable learners to begin with the *psychological* (human interests and concerns) and grow educationally as they pursue projects by moving back and forth on a continuum between the *logical* (funds of personal, public, and disciplinary knowledge) and the *psychological*. Thereby, learning and growth progress through meaningful connections between extant knowledge and evolving interests.

ENGAGING SMALL-SCHOOL EDUCATORS IN DEWEYAN REFLECTION

After role-playing as Dewey, and after seeing teachers rekindle their original interest in teaching, I try to build upon this rekindling with a number of small-group events that encourage participating educators to recall powerful learning experiences in their own lives (see McClain and Schubert, 1997). For instance, I ask them to begin by individually jotting down a skill or body of knowledge that they are glad to have—something they can do well or know a lot about that others recognize and tap. Or, I ask them to think of a deeply held value or belief that guides their life. Then, forming small groups, I encourage them to tell stories about milestones on the pathway to that skill, knowledge, or value. What experiences, in other words, helped them get to the place that they are now? The stories often begin with their earliest childhood memories, and gradually they reveal a timeline of events that refined and augmented the skill, knowledge, or value they are relating. As they reflect on the stories shared, I ask that they work together to excavate the conditions that have contributed to the development of the skill, knowledge, or value that is so meaningful to them today. I remind them that what they are doing in this activity is studying profound learning—their own and that of their colleagues. Through this reflection the participants begin not only to reflect on what has contributed to the profound learning that they have experienced, but they also start asking how they can provide conditions of such learning for their students in their small schools.

I have devised many such activities to move into this kind of questioning in different ways; however, the main point is that the activities (started by the role-played Dewey and other speakers) remind educators of their reasons for being teachers: namely, that they entered this profession because they wanted to help develop meaning, a sense of direction, and relevance in the lives of young persons. For many educators, I have found that preoccupation with standards, benchmarks, goals, tests, raising the bars, and accountability measures has pushed their original reasons for being educators to the sidelines. By opening teachers up again to these original motivations, I have found that they can release their imagination, wisdom, and insight to create small schools that in turn speak to the genuine motivations of students. It is not that easy, of course. Great struggle is required. So is great vision of what might be possible. At this point we can turn to the utopian vision described by John Dewey in 1933.

QUESTIONS OF SUBSTANCE BASED ON
DEWEY'S UTOPIAN IMAGE OF EDUCATION

While it is indeed valuable to say that smaller size in schools is a key to meaningful reform, this is necessary but surely not sufficient. Moreover, to have faculties that choose to work together, to have them be small enough to sit around a table, and to have them want to bring meaning to students' activities are all admirable. Still, this is not enough. To say that small schools can be of any kind, supportive of any ideology, is too lax a stance. I contend here that certain commonly valued images of what it means to learn and grow in worthwhile ways must guide the work of small schools. Small is form more than it is substance. Small schools must address the substance of their advocacy.

In Dewey's short statement on utopian schools (1933 [reprinted in Boydston, 1989]; page citations in following paragraphs refer to the Boydston volume), wherein he writes creatively as if he is a reporter who has just visited Utopia, I find a challenge that I now want to add to the deliberations of those who seek to design and build small schools. I will sketch salient dimensions of Dewey's challenge in the form of six central questions. In addressing these questions, I ask readers to further ask the haunting and overarching question: Can modifications of schools as the institutions we know meet Dewey's challenge, or are whole new and fundamentally different contexts needed for the kind and quality of education he characterizes?

1. Can schools be unschooled?   This is the most modest and least radical way in which I can present Dewey's first challenge, for Dewey begins his presentation of utopian schools much more radically, by asserting that "The most Utopian thing in Utopia is that there are no schools at all" (p. 136). To prevent readers from turning away, I suppose, he adds a slight disclaimer, saying: "Or, if this idea is so extreme that we cannot conceive of it as educational at all, then we may say nothing of the sort at present we know as schools" (p. 136). He goes on to characterize "assembly places" where young and old (e.g., parents, children of all different ages, grandparents, any interested in children's welfare) gather together to mutually enrich each other. Some of the characteristics of these places include large grounds, gardens, orchards, greenhouses, well-furnished homes, open spaces, historic museums, scientific laboratories, books everywhere, and a central library. Dewey specifies that there are "no mechanical rows of screwed-down desks" (p. 136). He indicates that there would be "a much greater variety of equipment," which makes me wonder, if applied to today's availability, what computer and multimedia configurations Dewey would favor. Situations, circumstances, and settings of Dewey's utopian vision seem more closely attuned to the "unschooling" of John Holt (1976, 1981) and his followers. Holt advocated a form of home education that did not resemble current schooling; its point was to overcome the limitations of schools as we know them and create new forms of public and private educational space.

2. Can schooling be based on mutual teaching and learning of all involved?
I refer here to Dewey's vision of utopian education as carried out within multiple age groups. By this he means not only older and younger children together, but also adults of varying levels of experience. He even suggests that having children of their own is a valuable experiential base for teachers. I recall from our Teacher Lore Project (Schubert & Ayers, 1999) that some teachers have indicated considerable transformation in their outlook on teaching occurred when they had children of their own— especially influencing their relationships with students and parents. Teachers, Dewey indicated, almost could be self-selected—it would be evident who among the older children and adults were "fond of children," and "who among them have the taste, interest and the kind of skill which is needed for effective dealing with the young" (p. 137). Too, he observed the need for "a very similar process of natural selection by which parents are taken out of the narrower contact with their own children in the homes and are brought forward in the educational nurture of larger numbers of children" (p. 137). Dewey likened their education to the ways "painters were trained in . . . Italy, when painting was at its height" (p. 137). Here, he saw "adult leaders . . . combine special knowledge of children with special gifts . . . [and] associate themselves with the young in carrying on some line of action" (p. 137). In essence, he suggests that the older members publicly *do* their interests, and the younger members gradually join the process in more complex and responsible ways. In special areas of expertise, capability, and experience, younger members could doubtless teach and inspire older members as well.

3. Can schools refrain from a preoccupation with preordained purposes, goals, and objectives?   Goal-driven schooling is almost the only kind of schooling we know. Dewey said he was programmed with that mindset, too, so he asked the Utopians about the purposes of their objectives, and here it is especially worth quoting: "Nothing puzzled me more than the fact that my inquiry after objectives was not at all understood, for the whole concept of the school, of teachers and pupils and lessons, had so completely disappeared that . . . my utopian friends thought I was asking why children should live at all, and did not take my questions seriously"

(p. 138). Does schooling, as we know it, even the bare-bones structures of it, live up to with the utopian response, elaborated as, "Of course, we, the Utopians, try to make their lives worth while to them; of course, we try to see that they really do grow, that they really develop." Dewey goes on to say that if he had to distort the fact that purpose was "ingrained" in the activities of children and youth in an attempt to restate Utopia's fundamental purpose in language that we could comprehend: "it might be said to be the discovery of the aptitudes, the tastes, the abilities and the weaknesses of each boy and girl, and then to develop their positive capacities into attitudes and to arrange and reinforce the positive powers so as not to cover up the weak points but to offset them" (p. 138). Dewey emphasized a major point throughout his essay that the Utopians discover and develop the *positive powers* of students. Can this be said of schools as we know them with their vast tentacles all designed to dissect and magnify deficits in students, comparing them competitively with one another? (See Ayers, 1993, for a stark critique of the deficit-mindedness of educators.)

4. Can schools resist and overcome the tendency to see education as subject-matter centered?   The proposed correction is not to make schooling bounce to the opposite or child-centered extreme, a prime deficit of too much practice in the Progressive Era. When Dewey reported asking about how methods of teaching he found practiced among Utopians would ever ensure subject matter coverage, he was met again by their disbelieving gazes. The Utopians asked in return "whether in the period from which I [Dewey] came for a visit to Utopia it was possible for a boy or girl . . . to grow up without learning the things which he or she needed to learn— because it was evident to them that it was not possible . . . to grow up without learning" (p. 138). Dewey inquired further if "it was true that in our day we had to have schools and teachers and examinations to make sure that babies learned to walk and to talk" (p. 138). As John Holt has also pointed out on many occasions, walking and talking are much more complex than most of the things traditional schools try to teach, and we have relatively few nontalkers and nonwalkers (as compared with those who, despite years of browbeating have not learned reading, math, grammar, or other school *staples*). This sorry state of affairs is precisely due to our propensity to decontextualize, overanalyze, and make meaningless these schooled skills. Can schools move away from this? For elaboration in a similar vein, I recommend Dewey's little-known book *The Way Out of Educational Confusion* (Dewey, 1931b), wherein he argues that the major culprit that prevents meaning and relevance is the artificial and arbitrary separation of subject matter areas. Although such separation may be a fine organizational device for the construction of encyclopedias, it is a patently improper basis for pedagogy.

5. Can schools overcome the larger societal mindset of the capitalistic ethos that makes almost every value into a thing to be acquired? In this consideration we re-open George S. Counts' (1932) question of whether schools dare (or even could) change the social order and its pervasive miseducation due to racial prejudice (so poignantly depicted in the little cited work of Carter G. Woodson, 1933). In this same period, Dewey drives to the quick of our basic values by providing a startling explanation of why the utopian education he admires never has been practiced deeply and widely. Dewey says, "It was during these conversations [with the Utopians] that I learned to appreciate how completely the whole concept of acquiring and storing away things had been displaced by the concept of creating attitudes by shaping desires and developing the needs that are significant in the process of living" (p. 139). Dewey goes on to indicate that the latter was almost impossible to comprehend with a 20th-century orientation, for "the Utopians believed that the pattern which exists in economic society in our time affected the general habits of thought; that because personal acquisition and private possession were such dominant ideals in all fields, even if unconsciously so, they had taken possession of the minds of educators to the extent that the idea of personal acquisition and possession controlled the whole educational system" (p. 139). Today, achievement is a test score rather than accomplishments in the world, education is a credential or certificate and not increased meaning and direction in life, and school is a place to autocratically hold and sort children during working hours instead of a place for them to freely grow personally and democratically in association with a diversity of others.

Dewey poignantly characterizes (through the lenses of the Utopians) our debased educational practices as "the kind of measure and test of success which had to prevail in an acquisitive type of society" (p. 139). This, he says, includes the competitive methods of appeal to rivalry, the use of rewards and punishments through examinations, promotions, and the like. Dewey's observation that "we had come to regard all study as simply a method of acquiring something . . . and thought of learning and scholarship as the private possession of the resulting acquisition" (p. 139) seems at least as true today as it was in Dewey's time, as is evident in the treatment of human motivation in the conflicting context of both our competitive ethos and democratic education provided by John Nicholls (1989).

Dewey then claims that the utopian form of education was possible only because of large-scale social reconstruction that displaced the acquisitive society. In his words, "the abolition of an acquisitive economic society had . . . made possible the transformation of the centre of emphasis from learning (in our sense) to the creation of attitudes" (p. 139). This "great educational liberation came about when the concept of external attainments was thrown away and when they started to find out what each individual person had . . . from the beginning, and then devoted themselves to finding out the conditions of the environment and the kinds of activity in which the positive capacities of each young person could operate most effectually" (p. 139). Dewey goes on to claim that in an acquisitive society education always defers enjoyment and satisfaction—the promises and rewards being brittle motivational constructs, myths always out of reach. He reveals that the Utopians "said that there was no genuine production without enjoyment . . . [and] the only education that really could discover and elicit power was one which brought these powers for immediate use and enjoyment" (pp. 139–140). This revelation alone explains the frustration, despair, rebellion, disappointment, apathy, and hopelessness so widespread not only among the inhabitants of schools today but also in the general citizenry.

6. Can the "sense of positive power" as the fundamental attitude that inspired Dewey's utopian education occur in schools devised in an acquisitive society?   Dewey concludes his essay, his challenge, by briefly characterizing dimensions of the attitude that enables positive power to develop and grow. He insists that this involves "elimination of fear, of embarrassment, of constraint, of self-consciousness . . . feeling of failure and incapacity." Moreover it fosters and inspires "the development of a confidence, of readiness to tackle difficulties, of actual eagerness to seek problems instead of dreading them and running away from them" (p. 140). To do this requires "a rather ardent faith in human capacity" and the "capacity of the environment to support worthwhile activities" (p. 140).

THE QUESTION OF HOPE FOR THE FUTURE OF EDUCATION, SMALL OR LARGE

Educators who want to create small schools to improve educational experiences for students must address the questions raised by Dewey's utopian vision. Moreover, they must ask what it is that can give them hope. Is hope warranted if the acquisitive society surrounds and interpenetrates all that we do in the name of education? In the society of acquisition permeated by mistrust, competition, contempt, disdain, control, and belittlement built upon deficits and detractions, how may hope be achieved?

To see schools as the hegemonic representation of the depths of an acquisitive society and, at the same time, as the torchbearer for the democratic prospect, is what David Cohen (1999) recently called the Deweyan Paradox. In light (or dark) of this paradox, can hope come alive? Where does hope reside at a time when we hear dedicated educators admonish parents to *Teach Your Own* (Holt, 1981) *Instead of Education* (Holt, 1976) in schools, to realize that schooling is a process of *Dumbing Us Down* (Gatto, 1992), to heed *The End of Education* (Postman, 1995) as we know it, and to learn from grass-roots cultures that offer insight for *Escaping Education* (Prakash and Esteva, 1999)? In one of his last books Paulo Freire (1994) called for *A Pedagogy of Hope* and Herb Kohl (1998) called for *A Discipline of Hope.* The message of both points toward a less acquisitive society. With hopefulness and purpose, Dewey pushes those who want to build small schools (or otherwise construct reform within the current practices of schooling) far beyond preoccupation with test scores, bridge programs, state goals and testing, the raising of "bars," and other facades of reform to the question of where we want to go and what we want to be as human beings.

So, beyond my personification of Dewey, and beyond the activities that encourage reflection on the examples revealed in our own best learning experiences, lies a great challenge. The challenge is to embody and extend the activist qualities of Dewey and struggle to overcome the pervasive acquisitiveness that entraps us. The question of hope for transformation through a less acquisitive society is a struggle already given impetus through the efforts of educators in small schools. Their example extends to a social and personal state of experience that furthers Dewey's utopian vision of educational settings that realize and enhance the positive power of individuals, communities, experience, and culture.

REFERENCES

Ayers, W. (1993). *To teach: The journey of a teacher.* New York: Teachers College Press.

Boydston, J. A. (Ed.). (1989). *John Dewey, the later works* (Vol. 9). Carbondale: Southern Illinois University Press.

Cohen, D. (1999, April 23). *John Dewey: The Chicago years.* Paper presented at the annual meeting of the American Educational Research Association, Montreal.

Counts, G. S. (1932). *Dare the school build a new social order?* New York: John Day.

Dewey, J. (1899). *The school and society.* Chicago: University of Chicago Press.

Dewey, J. (1902). *The child and the curriculum.* Chicago: University of Chicago Press.

Dewey, J. (1916). *Democracy and education.* New York: Macmillan.

Dewey, J. (1922). *Human nature and conduct.* New York: Henry Holt.

Dewey, J. (1925). *Experience and nature.* London: Open Court.

Dewey, J. (1927). *The public and its problems.* New York: Henry Holt.

Dewey, J. (1931a). *Philosophy and civilization.* New York: Minton, Balch, & Co.

Dewey, J. (1931b). *The way out of educational confusion.* Cambridge, MA: Harvard University Press.

Dewey, J. (1933). Dewey outlines utopian schools. *The New York Times,* April 23, p. 7. [See Boydston, J. A. (1989) for text citation.]

Dewey, J. (1934a). *Art as experience.* New York: Minton, Balch, & Co.

Dewey, J. (1934b). *A common faith.* New Haven, CT: Yale University Press.

Dewey, J. (1935). *Liberalism and social action.* New York: G. P. Putnam's Sons.

Dewey, J. (1938a). *Experience and education.* New York: Macmillan.

Dewey, J. (1938b). *Logic: The theory of inquiry.* New York: Henry Holt.

Dewey, J. (1939). *Freedom and culture.* New York: G. P. Putnam's Sons.

Dewey, J., & Bentley, A. F. (1949). *Knowing and the known.* Boston: Beacon Press.

Dewey, J., & Tufts, J. H. (1932). *Ethics.* New York: Henry Holt.

Dykhuizen, G. (1973). *The life and mind of John Dewey.* Carbondale: Southern Illinois University Press.

Freire, P. (1994). *Pedagogy of hope.* New York: Continuum.

Gatto, J. (1992). *Dumbing us down: The hidden curriculum of compulsory schooling.* Philadelphia: New Society Publishers.

Greene, M. (1995). *Releasing the imagination.* San Francisco: Jossey-Bass.

Holt, J. (1976). *Instead of education.* New York: Delta.

Holt, J. (1981). *Teach your own.* New York: Dell.

Hopkins, L. T. (Ed.). (1937). *Integration, its meaning and application.* New York: Appleton-Century.

Hopkins, L. T. (1941). *Interaction: The democratic process.* Boston: D. C. Heath.

Hopkins, L. T. (1954). *The emerging self in school and home.* New York: Harper & Brothers. (1970 reprint by Greenwood.)

Kohl, H. (1998). *The discipline of hope: Learning from a lifetime of hope.* New York: Simon and Schuster.

McClain, M., & Schubert, W. H. (1997). Rekindling a sense of purpose: The Curriculum Improvement Program. *Educational Forum, 61*(2), 162–171.

Nathanson, J. (1951). *John Dewey: The reconstruction of the democratic life.* New York: Frederick Unger.

Nicholls, J. G. (1989). *The competitive ethos and democratic education.* Cambridge, MA: Harvard University Press.

Postman, N. (1995). *The end of education: Redefining the value of school.* New York: Vintage.

Prakash, M. S., & Esteva, G. (1999). *Escaping education: Living as learning within grassroots cultures.* New York: Lang.

Ryan, A. (1995). *John Dewey and the high tide of American liberalism.* New York: W. W. Norton.

Schubert, W. H. (1986). *Curriculum: Perspective, paradigm, and possibility.* New York: Macmillan.

Schubert, W. H. (1987). What is citizenship education? And who is JD? *Educational Leadership, 45*(2), 76–82.

Schubert, W. H. (1997). Character education from four perspectives on curriculum. In A. Molnar (Ed.). *The construction of children's character* (1997 NSSE Yearbook, Part II, pp. 17–30). Chicago: University of Chicago Press and the National Society for the Study of Education.

Schubert, W. H. (1996). Perspectives on four curriculum traditions. *Educational Horizons, 74*(4), 169–176.

Schubert, W. H., & Ayers, W. (Eds.). (1999). *Teacher lore: Learning from our own experience.* Troy, NY: Educator's International Press.

Schubert, W. H., & Lopez, A. L. (1980). *Curriculum books: The first eighty years.* Lanham, MD: University Press of America.

Westbrook, R. B. (1991). *John Dewey and American democracy.* Ithaca, NY: Cornell University Press.

Woodson, C. G. (1933). *The mis-education of the negro.* Washington, DC: Associated Publishers.

CHAPTER 6

Education for Activism

MISSISSIPPI'S FREEDOM SCHOOLS
IN THE 1960s

Charles M. Payne

S MALL SCHOOLS ARE PART of an activist trend in education that takes much of its inspiration from the Civil Rights Movement of the 1960s and the Freedom Schools and Citizenship Schools in particular. Schools and students were of central importance to the movement, and many of its leading lights—Ella Baker, Charles Cobb, Charles Hamilton, Myles Horton, and Septima Clark, to name but a few—were focused on education as a liberating tool and a center for social activism and critical thought.

In 1927, soon after she arrived in New York fresh out of Shaw University, Ella Baker started a class in Negro history at the Harlem YMCA. In 1929, Charles Hamilton Houston (Phi Beta Kappa at Amherst and the first Black man to serve on the *Harvard Law Review*) became dean of Howard University's Law School and immediately set about making it an instrument of struggle. A lawyer, he liked to say, is either a social engineer or a parasite. He fired faculty who could not keep up and flunked out students in droves. Thurgood Marshall came in with a class of 30, 8 or 10 of whom made it to graduation. Houston's motto was "No tea for the feeble, no crepe for the dead."

The legal talent that made possible the Supreme Court's 1954 *Brown v. Board* decision was nurtured—if that is the word for what these educators endured—largely at Howard. In 1932, Myles Horton opened the

This chapter is a revised version of Chapter 10 from *I've Got the Light of Freedom: The Organizing Tradition and the Mississippi Freedom Struggle*, 1995, Berkeley: University of California Press. Copyright © 1995 by University of California Press. Adapted with permission.

For information on contemporary Freedom School projects, visit http://www.edliberation.org/

Highlander Folk School in the Tennessee mountains. For the next several decades, this school would train Blacks and Whites as union organizers, community leaders, and civil rights activists. One of the projects that best exemplified Highlander's spirit was the Citizenship Schools that Septima Clark developed while she was Highlander's Director of Education. At one level, the Citizenship Schools taught people how to register to vote, but Miss Clark always understood that as a means to the more significant end of developing community leadership (Grant, in press; Horton, 1990; Kluger, 1977).

Self-consciously activist education has a long history among African Americans, but it is one of the least well-understood aspects of African American struggle that could have significance for today's small-schools activists. This chapter addresses one aspect of that history: the Freedom Schools that operated in Mississippi during the summer of 1964 and for a while thereafter.

Organizationally, the schools were the creation of SNCC-COFO. The Student Nonviolent Coordinating Committee had entered Mississippi in the summer of 1961 and shortly thereafter helped form the Council of Federated Organizations, a coalition of the state's civil-rights organizations for which SNCC provided the bulk of the manpower. From 1961 to 1964, SNCC-COFO waged a valiant campaign for the right to vote. Mississippi Whites responded with violence, sometimes lethal, against individual civil-rights workers, with constant police harassment, and with wholesale firings and evictions of people thought to be associated with the movement. In effect, the Federal government shrugged at all of it, including the murders. For some in SNCC, the last straw was the January 1964 murder of Louis Allen in McComb. Allen earlier had witnessed the slaying of NAACP member Herbert Lee, and it was that which probably led to his own death. At the time Allen was killed, SNCC-COFO was in the midst of discussing the possibility of bringing large numbers of White students into the state for the subsequent summer, partly because they had noticed that when White students had been in the state that fall to help with a Freedom Vote, the movement got far more attention than usual from the press and the FBI. In the wake of the killing of Allen and several others, it was decided that something had to be done to make the Federal government take a larger hand (Dittmer, 1994; Payne, 1995).

The something turned out to be the Mississippi Summer Project, bringing nearly 1,000 young people to the state, mostly White and well-to-do—the kind of people, Ella Baker noted, who could bring the concern of the nation with them, and the kind of people the Federal government was likely to try to protect, and in protecting them officials also would be offering some measure of protection to the activists based in the state. The volunteers were expected to run voter-registration campaigns, operate community centers, and conduct Freedom Schools.

The idea for the schools came from Charlie Cobb, a Howard University student who had been in Mississippi since 1962. During one of the early planning sessions, Cobb proposed that the Summer Project do something to address the impoverished nature of the education typically offered Black students in Mississippi. The education the state offered White youth was nothing to brag about, but what it offered Black students was outrageously underresourced in every way imaginable—teacher salaries, length of the school year, instructional materials, facilities. The city of Hattiesburg was spending $115 for each White child and $61 for each Black child; in Magnolia it was $59 against $1.35; in McComb it was just $30 for every White child's education but only 76 cents for every Black child (Holt, 1965, p. 102).

Obvious inequalities aside, Cobb, very much in the spirit of SNCC, was also concerned that many Black classrooms were autocratic in tone, stressing rote memorization rather than offering the kind of teaching likely to stimulate intellectual curiosity (Cobb, 1991; Dittmer, 1995). As Cobb wrote:

> Repression is the law; oppression a way of life. . . . Here, an idea of your own is a subversion that must be squelched; for each bit of intellectual initiative represents the threat of a probe into the why of denial. Learning here means only learning to stay in your place. . . . There is hope and there is dissatisfaction. . . . This is the generation that has silently made the vow of no more raped mothers, no more castrated fathers; that looks for an alternative to a lifetime of bent, burnt, and broken backs, minds and souls. Their creativity must be molded from the rhythm of a muttered "white son-of-a-bitch;" from the roar of a hunger bloated belly and from the stench of rain and mudwashed shacks. . . . What they must see is the link between a rotting shack and a rotting America. (quoted in Howe, 1984, p. 9)

Thus, Cobb wanted a component in the Summer Project that would "fill an intellectual and creative vacuum in the lives of young Negro Mississippians, and to get them to articulate their own desires, demands and questions . . . to stand up in classrooms around the state and ask their teachers a real question . . . [to] make it possible for them to challenge the myths of our society, to perceive more clearly its realities and to find alternatives and ultimately, new directions for action" (Cobb, 1991, p. 36).

The schools marked a turning point in the radicalization of SNCC in that they became part of a larger discussion of parallel institutions. If American institutions do not work for Black people, let us create institutions—political parties, unions, co-ops—that will. The increasing focus on institutions meant that SNCC was moving away from understanding American racism as just a matter of some White Americans having backward attitudes (Dittmer, 1994, p. 259; Fruchter, 1969).

Cobb envisioned the schools handling perhaps a 1,000 students of high school age. In fact, somewhere over 2,500 students actually showed up—many without the knowledge or approval of their parents—and their ages ranged from 7 to 70. The number of schools was increased from 25 to 41.

Part of the classwork consisted of traditional academic subjects. In Mississippi, though, traditional subjects often were not available in Black schools. Publicly supported Black schools tended not to offer typing, foreign languages, art, drama, or college preparatory mathematics. Apart from whatever intrinsic interest they held, these subjects were popular with students partly because they symbolized equality (an interesting contrast to an era when some Black students equate academic success with "acting White").[1] Teachers were encouraged to use a Socratic style of teaching: asking questions that drew on the experiences of students and trying to help them develop a larger perspective. Volunteers who were professional teachers often had more trouble adjusting to this teaching style than did the inexperienced.

When the students at Mt. Nebo School in Jackson walked into their first class they were greeted by a tall White woman who pointed to herself and said, "Je m'appelle Wendy Heil," then walked over to a student and asked, "Comment vous appellez-vous?" The joy was electrifying as the first student guessed and replied, "Ida Bell Johnson!" From that small beginning, without a using word of English during the entire class, Wendy picked up objects, pronounced the French names in exaggerated fashion, and had the students repeat them. Class ended with a reverberating "We Shall Overcome," sung in Mississippi French (Holt, p. 111).

Sally Belfrage (1965) describes a Freedom School scene in Greenwood:

> The children sat in small groups under trees on the lawn or on the steps of the church. More than a dozen were learning to speak French with a drawl; nearby, half as many were studying Spanish; and a group of three, German. . . . A few yards away another half dozen were conducting a creative writing class. . . . Their teacher was asking them to describe the difference between two stones, a rough light one and a smooth dark one. By the end of the summer they had their own mimeographed newspaper, *Freedom Carrier,* and had written and performed a play. (p. 90)

At their best the schools were an electric experience for teachers and students alike:

> [From Holly Springs] The atmosphere in class is unbelievable. It is what every teacher dreams about—real, honest enthusiasm and desire to learn anything and everything. The girls come to class of their own free will. They respond to everything that is said. They are excited about learning. They drain me of everything that I have to offer. . . .

> [From Meridian] If reading levels are not always the highest, the "philosophical" understanding is almost alarming: some of the things that our 11 and 12 years olds will come out with would never be expected from someone of that age in the North. . . . (Sutherland, 1965, pp. 93, 96)

Elizabeth Sutherland, who edited a collection of letters from volunteers noted that

> Classes in voter registration work and political play-acting were a success everywhere. With innate sophistication about their own plight, the kids pretended to be a Congressional Committee discussing the pro's and con's of a bill to raise Negro wages and "the con's" would discover neat parliamentary tricks for tabling it. Or they'd act out Senator Stennis and his wife having cocktails with Senator and Mrs. Eastland, all talking about their "uppity niggers." Sometimes they played white cops at the courthouse, clobbering applicants with rolled-up newspapers. (Sutherland, 1965, p. 102)

Not only did they understand the positions of Southern racists, but some of the youngsters knew a little about the temporizing of Northern liberals as well. One Greenwood boy in a role-play got President Kennedy to a T, down to the Boston accent: "The Federal government is not empowahed to act." (Belfrage, 1965, p. 90). Another role-playing project had students study history by portraying three generations in the life of a Black family.

Role-playing was also an important part of the Citizenship Curriculum, the most distinctive component of the material taught. It was built around a set of core questions, including

1. What does the majority culture have that we want?
2. What does the majority culture have that we don't want?
3. What do we have that we want to keep?

One unit of the curriculum asked students to compare their social reality with that of others in terms of education, housing, and employment. One section in particular called for them to compare the adjustment of Jews to

Nazi Germany. The "Introducing the Power Structure" unit tried "to create an awareness that some people profit by the pain of others or by misleading them." The unit on poor Whites tried to help students understand how the power structure manipulated the fears of that group as much as it manipulated Blacks. "Material Things and Soul Things" was a critique of materialism.

The last area of the Citizenship Curriculum was a study of the Civil Rights Movement itself. The section on nonviolence made sure to present it as something beyond a mere refraining from doing anyone physical harm; students were admonished to practice nonviolence of speech and thought as well. Always they were encouraged to understand the relationship between their individual situation and broader societal questions. Always they were encouraged to develop a new understanding of their capacity for change. The curriculum reflects how far discussion within SNCC had progressed beyond a narrow concern with civil rights. A full analysis of society was embedded in the thinking behind the schools.

Belfrage, a volunteer in Greenwood, tells the story of Amanda, who had flunked the registration test five times before she came to the Freedom School to learn to read. She was out of work at the time and "so poor that she couldn't afford a cigarette and would take one of mine with the gratitude of one just handed a fortune." She finally found a job but was fired 2 days later. She had been hearing at mass meetings that people from distant places all over the world were supporting the movement. Her employer was from Texas, which sounded pretty distant to Amanda, so she asked her employer if she ever went to mass meetings. The White lady fired her on the spot. Amanda showed up crying at the Freedom School that night.

> By the end of the summer, she knew a great deal, though not much of it was reading. She would rush to finish the day's allotted letters, then ask me questions about the movement, FDP, the world; the questions had stimulated others by the next lesson, but she had forgotten the letters we had done and they had to be repeated. We never got as far as "w," but Amanda became a block captain. (Belfrage, 1995, p. 94)

The schools were more successful in rural areas or in those urban areas where the movement had been strong. With so little for youngsters to do in rural areas, the schools became the focal point of teenage social life and an activity in which whole communities felt invested. ("When the Freedom School staff arrived in Carthage, the entire Negro community was assembled at the church to greet them; when, two days later the staff was evicted from its school, the community again appeared with pickup trucks to help move the library to a new school site.") In urban areas with little movement history and alternative ways for young people to spend their time, places like Greenville or Gulfport, it was much more difficult for the schools to have an impact (Holt, 1965, pp. 317–319).

There is some suggestive anecdotal evidence about the political effectiveness of the schools. In August, students from around the state held a conference at which they worked on the platform for MFDP's youth program. The conference was held in Meridian in part because Michael Schwerner, James Chaney, and Andrew Goodman had been trying to establish a Freedom School near there when they were killed in June 1964. After the idea of a convention had been approved by the Freedom School "coordinators" (i.e., principals, a term that may have sounded too hierarchical for SNCC), the youngsters essentially took over the planning and logistics. During the actual convention, "there was a noticeable change in tone between the first and second days. By Sunday, these teenagers were rejecting the advice of adults . . . for they had discovered they could do it themselves" (Lynd, 1969). Bob Moses, one of the movement's staunchest advocates of teaching people to make their own decisions, was there. Staughton Lynd, statewide Freedom School coordinator (a position in which he spent less than $2,000 all summer, over half of that for films) said "it was the single time in my life that I have seen Bob happiest. He just ate it up. . . . He just thought that was what it was all about" (Dittmer, 1994, p. 260).

At the conference, the students developed guidelines for housing, education, and health programs; suggested that repressive school districts be boycotted; and, after a particularly bitter debate, decided not to endorse a boycott of Cuba. They further resolved:

1. The United States should stop supporting dictatorships in other countries and should support that government which the majority of the people want.
2. Whereas the policy of apartheid in the Republic of South Africa is detrimental to all the people of that country and against the concepts of equality and justice, we ask that the United States impose economic sanctions in order to end this policy. (Holt, p. 119)

In Philadelphia, where Schwerner, Chaney, and Goodman had actually been killed, students returned to school wearing "ONE MAN, ONE VOTE" buttons. In Issaquena-Sharkey counties, after the principal told them they could not wear their SNCC buttons, students launched a boycott that lasted 8 months.

The summer of 1964 represented a high point for this form of activist education. The Freedom Schools continued for at least another year in Mississippi. In the late 1960s and early 1970s, many radical political groups, the Black Panthers included, developed some form of liberation schools. The current popularity of Civil Rights tours for young people represents one contemporary parallel (Murray & Garrido, 1995). Boston's Freedom Summer Project draws explicitly on the Freedom Schools in its educational activities.[2] There are certainly some parallels between contemporary Afrocentric schools and the Freedom Schools, particularly in their common emphasis on community uplift and individual responsibility for it.[3]

It is interesting to note that within the movement, Freedom School work always had relatively low status. At least in part this was because women did much of the work in the schools and because it was not as dangerous as other activities. Voter-registration work, in contrast, held the highest status.

With 30 years of hindsight, we can say that of all the traditions, customs, and practices that grew out of the movement, it is a particular tragedy that we did not do more to build on this tradition of explicitly helping African American youngsters to construct a political identity for themselves. Why wasn't this approach continued more aggressively? The best guess seems to be impatience, a sense that more dramatic kinds of activism were more important. Early in the summer, a Freedom School teacher in Shaw wrote in frustration:

> Furthermore [the students] don't see how we can help them to be free. At this point, neither do we. Slow change is unthinkable when so much change is needed, when there is so much hurt. . . . Things are so terrible here that I want to change it all NOW. I mean this as sincerely as I can. Running a freedom school is an absurd waste of time. I don't want to sit around in a classroom; I want to go out and throw a few office buildings, not to injure people but to shake them up, destroy their stolen property, convince them we mean business. . . . I really can't stand it here. (Sutherland, 1965, pp. 100–101)

In part the Freedom School model got lost in the desire to do something bigger, something that would have more impact sooner. Associated with that, of course, in all probability, was the tendency to be seduced by media politics, a style of politics for which Freedom Schools are badly suited.

It would be interesting to have some discussion about how one would adapt the Freedom School model to our time. At first glance, I am struck by how little of the basic intellectual framework needs to be changed. The need for teaching Black history is certainly as strong as ever. The lessons about language and power that were taught in Freedom Schools were far more sophisticated than almost anything I heard in the recent exceedingly shallow discussions of "ebonics." Certainly, there is a much greater need now for young people to understand the causes and costs of mindless materialism. Mass media have become so much a part of our lives that perhaps a unit would be needed to cover that. We would certainly want to encourage youngsters to think about gender-based oppression: about the links and parallels between racism and sexism. In inner-city communities, I believe it is vital that young people be helped to be analytical about the patterns of interaction among themselves, often characterized by constant insult and personal attacks. They need to see, to paraphrase Cobb, the links between the way this country attacks their sense of self-worth and the way they attack each other.

One of the obvious differences might be the absence of movement context. Young people going to Freedom Schools were surrounded by activists who genuinely believed that they could change the flow of history. Such confidence must have been magnetic. They grew up wanting to be SNCC field secretaries. We would need to think very carefully about how to give young people some comparable sense of their own potency and comparably clear models for actualizing it.

The Freedom School as a model of social action may actually be more pertinent to our times than it was to the Mississippi of 3 decades ago. Strange though it may sound, young Black people probably had more opportunities for some form of political education then than their counterparts do now. To those of us old enough to remember the 1960s, the young Black people of today seem confused and rootless. To us it is obvious, whether one looks at it from the viewpoint of the NAACP or of the Black Revolutionary Army, that we should have been far more aggressive about continuing explicit attempts at the social and political education of our youngsters.

That we have not done so may suggest that we are still very much confused about the potentials and the limitations of the 1960s. The decade remains one of our major metaphors for social change, but we often preserve the wrong parts of it—the sizzle and not the substance. We remember the drama, the demonstrations—and forget the notion of individual development as being one of the keys to shaping a more just society. Radical-progressive-nationalist or whatever, we are still Americans, with an historical consciousness attuned to Hollywood, prone to understanding history as drama, prone to underestimating the long-term importance of determined and sustained nondramatic action. Perhaps the memory of the Freedom Schools serves us best as cautionary tale. Perhaps what we most need to remember is that the price for confusing the flashier manifestations of activism with its substance is a kind of self-alienation in which we lose the ability to do those very things that might sustain us. We lose even the ability to recognize them.

NOTES

1. Rothschild, *A Case of Black and White* (pp. 95–96, 112–113), suggests that the 1964 version of the schools was somewhat more traditionally academic and less political than had been intended, but that changed for those schools that remained through the winter of 1964 and the summer of 1965. The volunteers who stayed through that period, she contends, were more political than those available during the summer of 1964.

2. Boston Freedom Summer can be reached at 411 Washington Street, Dorchester, MA 02124.

3. A fair number of Afrocentric schools seem to offer traditional, teacher-centered pedagogy and in some cases exactly the kind of autocratic classroom ethos Cobb was trying to find an alternative for, suggesting a departure from SNCC's tendency to want to liberate both the community and the individual.

REFERENCES

Belfrage, S. (1965). *Freedom summer.* New York: Viking Press.

Burnet, J., & Nalls, C. (1995). Emancipatory notions of African-American education. *21st Century Afro Review, 1,* Spring.

Cobb, C. (1991). Prospectus for a summer Freedom School program. *Radical Teacher,* Fall.

Dittmer, J. (1994). *Local people: The struggle for civil rights in Mississippi.* Urbana: University of Illinois Press.

Fruchter, N. (1969). Mississippi: Notes on SNCC. In M. Teodori (Ed.), *The New Left: A documentary history.* Indianapolis: Bobbs-Merrill.

Grant, J. (in press). *Troubling the water: The life of Ella Baker.* New York: Wile.

Holt, L. (1965). *The summer that didn't end.* New York: Morrow.

Horton, M. (1990). *The long haul: An autobiography.* New York: Doubleday.

Howe, F. (1984). Mississippi's Freedom Schools. In F. Howe (Ed.), *Myths of coeducation: Selected essays.* Bloomington: Indiana University Press.

Kluger, R. (1977). *Simple justice.* New York: Vintage.

Lynd, S. (1969). The Freedom Schools: Concept and organization. In M. Teodori (Ed.), *The New Left: A documentary history.* Indianapolis: Bobbs-Merrill.

Murray, N., & Garrido, M. (1995). Violence, nonviolence and the lessons of history: Project Hip-Hop journeys south. *Harvard Educational Review,* Summer, 231–257.

Parker, C. S. (1994). The struggle for racial equality 1964/1994. *Boston Review,* December–January.

Parker, W. (1996). Advanced ideas about democracy: Toward a pluralist conception of citizen education. *Teachers College Review, 98,* 104–125.

Payne, C. (1995). *I've got the light of freedom: The organizing tradition and the Mississippi freedom struggle.* Berkeley: University of California Press.

Rothschild, M. (1982). *A case of Black and White: Northern volunteers and the southern Freedom Summers, 1964–1965.* Westport, CT: Greenwood Press.

Sutherland, E. (1965). *Letters from Mississippi.* New York: McGraw-Hill.

Tjerandsen, Carl. (1980). *Education and citizenship: A foundation's experience.* Santa Cruz, CA: Emil Schwartzhaupt Foundation.

CHAPTER 7

Where Race and Class Are Not an Excuse

REFLECTIONS ON EDUCATION IN BARBADOS AND THE AMERICAN EDUCATION DILEMMA

Pedro Noguera

FOR THE LAST THREE SUMMERS I have had the privilege of teaching a course in Barbados through the University of California Summer Session program. It is the closest thing to a paid vacation that I have ever experienced. My light teaching schedule provides ample opportunity for rest and relaxation and lots of time for my family to be together at the beach. When I return home to California and exchange stories with friends about our summer vacations, it can be difficult to contain the glee and utter satisfaction about the work I did over the summer. The euphoria usually lasts well into the fall semester before eventually being extinguished by the daily grind of life in Berkeley.

With the arrival of autumn, I also resume my work with urban schools in the Bay Area and immerse myself in grappling with the thorny issues that plague inner-city schools across the United States. It is at the point of reengagement that my trip to the Caribbean serves as more than merely a restful respite. Aside from enjoying a month of sea and surf, my travels to Barbados and other Caribbean islands provides me with concrete evidence that America's education problems have more to do with politics and the kinds of settings in which we educate students than with the ability of poor children to learn.

A Simple Justice: The Challenge of Small Schools. Copyright © 2000 by Teachers College, Columbia University. All rights reserved. ISBN 0-8077-3962-6 (pbk.), ISBN 0-8077-3963-4 (cloth). Prior to photocopying items for classroom use, please contact the Copyright Clearance Center, Customer Service, 222 Rosewood Dr., Danvers, MA 01923, USA, tel. (508) 750-8400.

You see, Barbados is an underdeveloped country, but like most of the other windward islands in the region, Barbados generally succeeds at providing quality education for all of its children. Evidence of this success can be seen both in its high adult literacy rate (98% according to the World Bank in 1998, much higher than in the United States, where it hovers just below 80%) and in the accomplishments of the relatively small number of students who enroll and generally excel at North American and European universities. Though far from perfect, schools in Barbados are not plagued by violence, inadequate facilities, or underprepared teachers. Instead, Barbadian schools are characterized by high academic standards (Barbadian children who migrate to the United States are typically ahead academically when compared with American-born children), universal access to quality programs regardless of income, and considerable public support.

For example, though not representative of the school-age population, it was recently reported that the average SAT score for approximately 300 Barbadian students seeking admission at U.S. universities was 1300 (*Barbados Nation*, July 16, 1999). What is particularly noteworthy about this score is that the highest achieving students in Barbados traditionally do not take the SAT because they tend to prefer to enroll at the University of the West Indies or at universities in Britain and Canada.

In the Caribbean region, Barbados's commitment to education is not unique. Students on even less developed islands such as Grenada, St. Lucia, Dominica, and St. Vincent attain similar levels of achievement, even though funding for education represents a relatively small percentage of the national budget. Of course, Cuba exceeds even these countries in providing access to education for its citizens at primary, secondary, and post-secondary levels. But Cuba's accomplishments in education generally have been dismissed by Americans as some sort of trickery or socialist scheme intended to embarrass the United States in a manner not dissimilar to its accomplishments in sports and health care.

So, rather than comparing the U.S. educational system with that in Cuba, let us focus instead on Barbados and ask why it is that in this small, underdeveloped country being poor and Black does not prevent one from learning and achieving at high levels? I have thought about this question quite often during my visits to Barbados, and have come up with four possible explanations, all of which have bearing on the problems and issues facing public education in the United States.

First, although Barbados and the other island nations of the Caribbean have a history of slavery, colonialism, and rigid racial stratification, since attaining independence these countries have made great strides toward eliminating racism and the stigma associated with African ancestry. Black children in Barbados grow up seeing Black adults occupy a variety of roles in their society. Sports and entertainment, rather than being what might appear to be the only option, are just some of the career paths available to them. Hence, children in Barbados come to believe at a young age that education can open doors of opportunity, and that racial discrimination will not be a deterrent. Moreover, because education is highly valued in the society, there is no stigma associated with high achievement and students are expected to be serious about their studies.

Second, while poor children in the United States are often relegated to inferior schools, the Barbadian system is far more egalitarian and merito-cratic, but it is also highly competitive. Funding for primary schools in Bar-bados is relatively equitable, and although there are significant differences in quality and standards among secondary schools, all aspiring students must take the rigorous Common Entrance Exam. While this is perhaps the ultimate "high stakes" test, in that one's future can be determined by the score one obtains, the exam actually favors poor and working-class stu-dents. Whereas access to good private secondary schools is guaranteed for middle-class and affluent children whose parents can afford to pay, work-ing-class children realize that a good score is their ticket to a good public school and, consequently, they generally outperform their higher-income peers. There is growing concern in the country about stress upon students induced by the exam, and its validity as a measure of intelligence and abil-ity has also been questioned. Even with its faults, however, the educational system in Barbados comes far closer than the U.S. system to the merito-cratic ideal embraced by many Americans. It is also more equitable because resources are more evenly distributed, at least among primary schools.

Third, whereas the educability and intelligence of Black children in the United States is frequently questioned by researchers and educators, in countries like Barbados there is no doubt that Black children can learn. In fact, there is a genuine belief in Barbados that all children, when provided with the opportunity, can achieve at high levels academically. There is per-vasive support for schooling as a social practice and, subsequently, teachers are respected and valued as professionals. The notion that race—or more specifically, being Black or of African descent—would somehow make a person less intellectually competent is largely nonexistent in Barbados. In the United States, such beliefs remain a consistent part of the public dis-course and national consciousness, and are used to rationalize the lower performance of African American children. As a result, the failure of Black children is normalized in the United States, whereas academic success and achievement are the norms in Barbados.

Finally, and perhaps most important, the relationship between schools and the communities they serve is characterized by what James Coleman has called "social closure." Like the students in the Catholic schools

Coleman studied, children in Barbados benefit from the fact that their parents and teachers share similar values and beliefs with respect to education and a range of other social norms. As a result of these linkages, students find themselves surrounded by a web of shared interests and priorities. They know that values stressed at school are shared by their parents, and they understand that a failure to perform at school will result in negative sanctions both at school and at home. In effect, there is an adult conspiracy at work to ensure that all children go to school and are held to high standards of behavior—circumstances that make it very hard for students to get lost.

Generally, the only U.S. public schools that show evidence of a similar degree of social closure are those that have consciously and deliberately created strong ties with the families and communities they serve. In almost every case, such schools tend to be small. Size matters because it enables the adults in the school to know the children and their parents. Such knowledge and familiarity make it possible for parents and teachers to work together as partners. Instead of the distrust and hostility that typically characterize parent-teacher relations, small schools make it possible for parents and teachers to work together through recognition of their common interests in providing for the education and well-being of the children.

When I leave Barbados and return to California I am compelled to ask myself the question: Why is it that education is so simple in a poor nation like Barbados, but so hard in a wealthy nation like the United States? Across the country, school reform, especially in urban areas, is increasingly regarded as a hopeless endeavor in which fads and gimmicks are given priority over the basic elements of sound educational policies (i.e., well-paid and competent teachers, clean and attractive facilities, productive and respectful teacher-student and teacher-parent relationships). In most places there is little evidence that the currently popular educational reforms in curriculum, assessment, or school structure actually have an impact on academic outcomes. Generally, the victories are far outnumbered by the defeats.

The situation is made even more difficult by politicians who have shown increasing interest in educational issues in recent years but who impatiently demand quick remedies to the complex problems facing public schools or, even worse, design half-baked solutions themselves. There is a frenzy of activity in public education: New policies that are untested and barely thought out are being implemented, new programs and initiatives intended to elevate student achievement are being introduced, and, of course, educational leaders—superintendents and principals—face new rounds of firings and public humiliation due to the extraordinary pressure to produce improved results. Unfortunately, some of the strategies that have proven most effective at improving the quality of education—creating smaller schools and quality career academies—do not receive the support they need and deserve.

As I contemplate my role in all of this I am compelled to return to the question I posed earlier: Why is it that Barbados can educate its children, most of whom are poor and Black, while the greatest superpower on Earth cannot?

The answer, I believe, is not that complicated. Children learn in Barbados because the society in which they live values education and because there is a genuine belief that all children can learn. In the United States, the failure to achieve academically mirrors other forms of inequality in society. This trend is so pervasive that it generates the expectation that some children are doomed to fail, even at birth. If nothing else, the experience of countries like Barbados shows quite clearly that race and class are not legitimate obstacles to academic achievement. It also should move us to see that the cause of the racial gap in student achievement has nothing to do with the children, and everything to do with the values and priorities of the society in which we live.

CHAPTER 8

Art, with Algebra, Guards the Gate

Susan Klonsky

I N A DISPLAY CASE at the Franklin Delano Roosevelt Library in Hyde Park, New York, one can study the handwritten verses, drawings, and personal messages exchanged annually between each student and alumnus and Endicott Peabody, Calvinist minister and headmaster of Groton Academy, the prep school where FDR was educated. This was the training ground for young men who were meant by their parents to run the world. The transmission of culture (or what was circumscribed as "culture")—exposure to grand opera, Shakespeare, Beethoven, the Greek philosophers, classical poetry, painting, and novels—was a crucial element in the legacy of familiarity and entitlement to which every good patrician son was treated as part and parcel of a "round and robust" preparatory education. This was "art appreciation," training not to *make* art but to be acquainted, to acquire through exposure a level of connoisseurship.

This training, conducted in small, intimate learning environments, was indeed preparation to move about in a world of wealth and power. No family of "breeding" would consider well educated a son who, while versed in calculus and chemistry, lacked the cultural background so essential for social and commercial networking. For children being raised for a life of factory work, educated in factory-like schools, such exposure was never considered a matter of necessity.

"The child," observes Judith Renyi (1993),

> needs to know the things that will enable her to converse in cultural settings beyond the neighborhood and family culture; the school needs to know the things that will enable it to converse with the child. The

A Simple Justice: The Challenge of Small Schools. Copyright © 2000 by Teachers College, Columbia University. All rights reserved. ISBN 0-8077-3962-6 (pbk.), ISBN 0-8077-3963-4 (cloth). Prior to photocopying items for classroom use, please contact the Copyright Clearance Center, Customer Service, 222 Rosewood Dr., Danvers, MA 01923, USA, tel. (508) 750-8400.

classroom, with its diverse children, is a place where many kinds of conversations need to occur . . . the place where the children engage in conversations with books and maps, pictures and music, dances and plants, mathematics and theater—*with each other.* (p. 217)

The current conservative accountability wave, however, with its one-sided
emphasis on standardization, has put the arts and art education out of
reach of the neediest students. An exception to this trend is the emerging
small-schools movement in cities such as Chicago.

A visit to the annual holiday *tianguis* at Chicago's Telpochcalli Community School of the Arts can give just a taste of what is unfolding. The week
before Christmas, the school is alive with parents and neighbors doing holiday shopping in a re-creation of a Mexican village market square. Teams of
students operate *tiendas* (little shops), selling products they have fashioned
over the semester: brilliantly colored papercuts, *piñatas*, and tin ornaments,
as well as handmade jewelry, woodcut prints, and many other items made
from found and recycled materials. All items are traditional Mexican holiday crafts popular in this port-of-entry neighborhood. The craft projects
are just one endeavor that students have undertaken, working with artists
in residence from the nearby Mexican Fine Arts Center Museum. Dancers,
musicians, and visual artists collaborate with teachers at all grade levels in
this tiny K–8 school.

The 240 students in the teacher-designed school enjoy a level of arts
education without parallel in the city. The school is small enough to permit, with the help of extra grants and volunteer artists, daily art activities
for all grade levels. Students in grades 3 and up receive weekly vocal or
instrumental music instruction, particularly in traditional Mexican instruments or dance forms. For the newcomers to Chicago who inhabit the surrounding neighborhood, the preservation of both language and culture is a
powerful attraction of the school, and one that has won it warm support
from parents, grandparents, and neighbors. (See also Chapter 11 for further discussion of Telpochcalli.)

To educate students to be able to move about in the world with a sense
of ease is one of those objectives rarely spelled out in the mission statements of schools. Yet it is that feeling of belonging and acceptance that we
adults prize. It is the sensation that we are on familiar ground, able to navi-
gate, negotiate, know our bearings, evaluate critically, and meet any situation with presence and self-possession—what used to be called "poise,"—
that we consider hallmarks of maturity, sophistication, and self-assurance.
Schools for the rich have always worked to cultivate that sensibility, while
schools for the general public, and particularly for children of the poor,

with rare exceptions, have given barely a lick and a promise to artistic education—whether broadly or narrowly defined by the classical canon.

Yet, with few exceptions, the arts stand, as they did in FDR's boyhood,
as a gatekeeper. The Mississippi civil-rights organizer Bob Moses has cor-
rectly identified algebra as a gatekeeper. Those unable to master it, Moses
insists, were and are doomed to exclusion from higher education, from the
mainstream of high-tech society and commerce, and from the possibility
of economic advancement (Klonsky, 1990).

The arts often play the same gatekeeping role. Children's ability to
express, share, and understand ideas and emotions, through a variety of
means and media, is severely limited when they have been deprived of
artistic training, exposure, and opportunity. These are exactly the skills and
habits of the mind that are requirements for information-age social interaction and many areas of employment—multilayered communication, both
verbal and nonverbal, empathy, sensitivity, and receptivity to ideas and
emotional expressions of others. Moreover, the appreciation of cultural
sweep, scope, and variety is a vital bridge between people—especially
young people, both in and out of school. The craft, complexity, and vital-
ity of hip-hop poetics is rarely part of *school*, yet here is a distinctive, high-
energy genre that absorbs the artistic imaginations of a huge slice of youth,
cutting across racial and ethnic lines.

Just as Bob Moses has identified algebra, and more broadly, numeracy,
as a civil right (Klonsky, 1990, 1991), one can argue that the arts are a
right—often squashed, suppressed, ignored, or gutted by urban public
schools.

Chicago's public schools, for example, have never given the arts their
due. What is accepted as passable is a couple of arts magnet schools—3 or
4 among 630 public schools—seats for about 1,000 of Chicago's 430,000
public school children, or less than 1%. One can hope that the small-
schools movement will add more schools of choice to the mix. Several
schools are already using their small size to create integrated curricula with
the arts a part of each content area. This effort is still marginal, however,
and Chicago's anti-arts pattern recurs with striking consistency in other
urban centers. Milwaukee has one arts specialty school each at the elementary, middle, and secondary levels. Washington's Duke Ellington Academy
and New York's renowned Music & Art High School (now renamed
LaGuardia High for the Performing Arts) stand out largely for their eccen-
tricity; these schools are not open to everyone—only those with demon-
strable talent or aptitude gain admission. This runs counter to the small-
schools approach of schools of choice and focus, open to all children. Even
Chicago's few arts magnet schools were launched as a result of civil-rights

decisions; indeed, the renascence of arts in Chicago's schools is inseparable from the movement for social justice in the city.

When it comes to art education, what counts and who's counting? Even today, more than 10 years since the advent of Chicago school reform, it is not possible to obtain reliable data about the growth in public investment in the arts in education. The nation's third-largest school system is unable to report, for instance, how many more art and music teachers are employed than in 1989, when the 10-year furlough of art teachers ended. The Chicago public schools are unable to produce such basic numbers as the number of federal and state antipoverty dollars and other public funds invested to this purpose.

This lack of attention and emphasis speaks volumes—that education in the arts is not considered worth counting. However, twice a year the *Chicago Tribune* reports the standardized test scores from every school in Chicago and surrounding Cook County, as well Lake, McHenry, Kane, Will, and DuPage counties—the "collar counties" of Chicago. We call them the "tornado counties," because the only times they are mentioned in the city press is when there is bad weather—*except* when comparing test scores of Chicago and suburban schools. The dailies report in painful detail all the scores of all the public schools in the Standard Metropolitan Statistical Area on local- and state-mandated tests of reading, writing, mathematics, social studies, and science—the *important* learning areas—the only ones we measure, the only ones on the public screen. The point here is not to advocate standardized testing in art and music, but to convey what the public discourse is about in Chicago. Reading, writing, mathematics, social studies, and science are still what we think is *worth measuring*. These areas are still where we think student engagement resides. And what we don't count, we don't invest in.

Benjamin Willis was Chicago school superintendent in the 1960s. His strategy for containing African American children in certain neighborhoods, regardless of the severe overcrowding and dilapidation of the schools, was to put trailers on the playgrounds, each with its own pair of outhouses (instead of more costly indoor plumbing). This was in the sixties—a full decade *after Brown v. Board of Education*—not in the twenties. These "temporary" classrooms, known as the "Willis Wagons," were hot in the summer and cold in the winter, and they stunk year-round. You did not have the space to teach dance or any kind of real movement. You could not teach music, because of the weird acoustics in an aluminum trailer and because there was barely room for the students, let alone instruments. You also could not paint or work with clay, because there was no running water, and the electrical supply was shaky at best. The majority of public schools on the west side of Chicago, where there was a large African American population, had Willis Wagons by 1975. How could a vigorous and effective educational system exist in separate and unequal schools?

Then, reality reached in and finished off the arts. Just like the 1929 stock market crash, "Black Monday" to the old-timers,the graft-ridden Chicago public school system collapsed financially in 1979. Among the first to be cast overboard were some 400 elementary art and music teachers, "furloughed" with the promise that they would be called back as soon as financial order was restored. Their return did not come until 1988, and then only a fraction of them were called back. The majority of children in Chicago's elementary schools received virtually *no* visual arts or music instruction for 10 years. During this long period of drought in the arts, a few activists built programs meant to fill the gap. The Urban Gateways program, for one, brought visiting artists into classrooms for brief workshops and residencies. Schools scrounged up the funds to pay them, in an attempt to stem the inequity. Urban Gateways artists—African, African American, Latin American, Asian, and Native American visual and performing artists—were frequently the only exposure provided for a whole generation of schoolchildren. Many of the furloughed art teachers maintained their ties to the schools as visiting artists through Urban Gateways. The principal of one westside school boasted, "We have a wonderful arts program—three Urban Gateways assemblies a year—one Black, one White, one Spanish." For educators who did not value the arts themselves, this was enough—the barest minimum.

In 1988, the Illinois Legislature passed the Chicago School Reform Act, the result of an enormous social and political movement that had lasted more than 10 years. In 1989, 6,000 parents and teachers were elected to sit on Local School Councils—site-based management bodies—at Chicago's public schools. Each LCS included parents, teachers, community residents, and the principal. One of the first tasks for these new bodies was to find the funds to put art and music teachers back into the classrooms. But the new School Board provided only enough funding to hire one half of one teacher, and The Local School Councils were directed to choose *either* an art teacher *or* a music teacher. Some choice.

The Local School Council at one westside school found a talented music teacher, but initially they had only money enough to hire him half-time. Marcus Love, a young African American in love with music and the teaching of music, had been laid off in 1979. Over the 9 years of his "furlough," he recorded more than a dozen gospel albums and played concert dates on weekends, working in a bank during the week. He accepted the offer of a part-time teaching position and quit the bank job. Then he went up the hill about a mile and found himself another half position at the nearest school. For 2 years he shuttled back and forth between the two schools with their combined total of 1,200 children, each of whom probably saw him once every 3 weeks if they were lucky. This was not an unusual arrangement, and it was the best those schools could do at first. As soon as they received their discretionary dollars under Chicago's reform legislation, the Local School Councils "bought" themselves "a whole teacher." Marcus Love went on to build a marching band and a concert choir that has performed at Walt Disney World, competed, and toured—100% African American and 98% low-income kids who would not have had these experiences were it not for a dedicated artist who kept up his fight for nearly 10 years.

The struggle now is not just for resources, staff, or good performance space. It's all of that, but it's also to change the way we conceive schools. We know we don't know the students. We don't know what they care about, what excites them. In his book *A Kind and Just Parent*, William Ayers (1998) retells a great story about Ella Fitzgerald. At 15, Fitzgerald was sent to a juvenile prison in upstate New York, a segregated facility where the typical punishment for kids was food deprivation and beatings. Her mother had died, she had been sexually abused by her father, and when arrested she was running numbers in Harlem and working as the lookout at a brothel. She was paroled after 4 years to the custody of bandleader Chick Webb, who knew her talent. Within a year of her release, Fitzgerald was a celebrated artist, with a bright future spreading out before her. A reporter biographer managed to locate Fitzgerald's English teacher from those years, and this elderly lady remarked that she had often wondered how she could have missed the fact that she had in front of her "the future Ella Fitzgerald." The former superintendent of the institution was a little more reflective, wondering how many *more* Ellas they had missed.

Too often, the way schools are organized *prohibits* us from seeing the children as individuals or recognizing their gifts. When we jam children into factory-style schools, it is impossible to view them as individuals. Our schools remain too big, too impersonal, too divorced, and it's too hard to see students as unique personalities.

To do the arts justice, schools must be smaller. We need to get our numbers down to a scale where students are not seeing an artist or an art teacher just once a month, but where the arts are a daily part of life in the classroom and in the school community. We need schools small enough that logistics and scheduling flexibility is a realistic possibility. We also need to provide meaningful choices—including more places where students can specialize in the fine arts if they choose. In factory-style schools that kind of personalization is not possible. The best intuitive teaching can take place only in a setting where children are seen and known as individuals. The bigger and more forbidding the school, the harder it is to attain that intimacy, to support that personalization, to sustain that vital bond between individual children and adults. Making art, both individually and in groups, requires a level of communication often prohibited by the very size and logistics of densely packed schools.

Today, however, there is hope for a renaissance in arts education in the public schools, a flowering that is inseparably linked to school restructuring. Some of this rebirth is already occurring in schools that have restructured and reshaped themselves and in the newest and smallest schools, products of community struggle and of organization by educators and parents to create new educational options in the poorest neighborhoods.

The neighborhood known as Bronzeville, located on the south side of Chicago, is one site of this kind of renewal. Bronzeville was once the center of jazz in Chicago—and maybe in the whole United States. From the 1940s, the local high school, DuSable, had an outstanding jazz orchestra. DuSable is the alma mater of jazz greats including, among many others, Dinah Washington, Nat "King" Cole, Gene Ammons, Dorothy Donegan, and even Bo Diddley (Black, 1998). *Chicago Tribune* arts critic Howard Reich (1998) termed DuSable "perhaps the most famous high school in the history of jazz." In its heyday from the 1930s to the 1960s, the school became "the Juilliard of jazz."

Today, DuSable High School serves the children of the Robert Taylor Homes, the country's largest housing project and the densest concentration of poverty in one census tract in the entire United States. Once the housing projects were built, DuSable began to slip academically, and in 1964 Benjamin Willis—the same villain who brought us the Willis Wagons—gutted the jazz program at DuSable because music wasn't a *hard* subject. It's a reward, a luxury, he argued, and you can only have dessert if you eat your vegetables. So jazz was rejected as "unaffordable," the rationale being that students did not deserve or could ill afford to spend time in such pursuits.

More than 30 years later, in 1996, DuSable High School was restructured into six small schools-within-the-school, among them a performing arts academy. A jazz teacher was again hired, and the school again possessed a student jazz performing ensemble. In June of 1997 DuSable sent four students to college on music scholarships.

However, DuSable, which was trying to improve student engagement by reviving its jazz program, loses 50% or more of its students by the middle of 10th grade. About 25% graduate. Fewer than 15% of 11th graders at DuSable can read at or above national norms on a standardized test. In August 1997, the school was reconstituted, placed on a sort of receivership by the system. Teachers had to reapply for their jobs, and about 30% of them were not rehired. The small schools were dissolved in favor of a stringent back-to-basics program. And the plug was once again pulled on DuSable's jazz program.

Don't doubt for a second that decisions about arts funding, inclusion, and emphasis in the curriculum, or the genres and kinds of arts offered are political decisions. They are nothing but politics played out in schools. When these kinds of high-stakes accountability measures are taken in schools, some new ways of engaging students must be put in place. Otherwise, the changes are just trashing, gutting, and pillaging the schools.

There has been a loud demand for "rigor" of late, heard mainly in the chambers of the Illinois Statehouse at education budget time. Top school leaders have referred to arts education as "fluff," a diversion from the basic skills education prescribed widely for poor kids. Should Chicago schools get more funds? Not without a greater show of "rigor." Marginally literate politicians press educators to "raise the bar" of academic performance across the city. Add to this the persistent notion that the arts are "frills," nonessential and undemanding. But, responds Renyi (1993), "The arts are tough, not soft; the arts are disciplined, not a free-for-all" (p. 219). The mission of our refashioned and renewed smaller schools, then, has to include demonstrating that the arts can help give voice to children and improve literacy and student engagement while reducing stress, conflict, and boredom.

This is an issue that deserves our attention, not because every child will be an Ella Fitzgerald, but so that every child *can* turn out to be *himself or herself*—an educated, expressive, and self-actualizing member of society.

REFERENCES

Ayers, W. C. (1998). *A kind and just parent: The children of the Juvenile Court.* Boston: Beacon Press.

Bernstein, N. (1996, June 23). The gap in Ella Fitzgerald's life. *The New York Times.*

Havighurst, R. J. (1964). The public schools of Chicago: A survey for the Board of Education of the City of Chicago. Chicago: Board of Education of the City of Chicago.

Klonsky, M. (1990, October). Civil rights leader promotes algebra for all. *Catalyst: Voices of Chicago School Reform,* p. 8.

Klonsky, M. (1991, May). Math reform = changing habits: An interview with Robert Moses. *Catalyst: Voices of Chicago School Reform,* p. 5.

Reich, H. (1998, September 8). The drill sergeant of DuSable. *Chicago Tribune Magazine,* pp. 10–19.

Renyi, J. (1993). *Going public: Schooling for a diverse democracy.* New York: New Press.

PART II

Portraits in Practice

Gabrielle H. Lyon

O N MARCH 6, 1999, at Chicago's first citywide showcase of small public schools, Public Schools CEO Paul Vallas declared small schools to be the "best-kept secret in public education." The unfortunate truth, however, is that there are many secrets in education. We know very little about what happens inside schools and classrooms. The most familiar pictures of teaching and learning have been "based on true stories," fabricated and manipulated by the media.

Our understanding of schools most often is grounded in individual experiences—our own, our children's, or those of other people's children. We rarely have an opportunity to examine the systematic nature of teaching and learning. Those who have tried to understand education and curriculum at a systemic level have encountered a complicated landscape.

Researcher Jean Anyon (1980) emerges from such an undertaking with a startling glimpse of the relationship between class and classwork. In her now classic study, "Social Class and the Hidden Curriculum of Work," she found that for children of the working class, schoolwork is routine and mechanical; for children of white-collar families, work in school involves planning and decision-making with no control over content; for children of the middle and upper class, work involves some conceptual assignments and creativity, but primary tasks are managerial; children of the elite, in contrast, work entirely on conceptual problems and control of enterprise.

Herbert Kohl (1995), who writes more frequently as an essayist than a researcher, speaks frankly to the question of "whose curriculum?" in his semiautobiographical piece, "I Won't Learn from You." He deconstructs failure in schools and links "not learning" to a sophisticated struggle for control and identity within a system that rarely probes deeper than report cards and standardized test score assessments of progress.

Lisa Delpit (1996) is another educator who has tried to see beyond the specifics of individual classrooms and teachers to understand how schools work—or fail to work—and why. For Delpit, the key question regarding teaching and learning across and through schools, classes, and races is one of the most piercing in education: "In order to teach you, must I know you?"

For small-schools folk the answer is, "Yes. I must know you." Some create curriculum to help students know themselves; some create schools with the knowledge that the needs of the community are not being met. And some do both, only to find themselves increasingly troubled by the knowledge that beyond the walls of their small schools is a society that may not support the students, their learning experiences, or their carefully practiced values.

The issue of control manifests itself acutely in the struggle for small schools. It is a multifaceted issue that appears at the level of school structure, culture, curriculum, and capacity for change. Large schools are about power—who has it and who does not; who is important and who is not; what work, skills, and experiences are valued and what are not. Many small-schools activists, as do many of the authors included in this volume, use the term *small school* as a metaphor—for knowing students, for working together as teachers and accountable professionals, for intimately connecting schools and communities.

Those who are building and sustaining small schools, disparate and diverse though they be, see themselves as part of a movement for systemic change. Because of this, the nature of the struggle changes—it is not just about the individual classroom, the 200 or so students in a particular school, the creation of a single small school, or even the collection of small schools in a large city. The struggle is to make the tensions and issues of teaching and learning public so that the critique of a de facto school system is commonly understood and can become the basis for restructuring a school system. The small schools are models of how things can be—not perfect, not a panacea—but a series of real, working pictures.

The chapters that follow are analogous to snapshots in a thick family album. As we look at each in turn, certain features become familiar: conscious construction of school culture and curriculum; examination and evaluation of relationships; particular emphasis on the meaning of work and assessment; and strategic crafting of internal contexts and external positionings. These are no flat portraits. Within them we glimpse the fluid dynamics of size and personalization, and the intense dilemmas of knowing and being known. Left in the wake are the eddies of teaching and learning, of commitment to communities, and to providing something other than a de facto school culture.

Within the stories offered by these authors are the details of what it takes on a daily basis to create more than one way to teach and learn. And, as these authors (and small schools) so well know, by opening the door to possibilities—and forging different kinds of relationships in schools—we challenge the hollow categories, stubborn status quos, and powerful hierarchies that have sustained education's not-so-secret history of classism, racism, and control.

REFERENCES

Anyon, Jean. (1980). Social class and the hidden curriculum of work. *Journal of Education, 162*(1), 67–92

CHAPTER 9

Social Justice and Small Schools

WHY WE BOTHER, WHY IT MATTERS

Rick Ayers

WHEN I STARTED THINKING about a piece on social justice and small schools, I immediately thought of that old bogeyman of teaching, classroom management. Or sometimes it is called discipline, structure, or behavior techniques. The following is a glimpse at these issues and how the size and intention of a learning community influence management. It is neither the whole picture of the problem nor the last word on discipline procedures at our school.

Now that we are in our third year of the Communications Arts and Sciences (CAS) program at Berkeley High School, however, we are experiencing a huge leap in the effectiveness of the program, and this makes me think a more interesting chapter might have been written on our development of a "social justice curriculum." This does not mean that the teachers stand in the front of the class and tell the students what justice is. Instead, we are working together to pursue an open-ended question, an essential question, that ties all the curriculum together.

For instance, the essential question for the freshman core classes in CAS is: "What are the characteristics of a just society?" This question is explored through literature: What is Prospero's idea of the ideal society in *The Tempest*? What does William Golding think of human nature and how we set up society in *Lord of the Flies*? What does Kenzaburo Oe suggest young people would set up as a community if left to their own devices in *Nip the Buds*? The question also is explored in world history: What were the various views of the Enlightenment philosophers toward human nature and

A Simple Justice: The Challenge of Small Schools. Copyright © 2000 by Teachers College, Columbia University. All rights reserved. ISBN 0-8077-3962-6 (pbk.), ISBN 0-8077-3963-4 (cloth). Prior to photocopying items for classroom use, please contact the Copyright Clearance Center, Customer Service, 222 Rosewood Dr., Danvers, MA 01923, USA, tel. (508) 750-8400.

the proper way to set up society? What kind of social norms existed in Ibo society in Africa before colonialism? What was the impact of colonialism? We can also create interdisciplinary papers addressing questions such as: Can people be trusted to govern themselves? For this, students decide their own position, develop evidence from history and English texts and discussions, and write out an argument. Of course, this essential question is also invoked as students work on issues in the program: What is the best way for our classes to be set up? How should we treat each other? What constitutes a just society?

This essential question is something that resonates with young people. How many times have you heard a teenager say, "That's not fair!" Fair, just, and honorable behavior is central to the ethics of young people. In a way, the social justice curriculum simply harnesses that concern and curiosity, making it part of the educational focus. This progresses each grade as students engage the questions at deeper and more complex levels.

The social justice curriculum is not limited to the academic course content, of course. In CAS we are committed to experiential learning, and we get out of the classroom, out of the school, whenever possible. A central feature of CAS education is that students are engaged in service learning at all grade levels. The freshmen will go as a group to help serve food at Glide Memorial Church or to work on building homes with Habitat for Humanity. The sophomores begin going out, alone or in groups, and volunteering with an agency. This will only be some 20 hours in the spring semester, but it gives them a chance to see what is out there. By the senior year, students are involved in a major senior project—an internship or a self-created task. They are not involved in these projects just to file papers or act as passive aids. CAS students are expected to bring skills and resources from their work and from the program to make a difference where they are working. For instance, they might help create a video or radio show that would help the agency. In every case, students are examining the society in which they live and imagining how it could be better.

As the small-schools program matures, as the teachers recognize the ways we can work together, and as the students and community members start taking ownership of the program, it begins to look like the kind of educational community we dream of. And it even begins to look like the kind of society, committed to social justice, that we would like to live in.

A TYPICAL MOMENT IN HIGH SCHOOL

As I was rounding the corner into the second floor of the C Building, something seemed wrong. There were dozens of students milling about and a tension was in the air. Jack and I were heading down to Phil Halpern's class to give him an award for the work his students had done in creating the Memorial Grove.

Then we saw it. A fight outside Phil's classroom had been broken up but both female combatants were still snarling, being held back by security monitors. One kicked out violently while flailing with both hands. At that, Joseph Harmon, the Berkeley police officer assigned to the high school, put a move on her wrist that landed her flat and hard on her belly. Then he knelt on her shoulder blades. He put on handcuffs. The other young woman was taken away.

The only responsible thing I could do was to help break up the crowd of gawkers, the inevitable group of teenagers getting voyeuristic satisfaction in watching a fight, even egging it on. It was a stereotypical moment in a big urban high school—fights, police, crowd out of control.

Jack and I finally headed back downstairs, deciding that this was not the time to visit Phil's class. Always the reporter, Jack remarked, "Damn, I have to get the background on that. It should be a story in *The Jacket*."

"What?," I asked. "Do you think undue force was applied?"

"Not really. Actually I'm glad there was someone there who knew how to bring that girl under control. That was scary."

I tended to agree with Jack. There have been complaints about the campus monitors in the past, undue roughness, use of handcuffs in minor altercations, rudeness. But this was different. Obviously, something had to be done, and Officer Harmon seemed to do it quickly and efficiently.

We got a severe wake-up some hours later when I finally did talk to Phil. He was incensed. "That violence on the student was not at all necessary," he remarked.

I was surprised. It had looked to me as if this student was completely out of control and needed to be subdued before any discussion could happen. Phil replied, "Well, you got there late. Much earlier, I had already come upon the fight. She is in Computer Academy. I don't even know what the fight was about. I was talking to the girl. I had made eye contact. She was calming down. Then the monitor came bursting in, shouting, 'Step aside, Halpern! I've got her now!' He grabbed her, she started to struggle, and the fight was on."

This was a whole new version of events. Phil was furious. "This is typical of how security is done at the school. No human interaction. Only repression and violence. Then later they shrug their shoulders and wonder, 'Well, what can we do?'"

We talked at some length about this and a half dozen other incidents that had occurred in the school. I reminded Phil of the struggle we had with the administration over Lisandra last fall. She was in the Communication Arts and Sciences program and making great progress. She was involved in a minor fight in the park one morning in October, and as a result the security personnel had her arrested and sent to juvenile hall. Deciding that this was "gang related" because it involved Chicana girls, the administration moved to expel Lisandra. In the end we won that one, getting her a suspended expulsion, but only because all the teachers stood up and spoke for her.

We talked about the case of Ann Pamanasong last spring. She had been involved in a sophomore prank in which a group of students simultaneously set off smoke bombs in all parts of the school. Ann got caught and also was put up for expulsion. She was told that the only way she would get leniency was to name names, finger others in the plot. Ann was stuck, facing the end of her dream of going to Harvard, standing alone with no one else coming forward. Finally she named another student, Nick, who denied everything.

Then we had a horrendous situation—everyone hating everyone else, one student up for expulsion on the testimony of another student who had a motive—to save herself by getting someone else in trouble. It sounds ridiculous. But, of course, this is the kind of case that marches through our courtrooms every day: This guy bought the dope, got busted, pointed to that guy, then he denied it but finally pointed to guy number three. Maybe these schools are just giving our kids a real-world experience.

Some of the faculty complained about this precedent of forcing a student to tell on others in order to get off for a crime, but their protests fell on deaf ears. Then this year during finals there was a great cheating scandal. Apparently one student had gotten a copy of the physics test, and dozens of students had programmed the answers into their calculators. Four students were caught, but everyone knew many more were involved. Again this most bizarre scenario was played out: Some administrators told the students that if they named others, say 10 others, then they would not have their colleges notified of this serious violation. The message was clear: Don't cheat, but if you do cheat you can get off by simply telling on others. Perhaps obtaining a "get out of jail free card" for informing is an integral part of an adversarial authoritarian system.

WHY DOES AUTHORITY = ORDER IN A FACTORY-MODEL SCHOOL?

All of these incidents push us to realize something very important about our efforts to set up a small-school experience for our students. We realize that we are not just trying to set up some classes differently. We are not just trying out some different approaches to pedagogy. Whether we know it or not, we are challenging the way power functions in the larger high school. We are experimenting with how communities can be built and how power relations—more just and more humane power relations—can be developed.

The large, factory-model school has its own kind of culture. It is a default culture. It exists because nothing else has consciously been put in its place. This culture parodies what is most absurd, most unjust, and most cruel about society at large. In a factory-model school, students are the products that are put out, just like a Ford automobile. You move down the assembly line and one specialist screws in the English, then the next bolts on some history, then a layer of chemistry is applied. Anything that disrupts the smooth operation of the factory is suppressed or arrested or removed.

You learn to lay low, stay out of trouble, and not stand out. No one is there for you. No group works on solving problems. No model exists of community values. Sure, there are little conflict resolution efforts at schools all over the country. And there are heroic teachers trying to soften the blows of the institution and its blind authority.

But is this the best way to expend our efforts? Is this the best way to set up a learning environment? The theory of the security personnel, and of the administrators in charge of discipline, is that "our job is to create order, to get their little butts sitting at the desks, and your job is to teach them." It is the politicians and the administration, not the students, who have set up the system of hierarchy and control. The idea behind the system is that order and education are two different things, and you achieve one and then proceed with the other. Or perhaps the institutional mind actually pursues order and discipline as the central theme of education.

This is the same thing that Michel Foucault has described concerning the engineering function of the prisons, and which also exposes repressive patterns in all of the institutions of modern, industrial society. The central elements are spatialization (a place where you should be at all times), minute control of activity (bells that determine when the next task is to be performed), surveillance (one of the school's great plans for use of technology money last year was the installation of surveillance cameras), repetitive exercises (designed to transmit bits of information, sometimes known as "downloading" in this era of computers), detailed hierarchies (students at different grade and ability levels, teachers, department chairs, administrators), and normalized judgments (grades that promote the illusion students have been ranked scientifically for acceptable achievement). In New York City, the circle has been closed with what Patricia Williams describes as Mayor Rudy Giuliani's policy of putting the police in charge of schools.

And what do you get if you are successful in this system? You get the proper socialization and the credentials to allow you to administer it to others.

Two years ago a student editor of the school paper, *The Jacket*, pointed out the hypocrisy of the administration. He remembered that when they instituted new security measures, built a fence around the school, and hired a new security chief, the explanation was, "There is a lot of talk about injustice and inequity in the school. But we cannot work on equity issues while there is chaos. So we are going to work on creating order first, then we will work on justice and equity." So far, the editor said, we have had 3 years of law and order. But once there is order, where is the impetus to work for justice?

How do we teach in this context? Shall we have a spirited discussion about the risks that Atticus Finch took in *To Kill a Mockingbird* while we ourselves are behaving like institutional automatons in the face of obvious injustice? Will we fail to model new ways of creating community, of solving problems? No wonder the kids find literature, especially great literature, boring.

Literature is boring because it is being pawned off on students as some kind of received wisdom, a flat series of homilies. Students have great insight and they do not hesitate to reject the hypocrisy of a teacher who walks them through a book on social justice while supporting structures that are patently "unfair" every day. In an alienated institution, the teacher's job is to act as codebreaker. The book is "hard." The teacher understands the code, the difficult language. The teacher unlocks the code and explains the meaning of the book. Then the student demonstrates this knowledge on a test or a paper.

But, in reality, great literature is much more problematic than this; it challenges assumptions and ignorance. If students have a chance to really engage with literature, all assumptions will be off.

HOW COULD THINGS BE DIFFERENT?

Communication Arts and Sciences is a pilot program at Berkeley High School, a grouping of three classes for students in order to create more opportunities for integrated curriculum and the building of community. We use video and computers as a hook, but we are committed to the broadest definition of communication as our theme—including writing and performance. We are now in our second year and far from being a small school, and CAS is moving toward more autonomy and a larger student day.

In CAS, we are working from a perspective different from that of the factory-model school. Education comes out of community, we believe, and out of community comes a way we can work together. We are operating from the idea that knowledge is socially constructed. We want students to respond to the text, to each other, and to their society with genuine engagement. Instead of learning to adopt a voice of false authority, the disembodied writing voice of the literary critic, they are getting a chance to engage with, struggle with, and develop ideas of their own and in their own community.

Young people need something to be passionate about, to care about, and instead of deadening this need we ought to be nurturing it toward their own creativity and capacities. If we seek to create a paradigm of democratic education, current models of administration and education are mutually exclusive. We believe you don't have to be an authority to teach. In fact, it is the opposite. You cannot be authoritarian and truly teach. True citizenship education in a democracy inherently forbids authoritarian education.

This may be ragingly idealistic, perhaps quaint and sweetly irrelevant in these hard and cynical times, but it is the only way we can teach the kids who need it most—the ones who are disenfranchised in society, who are alienated from school, and who have been told all their lives they are losers. If you want to round them up with armed police (as has been done) and march them into my class and stand over them glaring threats, don't ask me to "just teach." It can't happen. The rage, bitterness, and smoldering resentment smear my efforts.

When an administration creates an adversarial system in the drive for structure, they reap more and more resistance. Students call a forum on student rights. Students demand lawyers. One day the student body president is suspended because he refuses to give his driver's license to the head of security and demands to see a lawyer. Often administrators are blinded by the logic of their choices and they will suspend and expel and lay waste until, dammit, there is finally order. They don't remember LBJ or Birmingham's Bull Conner. You can hold all the weapons and still lose.

In a true community-building context, issues of equity and governance are given to the students. At the nearby middle school, Community School of the East Bay, the essential question of the fall has been "What is fair?" All 12- and 13-year-olds have a keen perception of what they think is fair and what is not. Why shouldn't their natural passion for fairness be brought into a classroom discussion? The students develop rules for the school and try them out. They discuss power relationships with teachers and parents. They study government at the local, state, and federal levels. And they read *To Kill a Mockingbird* and wonder what they might have done in similar circumstances.

After a number of conflicts, I have realized that what is most disturbing is that the factory-model administrators have not really based their disciplinary methods on systematic study or on any training they have received. It is just received wisdom in the culture, an adversarial culture with threats and punishments, expulsion and denial.

I had an argument with a vice principal last year when the school was trying to expel Lisandra. "OK," I responded to his decision to push for expulsion. Then I continued:

> Look at it this way. When I teach a lesson, I have been trained in educational theory, I have some pedagogical reasoning behind it. Usually there is research behind my teaching approach, usually there is countervailing evidence on both sides of a decision of how to teach something. I teach the lesson. Sometimes it works, sometimes it doesn't. But it is all embedded in some theory, some rationale and professionalism about teaching.

> When this administration picks up 14- and 15-year-old students, though, when it sends them to Juvenile Hall for four days without charges, when it moves to expel one for a brief fight in which minor injuries were reported, what is your penological theory? Did someone tell you that a trip to Juvie would do her good? What if I brought you evidence that a trip to Juvie would make her a criminal? But we aren't even at that level of discussion. This administration has no training in criminology. It has no theory. The theory is at the level of a couple of guys talking in a bar: "Yeah, if we weren't coddling these criminals, we wouldn't have so much youth crime." At this school, a person can't even argue with this. If you put forward an alternate point of view, they just look at you like you're crazy.

We all worry about what is on the other side of these walls. Some of these students will be going to college. Some will be going to jail. The state is building many more jails than colleges now. And they are mainly for African American and Latino youths.

Worse, though, is that what we offer our large urban schools is no more creative. If anything, the de facto curriculum acculturates them to a world of American criminal justice and American institutional control, a world that has proved to be so destructive to the human spirit.

IN PRACTICE, IT DOES NOT ALWAYS COME OUT THE WAY WE WANTED IT TO

Do we have any experience in creating engaged education through creating community? I wish it were so easy. I know that when we sided with Lisandra, when we did make her recognize her responsibility to the CAS community, she responded and managed to stay focused and productive.

Students will live down to our low expectations or step up to high expectations. That goes for academics as well as behavior issues.

Still, it is not so easy as to declare that we are "a community" and have everything magically fall into place. It is not all sitting around the campfire singing "Kumbaya." We have many experiences in CAS that are exasperating or that run counter to our expectations and force us to revisit our beliefs.

When these things happen, we could cop a plea that we are not yet a real "small" school—that we are an extended core program within a factory-model school, and the culture and methods of the larger school take precedence. In our current situation, we find ourselves always fighting border skirmishes to keep the program alive. We are either defending the creation of a new class, fighting over the assignment of personnel, or just trying to get the students together.

We recently took a field trip to Angel Island, where we visited the Chinese immigration holding station, had a picnic, talked, hiked, and bonded. Here the girl who had been suspended for bringing a knife to school climbed a cliff and dared the boys to be as nimble; there the guy who often fell asleep in class stayed back to help clean up litter around the picnic tables. But of the 160 students invited, only 80 came. The rest had to take a science test that the teacher would not reschedule, or feared missing math or the first 20 minutes of basketball practice.

It is difficult to build community when the main school, by its very inertia and size, exerts its gravitational pull on our world. We are working for greater autonomy, even considering secession in the alternative or charter model, to deal with the ongoing struggle. But we have to face our own shortcomings, even in the distorted structure we have.

Sometimes it seems our problems are worse. For one thing, many parents and counselors push their students into the CAS program precisely because they have had discipline and social problems: "Perhaps you can work with him/her, perhaps this more community structure will work better." Fine, but we can only absorb a certain number of students who already have conflicts with school. Otherwise, we reach the critical mass and there is no magic we can wield.

Then there is the fact that when students are together for more of the day, and over years, conflicts and evil behavior are only given time to take root and expand. Take the case of Marty. He has had it in for Julius for years.

We do counseling and meetings, but we have never been able to dig to the bottom of this conflict. Suffice it to say that Marty has decided that Julius is "gay," and that Julius deserves nearly constant teasing, occasional confrontation, and bullying from Marty. We have never been able to understand the root of the rage. We are not, after all, psychologists. And even if we were, could we really fix this conflict?

Marty's stance is so repulsive to most of the community that we wonder if we shouldn't just kick him out. What the heck? There have to be certain minimal values and commitments, some agreement to basic terms of decency, that students must agree on to be in CAS. Certainly you can't succeed with someone in the program who does not want to be there at all. But if we are angry at Marty about his behavior, what are we going to do about it? Kick him out and have him take that behavior to the larger school or to some prison camp?

And is this an isolated case? Is it just a story about Marty? Actually, there are a number of conflicts, a number of problems, that have festered over time. Have we failed to intervene properly? How do we intervene?

Recently, we were talking about the ongoing conflict between a group of sophomore boys. I was lamenting, "I mean, what the hell, shouldn't we have been able to overcome this by now?" As often happens, Phil put his finger on it.

"Well," Phil replied, "maybe it's just the downside of community."

The *downside of community*—the phrase is both dreaded and perfectly apt. We talk all the time about creating a sense of community among students as a way of making school more interesting, engaging, and safe. We act as if community is always succulent and sweet and nourishing. Nonsense.

When teens are together for a long time it is not just wonderful things that happen. Mean things happen. In fact, there are teachers at Berkeley High who argue that breaking the day into segments and remixing the kids for each class makes the school more orderly. Ellen Thatcher of the History Department once explained to a friend that keeping students together gives them time to build up a "head of steam." Another teacher described ongoing problems in a nearby junior high that has a school-within-the-school. It was a group of kids who were together for most of the day, and again the conflicts had time to get larger and more destructive. Students who are together so long form friendships, but they also form cliques, closer pals, and more vicious enemies.

So what are we to conclude? Should we go back to the repressive culture by default? The solution is at once easier and more complex than that.

WHAT DOES IT TAKE TO CREATE COMMUNITY?

Community, as Neil Postman (1997) points out, has been distorted as a concept by current fashions on the Internet. Virtual communities, connections between people with common interests, are all the rage. We now have communities of people who like begonias. There is the *Star Trek* community. Then you have the left-handed foot-fetish community. The term *community* has come to mean *commonality*. There is the lawyer community, the lesbian community, the disabled community. In a way, it seems that our era has produced less, not more, community. It has resulted in the creation of overdeveloped, narcissistic identities rather than fully rounded people.

But the core issue in community is difference. It is not that everyone is alike, but that everyone is different. And being in the community means having to deal with that person you dislike or disagree with.

The work of community is messy. It is frustrating. It means dealing with problems between people. If we have not solved the problem of Marty and Julius, it is perhaps because we have not given the time to it, the focus, the energy. The students have not had any mechanism to confront the problem. We also may not yet have the experience or wisdom to know how. We have only demonstrated that a quick fix, a reprimand, or short discussion will not do it. But the problem has to be solved. There is work to be done.

This need to confront difference, to figure out what to accommodate and what to struggle through, is evident in our staff. The culture of the factory school demands that you ignore a teacher you disagree with. Even if students are being mistreated, you shut your door and do your own thing. In the community of a small school, however, you have to face it. And we have wrestled with a whole range of conflicts. In our first year, we had a teacher who, to speak euphemistically, "did not work out." His philosophy was diametrically opposed to ours, and the students were in constant conflict with him. We had to deal with the problem. We had meetings with representatives of the students and the teacher, we had staff discussions, we set up agreements and plans to make it better. In the end, however, the main point was that we had to confront him. His department chair never had. No one ever had. But in this context, we had to face it, to do the uncomfortable work of discussing, struggling over, and resolving unacceptable behavior.

Richard Elmore (1996) talks about how school reform seldom gets to the "core of educational practice . . . how teachers understand the nature of knowledge and the student's role in learning and how these ideas about knowledge and learning are manifested in teaching and classwork" (p. 2). In small schools, however, we are compelled by our close work together to examine our own practices and those of others. Even small staff conflicts are more pronounced in CAS. If last year I taught sophomore English one way and then Jennifer Evans teaches junior English another way, the students pick apart the differences. They complain. They undermine morale. They make demands. And suddenly Jennifer and I have to look at what we each are doing. It is no longer a game of shut the door and do your own thing. This is collegiality—the "buzz word," the cliché of teacher-training programs—but something that never happens, not really.

This is the most difficult thing to confront and to discuss—our differences in approach, in philosophy, in expectations. We are pushed to have that pedagogical discussion, to open ourselves to reflection and evaluation. And at the end of the day, we can live with some differences and resolve others. In other words, we are forced to act like professionals.

SO WHAT ARE WE TO CONCLUDE?

The creation of community is not a simple slogan. It is hard work. But it is the only possible alternative to the mass society measures, the adversarial system, attacking our youth.

When we struggle to break down the boundaries and limitations that define education today, we are not simply rescuing kids. In fact, rescue is precisely what they do not need. The problem in our society is one of power—who has it, who wields it, and who benefits from it.

When we talk about social justice in our school, we are not just talking about security apparatus and rules. We are talking about how power is distributed in the school and society. We are really dealing with what we teach and how we teach. We are examining the most fundamental questions: What is education for? Who does it serve? How would we determine that someone has been educated? Why are we teachers?

Just like those students at the middle school, we have to put out to our community the questions: What is fairness? What is social justice? Are all people—students, teachers, custodians—treated with dignity? Are all given a chance to be their best selves? How do we decide to resolve conflicts? It is through struggling to create small schools that we can develop a paradigm of democratic education, one that promises to make a society that we want our grandchildren to live in. And, undeniably, within that struggle lie tensions that are forced by the existence of the community. We have to address and readdress what our values are and where we want power to lie.

One day in the junior class we were watching the video of *Obedience*, the famous Millgram experiment in which people were given power to administer shocks to others if they got the answers to memory questions wrong. The people being shocked were in on the experiment. The real test was being done on the shockers, to see how strong a charge they would progress to. An amazing 50% of the subjects gave the strongest shock, even when they heard the other person shouting in pain. They especially gave the shock when ordered to by an authority figure, the professor in charge of the test.

The discussion was spirited, as it always is after viewing this movie. It ranged from the Nuremberg principles, the defense of "I was only following orders," to the question of what the students would do if they participated in the same experiment.

One African American student, Shobab, had been sitting quietly, deep in thought, watching the debate unfold, when he raised his hand and said, "I just have one question. Do you think that you can go along with authority all your young life and then make the right decision, to resist authority, when an illegitimate order is given? Or do you think the decisions you make now, the patterns you establish, determine the type of personality you will have as an adult?"

That is a question we should all have to answer.

In the end, when we talk about students as the objects of a high school discipline plan, we are not just talking about high schools or students. We are talking about the people who will grow up and take over society. Will they reify the same values and assumptions? Will they be able to help us out of this mess? And, in turn, what communities will they know how to create?

AFTERWORD

Here is the overview letter to freshmen reflecting the social justice curriculum:

Communication Arts and Sciences (CAS) Core Program   September 1, 1999

Dear CAS freshmen,

Do you ever wonder why the world is so messed up? Do you ever think to yourself what kind of society you would create if you could just start over? Plenty of people have tried just that, either in writing stories or in actually remaking governments. This year, we are going to spend a long time considering our society and many alternatives. We will always be looking to answer the question: What are the characteristics of a just society?

We will begin with *The Tempest* by William Shakespeare. It is a play about a strange and magical land, an island. On this island, an exile from Milan has created his world, a regime of secret powers and spirits. Would you like to live there?

Of course, everything depends on your point of view: the world looks different through the eyes of the master and of the slave. In Brecht's poem "A Worker Reads History," he asks, "Who built the pyramids?" Not the Pharaoh, who did the actual work?

After we go see the play of *The Tempest,* we will read *Lord of the Flies.* Here is another island, and a group of children find themselves stranded on the island and have to make their own way. What kind of society will they create? What would you do? What are the characteristics of a just society?

During this same time, in history we will be looking at some of the Western political philosophers, Plato, Aristotle, Hobbes, Locke, Montesquieu, and Rossseau, and examining the radical transformation of the French Revolution. We will pursue the question, "Can people be trusted to govern themselves?"

After this, we will read and attend a play called *Galileo* by the great German playwright Bertolt Brecht. Galileo made great discoveries in astronomy, in understanding the nature of the universe. But he was forbidden by the church from publishing these ideas. Finally, faced with torture by the Inquisition, he renounced his findings. Brecht, too, asks what is a just society, what is the relation between scientific truth and the pursuit of power? He finds this question applies as well to the repression of the twentieth century as of the seventeenth century.

As we move into a study of the Industrial Revolution in history, we will look at the benefits and costs of this great advance in technology. As we are entering another great technological revolution with the Information Age, perhaps we can learn how to evaluate the great changes our world is going through. We will read the incredibly insightful science fiction novel, *Brave New World* by Aldous Huxley. The title actually comes from a quotation from *The Tempest.* Here society has been rescued from poverty and want, but are they free? Have they created a just society? Why or why not? These considerations will be tied to our study of the Industrial Revolution and imperialism and colonialism in history. And we will see how they led to World War I.

We will end the semester with an encounter with the Holocaust, the massacre of the Jews during World War II which brought together racist hatred and modern technology to produce one of the great crimes of human history. We will read *Night* by Elie Wiesel who survived imprisonment in Auschwitz, the most notorious of the Nazi death camps. And we hope to be able to travel to the Museum of Tolerance in Los Angeles. Is this where our society has come to? What can we learn from it?

During the second semester, we will visit the rest of the world, Africa, Latin America, and Asia. We will examine their encounters with these same questions, what makes up a just society? We will learn of traditional Ibo culture in *Things Fall Apart* and the disruptions caused by the arrival of the Europeans. What are the tensions between tradition and modernization?

We will experience Latin American writing, the magic realism which mixes western story telling with fantastic traditional worlds. We will read *Esperanza's Box* of *Saints* from Mexico and *It Begins with Tears* from the Caribbean. Again, how have the indigenous peoples coped with repression, how have they built a resistance and a culture, what kind of world do they want to live in?

And, when we get to Asia, we will read some of the poets of the T'ang Dynasty. We will encounter the Confucian Du Fu who was very concerned with the creation of a just society and we will read the poems of the Daoist Li Bai, who wanted to transcend and leave this world. And we will return to the island theme, reading a novel by Japanese author Kenzaburo Oe, who imagines a society established by abandoned children, but this one with a very different outcome than *Lord of the Flies*.

What would you do, what kind of society would you and your peers create if you were abandoned on an island? Perhaps young people are abandoned, in many ways, and have to figure out how to create a just society among yourselves. In our creation of the community for CAS, can we apply the lessons we are learning from our readings in English and History? What are the characteristics of a just society? Are we creating one? Is the school fair—in the way it establishes order, in the opportunities it provides, in the way it educates children?

By the end, we hope you will begin to feel more of a sense of responsibility, and more ownership, over the CAS program and over your own education. You will always be struggling on two fronts, to make yourself a better and more self-aware person and to make the society you live in one that is more just. This is as true in 9th grade as when you are out in the world on your own. It is a life-long struggle and so we can honestly say that we, the teachers, are investigating and learning in this class as actively as you students are.

We are excited to be starting this journey together. I wonder where it will end up in June.

Sincerely,
Rick Ayers

REFERENCES

Elmore, R. (1996). Getting to scale with good educational practice. *Harvard Educational Review, 66*(1). (Reprinted in *Working together toward reform. Harvard Educational Review*, Cambridge, MA).

Postman, N. (1997, August). Speech on media at conference: Media and American Democracy, Harvard University, Cambridge, MA.

CHAPTER 10

Practicing Social Justice in the High School Classroom

Deborah Stern

ARVIN[1] IS A 10TH-GRADER at a large urban high school in Philadelphia. A quiet boy, he does his schoolwork diligently and spends his free time in classes writing a spy novel, starring himself as chief international spy. One day in November, Marvin—never a troublemaker—gets suspended from school for a week. His offense? He lost his school ID. Without Marvin's identification badge, the guards at the front door of the school building will not let him in. He cannot be counted, and therefore he is not allowed to learn.

Marvin takes the suspension in stride. He says he plans to return to school after his week at home, scrape up $5 for a new ID, and start attending classes again. The problem is that when Marvin returns to school, he will, in a sense, be just as invisible to folks there as he was during his week at home. Marvin has not been assigned to one of the fast-track small learning communities at his high school that encourages and supports academically motivated students. He is grouped with other, academically average teenagers in classes where homework is rarely assigned and where teachers are mostly concerned with maintaining order. Only one teacher at Marvin's school has seen his spy novel. No one has talked to him about desktop publishing, about student literary magazines, about his espionage schemes, or about his sweeping, unconventional sense of narrative. Only a small number of adults at school even know who he is.

Maribel is starting 9th grade at another large urban high school, a school which is so crowded that students must attend in shifts. Maribel,

A Simple Justice: The Challenge of Small Schools. Copyright © 2000 by Teachers College, Columbia University. All rights reserved. ISBN 0-8077-3962-6 (pbk.), ISBN 0-8077-3963-4 (cloth). Prior to photocopying items for classroom use, please contact the Copyright Clearance Center, Customer Service, 222 Rosewood Dr., Danvers, MA 01923, USA, tel. (508) 750-8400.

who is in the afternoon shift, has no locker, because she did not learn about her school's locker lottery until it was too late to join the competition. She goes from class to class carrying her notebooks and her coat. Because there are not enough books to go around in several of her classes, Maribel can bring few textbooks home to study. Her schedule also has been changed twice since school started, so if she were to disappear from a class for a few days or even a week it is likely no action would be taken by her teachers. They would assume that the paperwork for Maribel's schedule change simply had not yet made its way to them.

Maribel loved going to elementary and middle school. A perfect attendance award from 8th grade is posted on her bedroom wall. But by the end of October, she is far behind in her schoolwork. For Maribel, high school is a bewildering tangle of events and policies that make her feel unwanted and unimportant. Invisible. By Thanksgiving, she has stopped attending classes regularly.

Will Marvin and Maribel make it? Or will they join the 40–70% of teens who drop out of public high schools in their respective communities? Both are caught in the gears of bureaucracies that exist to count, arrange, and control the large numbers of urban adolescents at their high schools. The teachers in these schools deal with up to 150 students a day, some of whom present alarming, profound problems that demand immediate attention. Marvin and Maribel do not represent obvious crises or threats. They demand little from their schools, and their schools are asking even less from them. Midway through their first and second years of high school, Maribel and Marvin are both on their way to becoming collateral casualties of urban schooling. Their schools are too big, too regulated, and too bureaucratic to be aware of their needs.

What would it look like if urban high schools were able to respond to students like Marvin and Maribel? If we want to give equal educational opportunities to all city kids, we will make urban schools places where their abilities and talents can be recognized, encouraged, and developed. If we want to make a difference in urban teens' lives, if we are committed to making our society more equitable, then we will work with young people in arrangements that allow them to be heard and seen.

How can we begin to do this? What can we do as adults, citizens, teachers? How can we connect school practices to urban students' voices, activities, priorities, and communities? How can we deal with students individually, rather than by type, by ability level, or by the hundred-count?

One way to take on this challenge is to create small, independent urban high schools committed to social justice. According to Maxine Greene (1998), teaching for social justice means helping young people deal critically with the world the way it is. It also means teaching students to imagine and experience the world that does not yet exist. School can be a place where students learn, proactively and productively, to straddle the gap between the world that is and the world that could be. Schools can allow students, administrators, and teachers to engage in this critical imagining—that is, to practice social justice—deliberately, every day.

SEEING CONNECTIONS BETWEEN INJUSTICE AND SCHOOLING, AND BETWEEN JUSTICE AND EDUCATION

One school where students are learning to engage in critical imagining, to see their lives and their educational possibilities in new ways, is Prologue Alternative High School in Chicago. Since 1975, Prologue has been a "last-chance" school for young men and women aged 16–21 who have dropped out of other Chicago public high schools. Before coming to Prologue, some students simply stopped going to school because they found it to be inhospitable and dangerous. Some were asked to leave after 2 years because they had not earned sufficient academic credits toward graduation. Some were told they could not go back to high school after being incarcerated or having a baby.

From the street, Prologue looks like anything but a school. It is located on the second and third floors of an old, decrepit building on a corner busy with drug traffic. Across the street is a popular concert hall; downstairs in the school building is a small grocery and liquor store, a bar, and a sandwich shop. At the back is open space that staff and students have cleaned up and use as both a sculpture garden and a vegetable garden, although efforts to keep the area clear of discarded bottles and trash have not always been successful.

Up in the 12 rooms that constitute Prologue, students gain academic and social skills by analyzing, demystifying, and critiquing the social institutions that have underserved or overlooked them in the past. They work on basic skills, they earn high school credit, and they examine some of the reasons why they were previously marginalized and made invisible at school.

> We learn to make our own expectations about ourselves here [at Prologue]. You cannot get education like this anywhere else. We don't just learn the nouns, verbs, and etc. But we learn about ourselves. I feel great about being in school for the first time since 8th grade. I am willing to learn anything and everything. I want to do much better for myself and my son.—Minette

I taught English at Prologue from 1988 to 1993, and I have served there in more recent years as a curriculum consultant and board member. Involvement with Prologue students and with the school has been the most important influence in my life as an educator. In its conception and day-to-day operations, Prologue models and teaches for social justice. Its incongruities and idiosyncrasies also bring up some of the stickier issues associated with teaching disaffected teenagers, using socially critical curriculum, and working both within and despite the mainstream public school system. We wrestle with important, difficult questions at Prologue: Can we teach young people not only to critique unjust social systems but also to confront and change them? Should we? How can we ask students to critique institutions such as their own school without inviting considerable trouble?

Questions like these play out in our courses, which are both traditional (biology, history, mathematics) and nontraditional (African drumming, parenting, peer counseling). Ideas for these courses have come from students as well as staff, and students also have proposed specific topics of study for the academic courses. For instance, students have suggested and studied topics including the following in English classes: racism, education, love, power, coming of age, AIDS, gender roles, justice, family, and dreams. In other words, students at Prologue construct curriculum around their own concerns and experiences. This arrangement demonstrates more than the Prologue staff's commitment to student-centered curriculum. It also affirms our faith in the abilities of students to teach and learn from each other. This is especially important to our students, who have previously been ignored and unheard at school, and whose knowledge and experience in the outside world have been consistently disregarded.

Whatever the topic of study, we try to ground our inquiry in questions that have relevance and meaning for us as individuals, as members of the Prologue community, and as residents of Uptown, one of Chicago's most economically and ethnically diverse neighborhoods. One way we do this is by locating our studies in historical, topical, literary, and local contexts. Another way is by putting students' questions at the center of our explorations.

What does a social justice curriculum look like in practice? How can classroom instruction simultaneously encourage students to problematize the status quo and develop academic skills? How do teachers teach critically so that students feel affirmed and energized rather than depressed and invalidated? It may be best to explore these questions by looking closely at a single topic of instruction in a single classroom.

A SOCIAL JUSTICE CURRICULUM IN THE CLASSROOM

Students at Prologue take the classes they need to round out their learning and fulfill the city of Chicago's distribution requirements for graduation. This means that most students will take several semesters of English while they are at Prologue. English classes consist of 12- to 14-week-long thematic units of instruction that develop reading, writing, and critical-thinking skills. Although the themes vary from year to year, students consistently name some of the same concerns when we are deciding what to study at the beginning of each English unit: power, love, money.

Almost every year, students at Prologue have said they wanted to study violence in English classes. In our investigations of violence we have found abundant opportunity to examine the world as it is now, and to imagine the shape and tenor of a more just, less violent world. While we all benefit from looking at our own and society's self-destructive behaviors, these urban students in particular need opportunities to make sense of the violence they observe and confront. Tragically, first-hand experience with violence has become all too common for urban youth. We cannot allow teenagers to accept the violence they have seen, been victimized by, and perpetrated themselves. When we approach violence critically, students can take time to reflect upon the surrounding circumstances, choices, and consequences of their actions. This unit has worked especially well at the end of the school year. The streets come alive during the spring in Chicago, and for many Prologue students, virtually all decisions and activities during May and June are predicated on avoiding or seeking out violence.

Once, as we debated the value of studying violence together, a Prologue student expressed her pessimism and frustration about the inevitability of aggression:

> Whether you seek it out or mind your own business these days, violence has a lot to do with growing up. . . . I don't see how things can get better 'cause there are more gangbangers and drug dealers in this world than good people. They outnumber the good people. So tell me, how can we talk about violence like we have a choice?—*Julia*

Shaped by students' interests and concerns, our inquiry into violence takes a different turn every year. One semester, a class consisting mostly of young women wanted to focus on domestic violence. Another class, with equal numbers of male and female students, led most class discussions to gang violence: How exciting, how stupid, and how inescapable it is for young people in Chicago's ethnic neighborhoods.

We begin by investigating the sources of violence. Students read scenarios depicting children and adults acting violently, and brainstorm possible motivations for their actions. One of my classes listed the following as causes of violence in these scenarios: self-defense, frustration, ego, entertainment, respect, principle, jealousy, no other way to express self, loss of power, built-up anger, impatience, brainwashing, desire to establish reputation, adrenaline rush, desire for retaliation, threats, fear, oppression, peer pressure. We debate and rate these findings. Are some reasons "better" than others? Which of these motivations do students find most compelling, personally? Are there any they believe should be dismissed as foolish or somehow inadequate?

We look next at theories that have been offered by different cultures to explain human violence, beginning with the Greek notion of aggression as stemming either from Dionysian abandon or Apollonian reason. After reading a few myths and briefly surveying the Greek pantheon, students write about a time in their lives when they did or did not choose violence as a way of resolving a conflict, and then apply this understanding of the human psyche to their own experiences. Here is one student's story of the events that led to his leaving a gang ("dropping flags"):

> I guess the turning point in my short life happened around June two years ago. It struck a nerve that made me think of all the shit I've been doing.
> I changed alot that summer I guess you could say I became aware.
> We had just gotten a case of Lowes' from Crown Liqures on Southport we headed to Addison Rocks to go meet the other guys. The we I'm referring to is Tito, Juan, Genaro, Shorty, and me. It was Genaros car and it was stolen so we could be chill. We got there early cause the rest of the boys weren't there yet. When a Broughem pulled up we payed it no mind because we were all ready fucked up. The two guys walked out with their ladies.
> Tito was like "That motherfucker is a Cobra. Straight up. I think he shot my brother."
> I was always down to serve someone but Tito had a .35 with, so I was scared not only if they had a gun but that one of them is going to die tonight.
> We walked up to the Cobras and Tito said "What's up, Folks! 'Eagle.'"
> One said I don't gangbang. The other said once a snake, always a snake. As soon as the words left his mouth a bullet went thru it. Tito shot him twice in the mouth and I think the eye.
> Two weeks later I dropped my flags. It was a head to toe violation,[2] three minutes of pain. It was worth it though. How could these guys be so dumb killing each other without flinching.
> Tito's in jail serving 30 years. Genaro got shot in the neck. He breathes thru a bag. Juan and Shorty dropped and got married. And I'm here.—*Michael*

Debate was hot when the class commented on this story in small groups. Everyone thought Michael's decision to leave the gang was courageous, but students were divided as to whether the boys in the gang were acting rationally or irrationally when they committed murder, whether these actions reflected Apollonian reason or Dionysian heedlessness. We never came to a conclusion, but Michael's candor allowed him and his peers to talk about life and death on the streets in ways that were critical, compassionate, and useful. This kind of writing and talking also makes students want to dig into other explanations for human behavior, other ways of thinking about creating and resolving conflicts through violence.

Typically, our next step in studying violence is to trace various cultural and historical approaches to aggression. Different societies have regarded violent natures as manifestations of the Devil or evidence of an inherent human weakness that must be transcended. We come to see our society's interpretation of violent action—as a natural drive more or less exacerbated by a person's environment and experiences—as just one of many visions.

We turn next to investigation of how biological and psychosocial forces combine to affect an individual's behavior. We read short excerpts from introductory-level college psychology texts about the "frustration-aggression hypothesis," the "social-learning theory," and the influence of mass-media violence, and we weigh these ideas in relation to personal experiences.

In early discussions, students regularly focus on issues of survival. They believe violence to be justified when an individual's life, family, or freedom is threatened. Prologue's social-justice orientation also invites us to think about whether or not society condones these same reasons for violence. As we regard individual experiences in social and historical contexts, we find ourselves asking a new question: When does mainstream society excuse or appreciate violence? Students often bring up "self-defense" legal pleas, and name police action or war as examples of socially approved violence. To test these hypotheses we read two particularly powerful texts—Tim O'Brien's "How To Tell a True War Story" (1991) and testimony of Bosnian rape victims from a short "Action Alert" in Ms. Magazine (January/February 1993). Both are wrenching accounts that reflect the senseless brutality of war.

We discuss these works in as much detail as we can tolerate. I ask students to explain the differences between war and interpersonal conflict. One year, one student defined war as "aggression motivated by outside orders." Another student said that if two people in a war fight to the death, or even if two groups fight to the death, it's not war if every person fighting is doing it for "personal reasons." Another student said:

> It is only when leaders give orders that conflicts turn to wars, because that's when people start to get disconnected from the violence they commit. Soldiers can then just say, "I'm doing my job." This is why raping the girls in Bosnia is war, not sex. The article even says "Serbian soldiers are under orders to use women's bodies as a primary battleground."—Chris

Figure 10.1.   *Noting Violence in the Media*

Title of film or TV show	Violent acts depicted	Apollonian or Dionysian impulse?	Psychological theory	Details of presentation	Consequences

This unit calls on us to think about the complicated relationships among social justice, social necessity, and violence. Why are some wars glorified and others excoriated? Are "just" wars any different from wars of conquest and greed? How or when can a good society allow and even endorse such brutality? We also look closely at the ways newspapers and television news programs report gang fights and street killings. Why are only some violent acts news? Why are articles written about neighborhood street violence usually so short and lacking in detail? These questions, too, lie at the core of this unit of instruction. They force us not only to confront the dehumanizing power of violence but also to consider the ways in which we are co-opted by this power, how we become inured to it, and how we sometimes benefit from it. These questions compel us to take a stand and ask ourselves what we are prepared to do about the powerful pull that violence exerts on each of us.

Our next investigation is into violence as entertainment. We watch a number of film scenes and/or entire films, and we analyze and critique their depiction of physical and verbal violence. We look not only at what is filmed but also at how it is filmed—camera angles, music, and so on. Does the movie condemn violence or celebrate it? How? Why? How do we punish those who commit violent acts? What are the consequences of glorified Hollywood violence for the perpetrators? For the victims? For the audience? Students use a sheet like the one shown in Figure 10.1 to note and comment on various acts of violence and aggression in popular films and TV shows.

Next, students read a major work, either William Golding's *Lord of the Flies* (1959), Trumbo's *Johnny Got His Gun* (1939/1983), or Tervalen's *Understand This* (1995). As they read, students generate discussion questions in small groups, imitate each author's distinctive narrative voice in short creative writing exercises, and reflect in journal entries on questions including the following:

- Have you ever believed in something so deeply that you were willing to sacrifice for it, maybe even die for it? What made you loyal?
- When have you been carried away on a wave of destruction or
  hatred? What does it feel like to be beyond reason? Why do you
  think this happens?
- What is our responsibility concerning the violence that is in our
  lives? Do you feel obligated to teach anyone what you know about
  violence? Who? Why?

For the students' final project in the violence unit, we all bring in poetry
and song lyrics addressing violence and aggression. Students have found
poetry written by soldiers especially moving, including the work of Wilfred Owen ("Dulce et Decorum Est," 1965), Thomas Gunn ("Innocence,"
1994), and Jan Barry ("Vietnam," 1976). Pop music ranging from Tracy
Chapman ("Behind the Wall," 1988) to Metallica ("One," 1988) to Ice
Cube ("Once Upon a Time in the Projects," 1990) has also yielded more
insights and more valuable questions about how to reconcile human violence with the struggle for a more just world.

As students evaluate each others' and their own presentations, they
consider new ways to think about aggression, manipulation, and representation. One student wrote on her class evaluation sheet that she learned
"not even the singers are taking all metal songs seriously," and that "young
White boys who listen to heavy metal are probably angry, and this music
gives them a release." We all come away with new insights into violence,
enriched by each others' experiences and perspectives.

A SOCIALLY JUST SCHOOL EXISTS NOT TO TRANSFORM
STUDENTS, BUT TO BE TRANSFORMED BY THEM

Students at Prologue do more than contribute to the curriculum in academic classes. Because we valorize student agency, we have created administrative arrangements that require students and the faculty to listen to each
other and make decisions together.

Our small faculty tends to be cohesive and self-selected. With few
exceptions over the years, Prologue administrators also teach. We divide
up scheduling, advising, attending outside meetings, and paperwork
amongst the staff. Weekly staff meetings are structured to allow staff to
keep track of students in the school. We hear who has been doing particularly strong work and who has been missing classes, and we learn the reasons behind individual students' struggles.

Twice a month we hold whole-school meetings with the entire student
body where we debate topical issues and school policies, listen to outside
speakers, and enjoy dance and musical performances. Students also use this

time to share projects and presentations originally prepared for individual classes. These group meetings bring teachers and students together intellectually and socially.

For better or worse, students also determine the social dynamics of the school. For instance, one year there was considerable tension between some African American and Latino students. By the spring quarter, staff members were the only ones eating their lunches in the usually full lounge area. Students had split into groups by race. African American students had lunch and hung out in the history room, and Latino students gathered to eat and talk every day in another classroom.

How would this situation have been treated at a large school? Would teachers or administrators have interfered? I am not sure adults would have known about increased racial tension among the student body at a large school, especially if there had been no overt conflicts. At Prologue, where the student body numbered about 75 that year, the tension was palpable. Still, as a staff we knew that our efforts alone could not fix the situation. We decided that students' responses to the division had to be everyone's starting point. One day a student posted a homemade, graffiti-style banner asking, "WHAT TIME IS IT?" which told us:

> This "he say–she say, I'm wit dis and you're phoney" mentality has gotta stop. Let people be who they are. We each have to know our culture, history, and destiny, so that we can respect each other, and rise up together to overcome this fucktup system. . . . With respect to the whole Prologue crew, including all Africans, Latinos, indigenous peoples (and all Brothers and Sisters locked up for Freedom): Keep your mind free! —*John*

John did not allow himself to be dragged down into his peers' negativity or feelings of powerlessness. Instead, he assumed a position of leadership and rose to rally the entire Prologue community to think critically about real issues of solidarity and oppression. This poster opened up substantive discussions among students and staff. In fact, two sections of English classes chose to study race and racism that spring. Students wrote in their journals about a time they experienced racial stereotyping. We read poetry and prose addressing race and racism. We conducted and tabulated schoolwide surveys about ethnicity, race, and prejudice, and when we role-played and discussed the effects of racism in our own lives, several students brought up the noxious tension among African American and Latino students at Prologue that year. Using this real problem as a springboard, students considered some of the underlying causes and sources of racism. Grounding our inquiry in our shared, lived experiences gave our academic studies immediacy and meaning, and stressed our mutuality and ability to look out for one another.

Saying that life at Prologue builds on student knowledge and experi-ence and develops according to student input means that we have to be patient with one another. We cannot ask students to imagine a more just world without meeting them where they are. We have to accept that not every student at Prologue is willing or ready to be a leader in the larger school. Most years, a few student leaders rise to lead their peers to critical action. Some years this does not happen.

What we do every year is try to help each student take control of his or her own education. This effort is put to the test at quarterly evaluations, a process we have tried to make as mutual as possible. We give no letter grades at Prologue. Four times a year we set aside a full day for students to come in and talk with each of their teachers. The student and the teacher sit down together and do a co-evaluation. The student reflects upon and writes about what he or she got out of the class, and the teacher reflects upon and writes about the progress the student has made, whether she or he has earned course credit, and what steps ought to be taken next. Both reflections become part of the evaluation.

This system does have drawbacks: Students either earn academic credit or they do not. It's all or nothing. Also, some students do not take advan-tage of the opportunity to look closely at their work or the course, and write only cursory comments such as: "It was OK. I deserve credit."

The evaluation process presents challenges for teachers, too. Looking at student evaluations I have saved over the years, I am struck by how I have tended to treat the form as a chance for me to tell students how I thought they could improve. I know I could have been more effective in eliciting students' feelings about school and their needs as students at eval-uation time. One year, for example, a student's evaluation in my English class included the following:

Course: Contemporary Literature

Student: Octavia

Student's Self Evaluation: I will hand in my work on time next quarter so you won't have to chase me down.

Teacher's Evaluation: A good final test on this quarter's theme, "Good and Evil," seemed to pull you out of the doldrums, Octavia. I hope you will be a strong and assertive force in class next quarter. We need a positive, articulate and mature female voice in here to speak out.

At the time of this evaluation, I recognized that Octavia seemed to be going through a hard time, and that she had potential to be a class leader. But I did not ask Octavia why I had needed to "chase" after her that quarter. Why had she been having trouble completing her work? In my efforts to affirm her good test performance and her leadership qualities, what wasn't I hearing that Octavia was telling me?

Prologue's cooperative evaluation strategies are not perfect. They do not cure teachers' tendencies to judge and sometimes misjudge students. What we want our approaches to assessment and curriculum to show is that we are committed to creating a school where staff and students are both engaged in inquiry. In Prologue classrooms, students and teachers search together for answers. We take on the complications that come with giving voice to different perspectives and agendas, and we reject the hierarchies and the certainties that we have come to associate with teaching, learning, and evaluating.

This is not to say that we are content merely to let our students discuss the injustices of school and society, pass them through classes, and then just give them all diplomas for sitting and talking. On the contrary, our intention is to help our students—for whom past instruction has consisted mostly of learning facts by rote—deal critically with the responsibilities and complexities of taking responsibility for their own learning.

Not surprisingly, student agency has enormous implications for us as teachers. The longer students stay at Prologue, the more active and critical their demands on us become. For instance, one year I asked students in one of my classes to write and tell me why they were falling behind on their schoolwork. One student wrote:

> No, no one has asked anything of me at Prologue that is impossible. To promote and educate people on change is good. BUT to expect—no matter how well intended—that a student will be able to change how he does school will lead to frustration 9 times outta 10. And if our instructors and role models are frustrated at our performances, your behavior will effect us. So even reasonable expectations can backfire.—*Simon*

I think I expected my students to admit that they just needed to buckle down and turn in some homework. But Simon had been at Prologue for 2 years and was capable of analyzing my demands and offering resistance to my prompting. If I was going to be serious about modeling ethical communication and cooperation in my practice, I also had to be serious about listening to what Simon was telling me. I had to hear Simon's reminder that even the most reasonable requests carry within them assumptions and have emotional consequences.

TEACHING FOR SOCIAL JUSTICE IN AN UNJUST WORLD

We cannot underestimate the difficulties of teaching for social justice in a world that is unjust. But we cannot become paralyzed by them, either. The crucial advantage that small, independent schools have is that they offer working alternatives to students' lived experiences with educational injustice and to teachers' feelings of impotence in the face of such injustices. The foundations of Prologue's program—all young people can learn, and we serve underserved youth best by treating them fairly and honestly as mature individuals—cannot help but make indelible impressions on students who are used to being ignored, abused, and oppressed in large urban high schools.

Prologue is not offered here as a model. We cannot ask how or whether all city schools could get small and political and be like Prologue. It is unrealistic to think that every school will transform itself into a small, politicized learning environment. It is unrealistic to think that any school could transform every former dropout into a radical activist against oppression and racism. We can ask, rather, what a place like Prologue can teach educators about opening all social practices, including those of the school, to critical examination and re-imagining.

At Prologue, we acknowledge the necessity of critical thinking and counter-discourse (Leistyna, Woodrum, & Sherblom, 1996, have defined counter-discourse as "critique, demystification, and agency capable of contesting dominant oppressive ideologues and practices" [p. 333]). We recognize that teachers always incorporate their own social and ideological values into a curriculum. We ask each other to interrogate our decisions about what and how we teach and learn. We do not contaminate the academic with the political when we teach for social justice—not only because there is no such thing as a ideologically neutral schooling but also because the connections among these domains are precisely what gives education meaning for disenfranchised youth.

Always, our work raises more questions than it answers. Every year Prologue students graduate and go out into the city, into higher education, and into the workforce. How is what they find affected by what they have learned with us? Teachers at Prologue are mostly products of traditional schooling. How are we de-schooling ourselves so that our work does not reinforce and reproduce existing social inequalities? How does knowing our students well change our relationships with them? Who is the student? Who is the teacher? Can changes in our classrooms, in ourselves, and in our students effect change in other schools and in our communities?

These are tough questions. Asking them in good faith requires us to consider the moral obligation that lies in every educational effort: We have to think honestly, creatively, and lovingly about what our young people need as they learn to take care of themselves and each other. We must encourage them to exceed our visions and create their own. The

richest and most useful education we can give our students is one that provides them with tools and opportunities to confront inequities in their
lives, one that will help them improve their own psychological and material conditions.

Above all, questions such as these call upon us to address the ways in
which schools are structured. When a school's policies, practices, and curriculum reflect students' realities, remarkable things start to happen. Students and teachers find new ways to think about ourselves and our relationships to one another, to learning, and to social change. Students teach
each other and challenge us to make school meaningful. Bringing students
like Marvin and Maribel into the conversation about the nature and purpose of their own education keeps them on track and keeps them from
falling through the cracks. They make greater academic gains, and they
help create a better, more just learning environment for themselves and
their peers. They bridge the gap between what is and what could be in
their own lives.

NOTES

1. All students' names are pseudonyms.
2. The "violation" Michael refers to is the ritual beating a gangbanger must
endure upon joining or leaving a gang.

REFERENCES

Action alert: Dispatches from Bosnia and Herzegovina: Young survivors testify to
      systematic rape. (1993, January/February). *Ms.*, pp. 12–13.
Barry, J. (1976). Vietnam. In J. Barry & W. D. Ehrhart (Eds.), *DMZ*. Perkasie, PA:
      East River Anthology.
Chapman, T. (1988). Behind the wall. On *Tracy Chapman*. New York: WEA/Elektra
      Records.
Golding, W. (1959). *Lord of the flies*. New York: Turtleback.
Greene, M. (1998). Introduction: Teaching for social justice. In W. Ayers, J. Hunt,
      & T. Quinn (Eds.), *Teaching for social justice* (pp. xxvii–xlvi). New York: Teachers
      College Press and New Press.
Gunn, T. (1994). Innocence. In T. Gunn, *Collected poems by Thom Gunn*. New York:
      Farrar, Strass, and Giroux.
Ice Cube. (1990). Once upon a time in the projects. On *AmeriKKKA's most wanted*.
      Hollywood, CA: Priority Records.
Leistyna, P., Woodrum, A., & Sherblom, S. A. (Eds.). (1996). *Breaking free: The trans-
      formative power of critical pedagogy*. Cambridge, MA: Harvard Educational Review
      Reprint Series.
Metallica. (1988). One. On *And justice for all*. New York: WEA/Elektra Records.

O'Brien, T. (1991). *The things they carried.* New York: Penguin.

Owen, W. (1965). Dulce et decorum est. In C. D. Lewis (Ed.), *The collected poems of Wilfred Owen.* New York: Norton.

Tervalen, J. (1995). *Understand this.* New York: Anchor.

Trumbo, D. (1983). *Johnny got his gun.* New York: Citadel. (Original work published 1939.)

CHAPTER 11

When *Jamas* Is Enough

CREATING A SCHOOL FOR A COMMUNITY
(A CONVERSATION WITH TAMARA WITZL)

Gabrielle H. Lyon

IN 1994 A SMALL PUBLIC SCHOOL OPENED in Chicago's Mexican American "Little Village" neighborhood. A staff of 15 teachers, 3 artists, musicians and dancers, 250 students, and their families embarked together on a journey to create a school for the community in which it was located. At the helm—although at the time informally—was Tamara Witzl.

Witzl's dark hair is cut into a pageboy, and her expressive eyebrows frame dark brown eyes. As she speaks her eyes are bright and sharp. Witzl learned Greek before she knew Spanish, but once she moved to Little Village with her husband she became immersed in the struggles of the working-class community and the issues of living in a gateway for new immigrants. She learned Spanish in the neighborhood, working, shopping, and raising children alongside her neighbors. When she started teaching at the local neighborhood school, she found colleagues who shared some of her educational goals and philosophies.

Witzl and a few other teachers birthed Telpochcalli—pronounced "tell-poach-coll-ee", meaning "House of Youth" in Nahuatl, a language spoken by indigenous groups in Mexico—out of the local neighborhood school. The 2-year battle was rooted in frustration with inadequate language programs and with watching students and families who were being affected by the racism of language and culture.

The walls of Telpochcalli are drenched with artwork. Technique, style, color, and materials echo with refrains of Mexican culture and tradition.

A Simple Justice: The Challenge of Small Schools. Copyright © 2000 by Teachers College, Columbia University. All rights reserved. ISBN 0-8077-3962-6 (pbk.), ISBN 0-8077-3963-4 (cloth). Prior to photocopying items for classroom use, please contact the Copyright Clearance Center, Customer Service, 222 Rosewood Dr., Danvers, MA 01923, USA, tel. (508) 750-8400.

As you walk through the bowers of paintings and projects, you will be drawn to listen at a door where recorders are piping. Farther along you hear the shuffle, shuffle, stomp of young feet learning ancient patterns.

For Telpochcalli, integrating arts into the curriculum through a unique partnership with the Mexican Fine Arts Center Museum is based on more than a creative idea. Culture *is* the curriculum, and validating the culture of the school community is intimately connected with language.

In the summer of 1999, Principal Tamara Witzl spoke with me about Telpochcalli and about Chicago's small-schools movement.

What was it like at the beginning? To me it seemed like small schools weren't going to work. First we wrote a proposal to break into small schools and it didn't get funded. That really took the air out of the balloon. Then in November the Mexican Fine Arts Center Museum held a meeting. I went with another teacher and the Local School Council chairperson. Right away we looked at each other and said, "Hey, this is an idea for a small school." We went back to our principal and said, "This is what we want to do." He agreed. So we presented an all-call to the staff at the next faculty meeting and handed out a fact sheet. We had to print the words in red because the black ink ran out on the printer. We said, "The Mexican Fine Arts Center Museum (MFACM) wants to form a partnership with CPS to integrate Mexican arts and culture into classrooms. The museum is going to write a funding proposal that would support Mexican art and culture by bringing artists, dancers, and musicians into the classrooms to work with students. If we get a significant number of people, we'll tell the museum and they'll write us in and we'll go from there. There'll be a year of planning to build a small school."

At the time were you talking about it in terms of language and culture? Oh yes, from the very beginning. We hung out our shingle right away. We said, "We want to do this and anyone else who wants to do it, come on." Ironically, a monolingual parent of one of the only Anglo kids in the school was one of the most supportive people. She didn't really think it fit for her child, but that didn't sway her. She would say things to me like, "Tamara, I understand. I was just watching this program on cable about Native Americans, and a girl was talking about how it only took a generation for them to lose their culture and their language. What you're doing sounds similar to me and I understand how sad it is." Somewhere in her background she has some Native American roots and that helped her to see a little farther.

From the beginning, the principal would entertain my ideas to push for the fact that we needed to have control over budget and staffing. He would entertain those and say, "Yeah, OK, just wait. We'll get there. You're trying to move too fast." But he would also say, "Try it this way. Or try it this way. Put out the proposal for funding artists, see what happens, just try." All along I wanted to demand the part of the budget that belonged to our students. I wanted to demand, "This is ours to decide because it belongs to our kids."

Also, there was an opportunity to decide who would teach in our school. That seemed vital to its success. These issues, as well as the focus on Mexican art, language, support for full bilingualism made our school mission controversial.

As we started to have politically hot discussions, people began to drop like flies. What some thought originally to be a "neat idea," grew into a school focused on giving students and kids the opportunity and support to look at themselves, their roots, their community as a way of learning about their important place in it.

What did those discussions sound like? "There's not enough in Mexican art and culture to make it the focus of a school." "What about all the other places in the world?" Some people reacted to us in a narrow way. What we were suggesting was seen as a reductionist vision. Our feelings were the opposite. We felt, "Start here with who you are and that will give you the understanding, the template to look at everything else in the world. There's never anywhere specifically in the curriculum for our kids to look at themselves—with themselves as the focus, the reason for investigation, the reason for celebration." Some people had a hard time envisioning or supporting that.

What was it like when you decided to move ahead and become an independent public school rather than a school within a school? We felt strongly that our school needed to continue to move forward. Fortunately, we were able to participate in a request for proposals put out by Chicago Public Schools in 1996. In that proposal we asked for the $10,000 Chicago Public Schools were offering as part of the request for proposals, a unit number, control over faculty and staffing, our own budget, and a space which was located across the street from our original school. We asked for all of that and got all of that. The small schools coalition played a major role by encouraging us. They kept saying, "Be strong and just ask for it."

Our proposal to the Board of Education was accepted in the context of a commitment to accept a number of proposals for new small public schools. We were all going to form new schools with our own unit numbers. We found out in March 1996 that our proposal had been accepted. We had to open on August 28. All the new small schools had very similar issues—we all needed a budget, to be staffed. We had to find out how we were going to get books, desks, and chairs. At one point we got a call and the Board told us our building was going to be rehabbed—well, when? It was wild and crazy, and it was *July*. We ordered supplies, and did all kinds of stuff and worked for weeks and weeks, day after day.

In the first year we were assigned a principal, but he was the principal of three of the new small schools. In our second year, they assigned us our own administrator, but it was a person who wasn't at all on board with our vision of the school. The person was autocratic, disrespectful, and tried to move us in the opposite direction of where we wanted to go. The parents wondered why I wasn't the principal, and the staff encouraged me to get the necessary credentials. After a while I willingly accepted the draft and went after a Type 75 so that I would be eligible to serve as principal.

That was a good decision. We saw what we needed, and we moved forward to do it. When we look back now, we realize we did some very strategic things at important points in time when we were first getting started.

In terms of getting from that place to the place where you are now, what are the elements that have been the most crucial? There are so many elements. If you have a vision of what you want to do, it's important you put together a group of people who want to do it with you and who can support you. While we were working to create Telpochcalli from the inside of CPS, it was vital that the coalition outside was pushing this along.

For us, the small-schools coalition was crucial. They were willing to push on different sides from all different ways. They talked about issues that were pertinent to us to other people, and at the same time worked to understand, and help us to understand, what we need to be able to do to move ourselves forward.

When we were first establishing Telpochcalli I was *persona non grata* on the inside of my own building—the unwanted in my own land, so to speak. I'm not one to feel I need a gazillion friends. As long as I feel I share a mind and vision with a group of people I'm fine. The group of teachers that formed Telpochcalli became a very cohesive and cooperative group of people.

Being part of a coalition helped me because it kept me abreast of the bigger picture and focused the work on the inside. It gave me energy. At the same time, our partnership with the Mexican Fine Arts Center Museum helped us develop our curricular focus and commitment to our students' and parents' language and culture.

The Small Schools Workshop at the University of Illinois at Chicago has also been a steady support and helped us from the start by facilitating, providing feedback, staff development.

These are the kinds of supports that have been crucial for our development.

What is the vision of Telpochcalli? Why does Telpochcalli need to exist?
That's a heavy one. Our vision is to integrate Mexican art and culture into an educational experience which is challenging. At the same time, we want to develop fully biliterate students who have an appreciation and respect for themselves, their families, community, and the world.

Telpochcalli definitely needs to exist because it needs to provide a cultural and linguistic basis for the kids that we serve. We need to do it first for our kids in the community and the parents that we serve. Second, we need to exist for the city and for the country as a whole—and do well—because there's nothing like ours as far as I know.

The combination of a small school and the focus we have is what I think is unique and needs to thrive. Our view is that curriculum is something dynamic and creative and that a certain set of standards or goals are the mainstays. The interesting and creative part is how you actually get there. That's the curriculum part. Those things are things so broad and open that you can do it in any given way, including weaving Mexican art, history, and culture through the curriculum.

Another thing that makes us unique is our commitment to our student population. We have parents that have obviously showed their faith and belief in us, taken a real risk in coming along with us on this uncharted ride. When I think of that I am continually in awe. As a parent you know how important education is to your kid, and to be willing to put your kid on a journey that is unmapped—those are really strong, committed people, people who have a lot of heart and believe that something different can come from their kid. It's humbling to me whenever I think of it.

What are some of the struggles for you outside the school?   One of them is just trying to explain to other people our commitment to integrating Mexican arts and culture and our commitment to total bilingualism. We call ourselves a "maintenance bilingual program." From our perspective, children bring a language other than English to the school. We try to use that to teach academic concepts and teach English as a second language. We want to build on what students bring—not take away from it. We see it as an "additive model." Eventually the two will become developed and the students will be bilingual.

How is that different from "dual-language programs"?   In "dual-language programs" you have two different language groups, and then you build literacy in their home language while you create interesting ways for students to learn the other language. We don't have two different language groups at our school. For the most part, our students are more dominant in Spanish when they come to us. We have very few kids who come as balanced bilingual or kids that are dominant in English.

The goal of dual-language programs is to create fully bilingual/biliterate students. It's how you get there and how the programs work to fit students' needs that is the difference.

How does this difference come out in practice in schools? We're looking for a way to name our road to bilingualism. In the meantime, my question is, What's wrong with maintenance bilingualism? The problem is that it's not politically palatable right now. All of this is in contrast to transitional programs which, for most kids, end up being "English-only" programs. The emphasis is entering monolingual English classes as soon as possible. This is subtractive—"Let's work as hard as possible to move students away from what they already bring and know because all they'll need is English."

For example, you have a kid that doesn't read in their home language in first grade and then is transitioned into a monolingual program. By third grade the teacher says, "Hey! This kid can't read." Well, the kid couldn't really read in Spanish when they were transitioned out of a bilingual program. Most kids develop what are called "BICS"—basic interpersonal communication skills—things they pick up off the street, from TV. They appear to be proficient speakers in the language because they can say, "Hi. How are you? Last night I watched. . . ." And people think, "That kid's really conversant in English," not knowing that the deeper language structures that are needed to do well academically haven't begun to take root.

In discussions about schools and language what gets me most is the facade. Most often the real end result in schools that say they have a bilingual program is that the kids will be English-only speakers. There's no intent to make kids bilingual. People explain it by saying, "Oh, they'll get it at home." I think that's a dubious notion. We know that our families are stressed in so many ways. They're economically stressed. Culturally, it's very difficult for them to maintain connections to kids because of time restraints and job demands. It's especially hard for families. When you add them all together, you've got a hit-or-miss situation. Furthermore, the parents themselves have mixed feelings about what it is to be bilingual and what it will mean for the long-term success of their child. Because the society is giving the message that if you are an immigrant of modest economic means you have to leave your culture and language behind to "make it."

Given that, how do you present Telpochcalli to parents? We try to tell them in a clear, logical way what an advantage it is to be bilingual and how we view bilingualism at Telpochcalli. Parents usually agree with us. Initially you do have families that think their child is coming to school to learn English—not necessarily to learn how to read, write, do math and social studies, and that they will also learn English and continue to develop their Spanish.

We emphasize from the outset that we have a maintenance bilingual program and that we have a Mexican art and culture focus. Not to the exclusion of any other culture—but it's something we weave throughout the curriculum because it's who our students and families are. I always say, "You don't have to register your child today. Go think about it. Come back and ask questions. If you or your other family members won't be able to support your child in this endeavor, you really need to think about not enrolling your child. However, if you think and support this idea, please come and register."

In the last 3 years there have only been a couple of families that have come to take their kids out of the school. In one case the mother really wanted to keep the child in the school, and the father wouldn't come to the school to meet us. He just kept insisting that she take the child out because the child wasn't learning English quickly enough. The mother was more bilingual; he, ironically, was less bilingual and mostly spoke Spanish. The mother felt too much pressure. It was very sad for the student and the mother.

Why not just have a good language maintenance program? Why the cultural and arts element? I feel very strongly that kids need to get a good foundation in their home language. I also think that the kids who have an opportunity to be bilingual need to be supported. The connection between language, culture, family, and community is a direct link. When you take away people's ability to communicate with their parents, uncles, grand-parents, you break down a very human element—for that individual, as well as in communities and society as a whole. At the same time, no one who works at Telpochcalli wants to deny the fact that kids need to learn English and be proficient and truly bilingual. A K–8 experience embeds that kind of feeling. Biliteracy is the key to the long-term success of those kids.

I feel very strongly that our kids need to leave us with a strong sense of self, character development, and what they're about. They know they've been in a place that has honored them and their families. I think those things for the long term are what are going to carry them through. They're with their families forever; they're only with us for a short period of time.

I also think our parents feel strongly that at the school their opinions, ideas, culture, and who they are, is celebrated, worth asking about, worth studying. Those are the kinds of things that are tremendously powerful in terms of transforming a school, a student, a family, a community, and society.

What are some moments in this process that stick out in your mind as particularly meaningful?   One thing that sticks out in my mind is when a parent was thanking me for starting Telpochcalli. She said, "It is important for me what you're doing. I sit on my porch in the evenings when it's warm and the neighbors have two adolescent girls and I hear them talking, 'Those Mexicans! Those Mexicans!' I say to myself, '¡*Jamas* [Enough]!' What do they think? When they leave this neighborhood and they go to someplace, everyone sees them as being Mexican. They are Mexican. But they're a lost people because they themselves don't know who they are. They have no connection and no identity." That always sticks with me. I think that speaks to the heart of what Telpochcalli is, wants to be, and believes strongly. It is something that's core to its educational process. Kids need to know who they are.

Another thing I think is powerful is that we have a number of Mexicano teachers on staff who were educated in Chicago public schools, went through the university, came to Telpochcalli, and said, "Finally! It's time for me to learn along with the kids who I am and where I came from, what's important about my history." For them, they were never there. They were never included. They were the last chapter in the book. They were the book that you never got to, the course that was never offered. Is it not vital that people see themselves reflected in positive ways? That we recognize the contributions that our kids, families, and ancestors have made in a real way? Not just as "Latino Heritage Month."

What's your stance on standardized testing?   I would say that I believe tests are a piece of what happens in schools and that we should be accountable in some way to them.

But I don't want to get too hung up on them because we could sit here all day and debate whether test scores are bad. Test scores are not the only reason we exist or the only indicator that will validate us. I have a lot of issues and questions when they become the veto power to any child's individual progression in school. I also wonder what they tell you about any child. It's apparent that our kids, no matter where they are when they come to us, are making a year or more gains in reading and math. If you want to use growth as a measure, our kids are making gains.

What is one of the things you are focusing on right now?   Developing self-disciplined students is one thing. It's taking a lot of our attention right now.

Not many people have the experience of having gone to a school that tries to develop self-discipline in their kids. Most people go through dogmatic and autocratic systems, and when push comes to shove, there's nothing else out there that they know. We're pushing into the dark to try to come to some real understanding about how things can be different. It takes time, focus, and commitment. It's hard for us not to have everything in place all at once. At a new school everything is on our plate at once. We can't take bits and pieces of everything and we can't gorge ourselves on any one thing.

One of the ways we're trying to get there is by appreciating one another's differences. I am lucky to have the experience of being in everyone's classroom and am humbled and impressed with the people I'm working with. We want everyone to have that experience, so we're developing Critical Friends groups of triads of teachers who work together. It's an important step for us. In these groups teachers at Telpochcalli will do a year of observing each other, giving feedback on their work. After a year they'll switch and will be with a different group. I am excited about this and its development over the next 5 years. It's so critical that we have the ability to build a professional community with respect for the work and criticism.

How is leadership manifested at Telpochcalli?   Everyone who participates in our school is a leader in some respect. Leadership is a shared expectation at Telpochcalli. We all have different vantage points that we bring from those things that are closest to us. I think what's important to all of us is that we have a professional community, respect for one another. There has to be that basic element in place.

Right now the way it exists is that I'm largely the person who has the responsibility to ask those questions. I would love for the community to come to a point where they say to a person, "Yo, we're moving here and you seem to be stuck there. You seem to be disrespectful of the way we're moving." But right now it doesn't exist like that. For one, the teacher contract doesn't really allow for that, and you get into all kinds of sticky wickets with procedures.

We're intent on making sure that everyone is heard, that things gradually unwrap themselves. I think that is crucial so that people aren't alienated, and so that some people who are not used to criticism and critique can experience it in a way that is useful and effective.

I would say we're a group that does. We don't sit around talking about what we can't do a lot. We do what we can do, and there's a great sense of satisfaction.

Above all, it manifests itself in a shared vision. We have retreats and staff development that are decided on by the group. We also work to maintain our focus with a common prep time, a common area, a summer institute. Without those things, vision gets fuzzy and lost.

How do you see Telpochcalli within the realm of small schools? Are you fulfilling a very specific need? Or would you like to see more schools like yours?   We are a school which was created in the Mexican community to serve the students and families who attend our school. As far as I know. there isn't another school around like ours. However, I know there is a need for more schools like ours. Every year we have had student teachers with us. When they leave they always want to teach in a school like ours. Obviously, everyone cannot stay and work with us. At the same time, many parents who hear about our school wonder how we created it and if they could have something like that for their children.

I think that most small schools come under a lot of pressure not to make something as focused as Telpochcalli. We are not just a happenstance or result of being at the right place in the right time. We are the result of a vision, support, and struggle to improve education for students and families. It can and should be done over and over.

Where should the small-schools movement in Chicago be heading?   I believe we need to keep pushing for small independent schools—schools which can exist as schools-in-schools and independent schools. The CPS needs to keep looking to small schools as a way to reform and transform the system. Smaller, more intimate learning communities are what have the potential to put theories and ideas into practice and to transform a school on every level—test scores as well as safety, achievement, student retention, and faculty/staff collaboration and satisfaction.

What do you think the movement needs in order to sustain itself?   Well, one thing I think we need to do is continue the work in coalitions and stay connected to work in the schools. People say, "This is about systemic change. We have to go into schools and everyone is all of a sudden going to start restructuring."

I obviously believe in small schools and the power of them to transform a school. I don't want to claim that the way we came into existence is the only way to do it. I just see other people getting sucked into doing more programmatic things rather than something profound that goes to the roots. That's why documentation, publications, and events which highlight the accomplishments and possibilities of small schools are very important. We need to work to find the leaders and teachers in schools who are willing to do things—and support their efforts. And policy issues are critically important in terms of sustaining the movement.

For us, it's about doing something different. What *we* want is to work better, more closely, develop collegiality, create a school that is in tune with families and culture and language, create different kinds of relationships and power dynamics. That's what we want to do. Is everyone else who isn't doing this bad or wrong or not real? No. But do something. *Something.* And if you're not going to do something, at least don't get in the way. That's more or less our message.

PART III

Landscapes and Lessons

William Ayers

TOO MANY OF OUR CHILDREN ARE DYING. Too many others are living lives of hopelessness and despair. They don't know where to turn. We must say—in our work, in our advocacy, in small and large ways—turn to us. We will not abandon you. We will not let you down. And the largest voices should come from teachers and parents and citizens building powerful and innovative small schools: TURN TO US.

We have seen now exciting, exemplary cases of small schools in practice, and we have tried to locate small schools in the ongoing struggle for justice. It is time to turn our attention to lessons learned in an attempt to sum up in the interest of moving on. In this section we will consider problems and potentials, pitfalls and difficulties in the search for strategies for success. We will point to unfinished tasks and offer tentative conclusions.

"We love our children," observed Martha Gellhorn in early 1967 in the *Ladies Home Journal.* "We are famous for loving our children, and many foreigners believe that we love them unwisely and too well. We plan, work and dream for our children; we are tirelessly determined to give them the best of life. . . . Perhaps we are too busy, loving our own children, to think of children 10,000 miles away, or to understand that distant, small, brownskinned people, who do not look or live like us, love their children just as deeply, but with anguish now and heartbreak and fear."

She was writing, of course, about the children of Vietnam at the time of the American war, but her words are as descriptive and incisive today as ever. We Americans love our children—famously. We salute "family values" and promote "child centeredness." The difficulty arises in the open spaces of those commonplace proclamations. We are driven, then, to a set of urgent questions: What of families beyond our own? What of other people's children, children far away or across the tracks? What is fair and just and moral for them? Small schools as a strategy for change emerges in sustained engagement with these questions.

CHAPTER 12

Small Schools Are Not Miniature Large Schools

POTENTIAL PITFALLS AND IMPLICATIONS FOR LEADERSHIP

Nancy Mohr

I BEGAN AND RAN A SMALL SCHOOL for 10 years, and it took me a long time to appreciate how smallness was in many ways making my work as a leader more difficult, not less difficult. Lately I have had occasion to spend time working with principals in both small and large schools in New York City and across the country. My conversations with these leaders have revealed many significant differences between large and small schools. Complicating these differences has been a tradition of separation—instead of learning from each other, small and large schools, each has been scornful of the other. Small says, "You're too traditional, big, stuck-in-the mud to understand." Large says, "You can't know what it's like to have 2,000 (3,000, 4,000) students; your world just doesn't compare."

One assumption has been that running small schools is easier. Generally, principals of larger schools believe that the larger number of students they have means they have more to do. They brag about their size: Mine is bigger than yours! Principals of small schools, finding themselves frazzled most of the time, would argue that their jobs are not easier. One New York City chancellor, years ago, when hearing from a principal that a school had 350 students, burst out laughing, as though it was not even possible to take such a school seriously. Principals in some cities are "promoted" from

A Simple Justice: The Challenge of Small Schools. Copyright © 2000 by Teachers College, Columbia University. All rights reserved. ISBN 0-8077-3962-6 (pbk.), ISBN 0-8077-3963-4 (cloth). Prior to photocopying items for classroom use, please contact the Copyright Clearance Center, Customer Service, 222 Rosewood Dr., Danvers, MA 01923, USA, tel. (508) 750-8400.

smaller schools to larger ones. And then, often, they are paid more in larger schools. The message has been clear. Yet, with a growing emphasis on standards and quality of education, it also is becoming clear that "running a school" is not sufficient. Students have to be learning in powerful ways or else the school is running on empty.

Small schools have the potential to be powerful places for students to learn and for adults to grow and flourish. Community can more readily be built based upon commonly forged values, and teaching and learning can be integrated more fully throughout the life of the school, not limited to the "periods" of learning. Small schools have the potential to be places where social justice is practiced, not just talked about. It is no coincidence that small schools attract educators whose interest is in finding a place that is different from the larger school environment. The smaller structure allows the kinds of interactions among adults and students that many teachers dream of (and others are appalled by). Smaller scale provides the opportunity to work through the complexities that a dynamic community requires. It teaches students about society by example—by being a society that works through its issues in real time instead of talking about them. It magnifies problems and allows them to become fodder through which the whole school can learn. However, if these opportunities are not tended well, they can backfire and can consume rather than inform the entire community. And even the most well-intentioned sometimes find themselves using "old" tactics, controlling and directing, instead of realizing that a whole new set of rules is needed. The wrong responses can be counterproductive to the delicate ecosystem that characterizes the small school.

Small schools will not be better just because of their size. They will be better if they are purposefully designed to be different, if they systemically respond to the needs of each individual member of the community, and if they radically change some of the "standard operating procedures" in order to take the incredible potential that resides in their small size and turn into powerful learning communities. If, for example, a small school organizes itself around a set of rules and regulations, it will be teaching obedience and shallow thinking, instead of encouraging the kind of complex thinking and application of critical decision-making that takes place when the school is organized around policies and norms that require constant individual and collective judgments.

When my school, University Heights, Bronx, New York, began, we were concerned about safety and wanted to provide a violence-free environment for our students. We began with a nonviolence policy that was quite strict—"If you fight, you're out." It didn't matter who started it, it didn't matter if it took place on the school grounds or not, it didn't even matter if it happened in the middle of the night. If it involved members of our school community, that was that. We followed through, and it was painful to lose students for whom we cared so much, even though it did not happen often. After a while, however, I had an awful realization. We were not teaching students much about the possibility for building a community that was safe; we were teaching them that the only reason they were safe was because of the fear of being asked to leave. And it was not only the students who believed this was the only thing preventing the violence many other schools experienced.

So we began a schoolwide dialogue, among parents, students, and teachers, about whether or not we could move into a new way of being— one that substituted judgment for the blanket rule about fighting. One argument was that it was not the rule that kept us safe as much as it was the constant attention to conflict resolution (no matter how small the argument) and our norms of respect and trust. One counterargument was that we were fighting the outside community, whose norms encouraged standing up for your rights, getting revenge, and not backing down. Finally, it was agreed that we would take a collective breath and risk changing the policy to allow for extenuating circumstances and to judge individual fights on criteria such as: Had they sought mediation? Were they new in the school? Had the adults in the community done everything they could have to prevent this from happening? Happily, it worked. There was no outbreak of violence, and we were able to practice real justice and keep our community safe at the same time. As a leader, I am not sure we could have done this earlier. Perhaps we needed to establish the principle of safety first before we could trust ourselves to employ judgment. One lesson I definitely learned is that engaging in social justice is not just a decision you make. If you do not learn *how* to do it—develop the skills that it requires— then you are demanding something that few of us know how to do automatically. The adults and the students in the school community had to learn how to communicate with genuine respect, how to manage conflict effectively, how to respect judgment, and how to learn and grow together. They also had to learn how to have the courage to act in ways that went against the norm. As a leader, I had to be sure I was grounded in core values, which included collecting the wisdom of the community and at the same time being true to myself—not an easy mixture.

There are some pitfalls that await unsuspecting small-school designers. A small school is not merely a change of scale; it is a change of intensity and it requires a whole new set of responses. If that is not realized by everyone embarking on the journey, there will be a terrible lot of energy expended with little gain. A significant factor will be having leadership that is sensitive and caring, yet strong enough to say, "We all are going to go through some minefields here and this is what we have to do, and we have to do it together and be unafraid." Because without that, there will be a lot of wheel-spinning, and no one can afford to lose any time in this race to do better for our children.

One thing that is clear: Small schools simply cannot be run as miniature large schools. If they do not take advantage of their smallness to be *different*, they can be doomed to mediocrity—having the worst of both worlds. It might be argued that if a school is small, even if nothing else changes, it will allow its teachers and students to know each other better. And that would be true. But toward what end? Without ways of addressing what happens when you know each other better, the close members of a community can become fast adversaries who will not be building community but will be spending much of their time skirting a pervasive sense of a lack of stability.

There is greater fear of the impact of an "event" in a small school. In the early days of University Heights, a teacher came to me to inform me that she was to appear in a week on a television show about her life as a lesbian. I was pretty new at being a principal and certainly had no precedent for how to handle this news. Luckily, I had no choice but to deal with it head on, because it was clearly going to happen. However, there was considerable trepidation among the staff about what parents and students would think. Would this result in an upheaval we could get beyond, or would it be so disruptive that we would tear ourselves apart? I decided that since we had little time to waste, we would embark on a step-by-step process to inform and include the community. The teacher began by talking with her own Adviser Group, the students she was with every day and for whom she was responsible, telling them about her sexual orientation and the upcoming show. Immediately after that, the other Advisers talked with their own groups, engaging them in questions that helped the students think about their values and attitudes about homosexuality. And, taking the most bold step, the Advisers asked the students to go home and talk with their parents about what they had learned and about the program coming up. Thus, all students were teachers going out into the community to talk about their own learning and to engage their families in the conversation.

Was this successful? For one thing, we got no complaints. But more important, we all learned that we could not keep quiet about issues that mattered to us; the sooner they were made public in a way that engaged the entire school community in conversation and learning, the sooner they would be dealt with in a way that was respectful to all and defused the possibility of fear and anger taking over. In a larger school we might have been tempted to keep the incident quiet. Instead, our entire school community benefited from having this teacher and the richness she brought to us, because we brought the issues out in the open and used them to learn. Students who were exploring their own sexuality benefited particularly, but we all grew through having the experience of learning how to value difference and make that value explicit.

Through this all, I learned a lot about the dangers that awaited burgeoning small schools, landmines waiting for the slightest misstep to set them off. I also learned to take advantage of the potential of small schools. For every possible pitfall there are clear preventive steps based on principles of social justice that work. Small schools, which historically have had a strong commitment to democracy, can no longer imagine that they need leaders less. "We're democratic, we just decide things together, we're all leaders." Democracy does not mean nobody is in charge. It means *somebody* makes sure that things run democratically. And somebody sets parameters and keeps things on course, helping to avoid pitfalls. Democracy requires strong, not weak, leadership.

- It takes strong leadership to make sure that all voices are heard.
- It takes strong leadership to set and hold to the parameters within which collaboration can flourish.
- It takes strong leadership to teach, direct, and influence the development of social justice.
- It takes strong leadership to keep the focus on student learning, not just on individuals' rights or needs.
- It takes strong leadership to hold oneself and others to core values.
- It takes strong leadership to hold oneself and others to a level of courage that regularly goes against the status quo.
- With strong leadership, the leader and the group are not competing for power; together they are all more powerful.
- With strong leadership, children can learn what responsible and humane leadership looks like so that they can start practicing it themselves.

Successful small schooling means avoiding some inevitable pitfalls, and that does not just happen by itself. There has to be someone in charge, someone who can anticipate the dangers, read the terrain, collect the wisdom, and inspire confidence, especially when not feeling very confident herself or himself.

Pitfall 1: Forgetting that *everything* in a small school has an amplified impact

To help avoid Pitfall 1, good leaders

- View all problems as schoolwide, not idiosyncratic; every solution should build toward a systemic, coherent culture.

- Value and nurture personal relationships, and at the same time take things less personally.
- Create and take advantage of multiple lines of communication.

Large schools are ocean liners on a steadier course—for better or worse, they keep on going. Small schools are little sailboats, maneuverable but easily tipped. If graffiti is found in a large school, the custodian removes it, and perhaps it is addressed on the loudspeaker, but it is not considered a threat to the school culture. In a small school, the same graffiti can cause the community to believe that things are falling apart. However, in the smaller school, the subject can be addressed by schoolwide conversations about the meaning of disrespecting the community. As a principal, I constantly talked about the disrespect that graffiti represented, and at the same time, I went around and cleaned it up, making it clear that I cared about the school environment. In a small school it is also more likely that the culprits are known and can be identified by most students, making it more important that there be a schoolwide response—outrage and a sense of "We don't do that around here." If the problem is ignored in the small school, the resultant increase in graffiti could lead to a sense of breakdown: "Why doesn't anyone care about what happens around here? This school is not what it used to be. "More important than punishing the offenders is the development of collective outrage. If everyone is upset, not just the administration, then there is a strong group norm developing, and that can be a powerful deterrent.

Effective small-school leaders learn to view all problems as schoolwide, not just as isolated occurrences; therefore, every solution is geared toward a systemic, coherent culture. In a large school, a student misbehaves and is punished or reprimanded individually. There is rarely a schoolwide response that recognizes individual misbehavior as an opportunity for learning. Good small schools have vehicles for getting these messages discussed throughout the school—adviser groups, town meetings, frequent newsletters—that all ask the school community to engage in discussions of what we expect of ourselves, how we are different, and why certain kinds of behaviors are intolerable. Students are involved in the discussions not as recipients of lectures but as participants in the building of moral communities that continually ask: What are our beliefs, and are we practicing them? A larger school can tolerate small perturbations with less damage. In a small school, however, behavior contrary to the norms of the school can have far greater negative impact if not addressed. Therefore, small schools that are not prepared to see student conflicts or acting-out behavior as a signal for a communitywide response will suffer far greater consequences and can find themselves with ever-increasing disruptions. The typical course corrections —increased attempts to control and be controlling— will result in an escalation of tension and anger. Responses of this sort do not belong in a small school; they are no more desirable in a larger school, but they are not as devastating. Small schools must use the community as a vehicle for dealing with issues and not revert to familiar and inappropriate consequences, such as automatic suspension.

Following the Kohlberg "Just Community" model (Power, Higgins, & Kohlberg, 1989), University Heights had a Fairness Committee—a group of students, one from each Adviser Group, that dealt with infractions. The goal was to find a solution to a problem as opposed to a punishment for a crime. Although the solutions sometimes looked a lot like punishments, at least their intent was different. When a student who had been drinking came to a school dance, he was sent to the Fairness Committee. The consideration of the group was that he had two problems. One was drinking, and the other was not respecting the school community. For the first, he had to see a counselor. For the second, he had to go to each Adviser Group and apologize for his behavior, explaining that he understood the insult to each of them. In a large school, this student probably would have been sent to the dean, who would have called the parents and/or suspended the student. This may or may not have helped him learn a lesson, but the more important question is what the rest of the students would have learned. Most would not know what happened. If they did, they would learn that punishment oftentimes means staying home from school. The thing I remember most vividly about the student who went to the Fairness Committee is that after his apologies, he was applauded by the other students— for having the courage to atone for his behavior publicly and for having shown them that he understood that he had done something that hurt the school community, not just the school's administration.

It is hard to value and nurture personal relationships and, at the same time, learn to take things less personally. Principals, teachers, and students can invest more in relationships and in caring about this community. However, when the inevitable disappointing event happens—people being people—there is a deeper sense of hurt and disappointment. "I'm treating you differently—why are you treating me as though I'm not?" When a teacher really spends time caring about students, their lives, and their minds, and the students still behave like students—blaming the teacher, not coming to class, and so forth—the teacher feels grievously wronged. When a principal is working to be humanistic, nonbureaucratic, *different*, there is a feeling of betrayal when the staff is not automatically appreciative and grateful. I brought bagels every Friday for the staff. It started when the staff was small, but continued for 10 years, and each Friday called for more and more bagels. Sometimes students asked if they could have a bagel, and I would say, sure, of course. One Friday, the union leader raised her hand at our morning meeting. She said she had noticed that some students were eating bagels and wanted to propose that only staff could take them. I said I understood her concern, but pointed out that I bought and paid for the bagels. This did not stop her from thinking that although it had somehow become my obligation to buy the bagels, it was their decision about what to do with them. She went on to suggest that I buy regular cream cheese, not the fat-free variety! Even the most enlightened teachers and principals can still be locked in a dance they did not choreograph. And without getting too involved in Freudian interpretations, it is pretty clear that we still act out our habits of family relationships and feelings about hierarchy with one another.

Strong messages can be embedded quickly in the small school because there are more crisscrossing lines of communication and because a small number of voices can influence the whole with a disproportionate effect. This can, of course, work for better and for worse. Social justice requires these conversations because, without constant questioning and examining of controversy, justice is not learned by the school community. And justice must be learned and practiced—it cannot be mandated.

Pitfall 2: Teachers and principals are unprepared for new demands

To help avoid Pitfall 2, good leaders

- Help smooth the balancing act needed between a top-down system and a "flattened" organization.
- Replace bureaucratic responses with democratic responses.
- Develop and maintain strong professional development networks.

Sometimes it is tempting for small schools to think, "The students in this school are especially needy, problematic, crazy." In reality, the students probably are not very different from other students. The teachers just know them better. They can discover a lot of things they did not necessarily want to know. When deeper relationships are developed, there is no escaping them. No longer does it work to go to the staff room during a break. The students are out there demanding attention. Lunchtime is consumed; there are always the kids' needs. And *all* kids have a lot of needs. This is not "new," because kids always have had these needs; it used to be that we just hear or know about them, and the students didn't think we cared. The most common response students give when asked what is different about their (small) school is, "Here they care about me." To one degree or another, teachers everywhere care, but schools are not always set up to demonstrate that caring.

In small schools, teachers share in leadership tasks and roles in the leaner organization. They often want it this way and yet, of course, find it results in a sense of overload and energy loss that can be overwhelming. While the joy of having more control over things and more involvement in governance is greatly desired, there can be such a huge cost to all of the adults. They put enormous amounts of time and energy into the running of schools and are so consumed, oftentimes, by the endless demands put upon them that they end up questioning their own judgment in taking on such an enormous task.

Principals can find themselves in a small-school sandwich, which puts them between the school community and the outside community. The principal has to translate demands, standards, and regulations from a large system into the language and culture of the small school. The principal has to buffer the school from the bureaucratic minutiae and cannot be intimidated by the responsibility nor be tempted to blame the outside world, turning the situation into "us" versus "them." The principal has to be able to say, "This is what we must do; some things we have no choice about." The other side of the sandwich is the pressure from within: the students, staff, and parents continually pressing—"Why aren't you listening to all of our voices? Isn't that what a small community is all about? Why can't we do it our way?" The principal is somewhere between the slices and is always trying to keep from being squashed. Principal preparation programs do not talk about what to do when your staff accuses you of being too top-down while your superintendent thinks you take too long by being bottom-up. And they do not tell you what to do when you are the only one who can attend all of the meetings that come up outside the school, and then when you're outside of the school, there is no one to take care of what's going on inside the school. Principals of small schools are much more immediately important to the day-to-day running of their schools, and their presence is highly significant to both teachers and students. This is not a sign of a deficiency on their part or of poor organization; it is a sign of the different way the small-school community relates to its leaders.

Why can't a small school be run in a traditional top-down manner? If one major advantage of a small school is that everyone can know everyone else better—staff, students, parents—then it is imperative to find ways for this to happen—ways for dialogue to become a way of life, ways for voices to be heard regularly and equitably. Otherwise—if the parent-teacher conference is still one where the teacher is the expert, if the administration always has the last word, if the students are expected to sit quietly in rows and listen—then there is little point in having a small school. Smallness is not about better control. Building a small school is too much trouble unless an integral part of its mission is creating new ways of working together and shifting power and authority. If democracy means everyone gets to vote on everything, endlessly, instead of everyone working for the inclusion of all voices and ideas, then it will become an albatross instead of a road toward greater justice and equity. Equitable decision-making has to be focused not on the right to make the decision but on making the right decision.

In order to do this, schools need professional development networks. Teachers who work on teams not only improve their craft but also begin to see the patterns in their work and relationships. They learn together, critiquing one another's practice by looking at student work. Principals who have their own networks learn from and with each other, building professional knowledge. Having a regular time to talk with other school leaders about their work means improving their craft, developing intellectually, and seeing the similarities across schools. This then allows them to begin to let go of the sense that this is happening to me and I am alone. The school becomes more powerful, as it weaves not only a safety net but also a strong fabric that holds the norms and expectations of the community tight.

It was important for me to learn and believe that when the adults in a school do not act the way we hope they would, it does not mean that they are being obstinate. More often than not the problem is not their attitude but their knowledge of what to do. We cannot assume that once we point out the goal it becomes automatically clear how teachers are supposed to reach it. Social justice requires a level of trust that most people's motives are good and that they are educators because they truly want to help students to learn and grow. It is no surprise that they do not always know how to do that—none of us has all of the answers about how that mysterious learning process works. As a result, responses designed to "force" teachers or students to change only perpetuate the sense that schools are coercive places whose purpose is to set people straight. If we truly believe that neither students nor adults come to school hoping to mess up, but wish to have meaningful experiences, then we must conclude that they are in school to learn and that it is everyone's job to keep that focus and act on it.

Pitfall 3: Thinking it is essential to provide a huge variety of courses and activities

To help avoid Pitfall 3, good leaders

- Promote a cultural message that is a positive affirmation: We *choose* to be small.

- Do not confuse choice with variety.
- Recognize that groups are "mixed groups," requiring individual needs to be met within them.

It should be pretty obvious that course offerings in small secondary schools cannot be like those in larger schools. You cannot have a hundred students in a grade and offer many electives. You cannot have multiple sports teams with junior varsity and varsity squads. You cannot offer many advanced placement courses and at the same time address the needs of all students. Yet, some small schools try to differentiate course offerings, mistakenly confusing intelligent choice and control with variety. If we do not educate them otherwise, students (and parents) will assume that a large menu (as in a glitzy diner) is better than a thoughtfully chosen bill of fare (as in a tiny restaurant). This has a lot less to do with what goes on within each course: Is the teacher paying attention to each student's previous understanding of the subject at hand? Is the classroom organized into groups that value the differences and contributions of each member? Are there opportunities for a variety of responses to assignments? Does assessment give fair and appropriate feedback regularly so that each student knows what has to happen next?

If teachers cling to their areas of "expertise" and specialization, they are focusing on themselves, in essence, and not on the students and what they need. Sometimes this comes from a deeply felt love of a certain discipline or subdiscipline. Sometimes it comes from not feeling capable of moving beyond what one was "trained" to do. In either case, change can lead to a devastating loss of confidence. Consequently, some small schools attempt to acknowledge the teacher's "need" to specialize and at the same time claim to be moving toward an interdisciplinary curriculum. The result is that instead of spending their time creating meaningful and valuable curricula for students, teachers are spending their meeting time trying to satisfy the needs of their separate disciplines, with the result being "pseudo-integration," such as we see in many so-called math/science courses. What is wrong with this? Besides the lost opportunity, there is the time wasted planning together. The most avowedly student-centered teachers sometimes base their curriculum decisions on the wishes and comfort levels of the adults. The truth is adults do not *need* to specialize— they want to. Students do need to have learning be made meaningful. They do need to have engaging work, and they do need to feel cared for in the process. Creating a community that is founded on social justice means focusing more on the greater good rather on individual preferences—adults who specialize in children and their learning. If the teachers cannot do this, then how can they persuade the students that they must look after the good of the entire school and not themselves behave selfishly?

Many effective small schools are organized in heterogeneous groupings within which individual needs are met. This takes a lot of re-learning for teachers and administrators accustomed to thinking that teaching must be "aimed" at a certain "target." Teachers can begin to learn how to meet multiple needs of students with multiple abilities through the use of groups, anecdotal evaluations, and individual conferences. This means knowing students in a way that is much more thorough and much more personal than is possible in large high schools, where teachers might have five classes of 35 students, for a total responsibility for 175 students and often get an entirely new group of 175 every six months. A small school can change the ratio of student-teacher contacts drastically, and if it does not, it is losing an invaluable opportunity. The Coalition of Essential Schools suggests that the student-teacher ratio be no more than 80:1, and it is equally important that student-teacher relationships last for longer periods. Some schools keep groups of students together for 2 years, some even longer. If small schools do not create the structures that allow more powerful relationships, then they are missing the point.

One of the most powerful, and most overlooked, advantages of small schools is that all members of the community know each student over time. This means that they remember the student and have seen progress: "Do you remember when John came here 2 years ago, what a pain in the neck he was? And look at him now. If we hadn't given him those extra chances, he wouldn't still be here and that would have been a real loss." The organization learns about student learning by having so many powerful examples of what can happen over time. In large schools, if students are only in a class for 1 year, teachers never get to see the changes that take place over the long haul and thus do not appreciate how much students can learn over time.

As a leader, I learned how important it is to promote a cultural message that is a positive affirmation: We *choose* to be small. The small-school community has to be clear—and nonapologetic—that it values its smallness. "We offer a community in which you will be known well. Your teachers will give you extra attention and help. But, we cannot have a football team. We cannot offer five languages. We do not have a vast number of electives. We have chosen this trade-off and are firmly behind it. We are going to try to meet more of the individual needs of students by personalizing our classes, rather than trying to create more specialized classes." In fact, negotiating the relationships and issues that arise in a school can be an interesting intellectual process in itself, one that can engage the entire community in a powerful learning experience. Students can research school issues, have productive dialogues about them, learn how to problem-solve, and look at multiple points of view.

It is useless to rant about how our job is not social work. Of course it is. Intellectual growth cannot be separated from the rest of our lives, and current research on the brain makes that clear. That means we are there to help students understand their own confusing responses to a changing world and to their own lives, which are constantly in turmoil. It means that teachers both love and hate being needed this much, and they need help in learning how to keep the balance. Real choice is a higher-order thinking skill—learning how to weigh alternatives and prioritize. We want students to learn how to choose projects to work on, how to choose appropriate books to read. We want students to choose smallness because they understand that stronger relationships help them learn better, not because they have the same variety of options they can have in a larger school.

If we want students who will build a more just society, then we have to teach them how to do it. Among the lessons are how to make critical choices, how to sustain family and community relationships, and how to appreciate multiple points of view.

Pitfall 4: Not realizing that small schools are "like family" and, therefore, like many families, can be dysfunctional

To help avoid Pitfall 4, good leaders

- Deal regularly with issues of race, class, gender, and homophobia; "embrace" discomfort.
- Remember that this must be more like marriage than dating.
- Realize that conflict resolution is about more than breaking up fights.

Members of the small-school community develop relationships they often describe as being "like family," which is what the school is working hard to achieve in the first place. Not only do teachers and students have opportunities for deeper relationships, through adviser groups, for example, but these relationships also have the advantage of continuing over time. Although adviser groups are possible in a large school, I have yet to see an example where they have been effective avenues for building community. In small schools, adviser groups are not just independent minicommunities; they also are the means by which the school creates the larger community. They connect with each other, forming a larger network that provides the means for a web of connections. The resulting relationships are the foundation for different relationships in classrooms, which are what make the learning and teaching dynamic really take off. Staff members know how and why each student learns best, they know the students' histories, they see the students grow over time, and they are a part of the process. However, this closeness also can lead to endless, paralyzing conversations and issues among staff members, issues between the staff and the administration, and issues between students and staff. The fact is that everyone does care about everyone else, and so it is hard to say, "Just do it," or "Let's not pay attention to someone's feelings," or "This is about academics, nothing else."

As a White principal in a school that had mostly students of color, I had to learn to be proactive and put issues of race, class, gender, and homophobia on the table. I could not wait for them to come up "naturally," and I did not want to wait for them to become eruptions. We learned how to develop curriculum that addressed these issues by putting them in contexts that were both important to our youngsters' lives and addressed their academic needs. As a staff, we began to address our own attitudes, beliefs, assumptions, and actions. This was most difficult in our early years, when we were working out our trust in one another. On one inauspicious occasion, we hired an outside facilitator to help us look at some racial tensions within the staff. Highly touted (and expensive), this facilitator managed to make things worse. After that we all were reluctant to try again, and there was a time when we all had a complicit agreement to just let it alone. However, that was no solution, and so bit by bit we got back our courage and readdressed these issues. Families like to hide their secrets, and we were no different. But the thing about secrets is that they lurk about, and everyone knows it. We learned that conversations about tough topics do not have to be confrontational and that we can tolerate more discomfort when we create a safe environment for ourselves and our students. Sometimes discomfort is what it takes if we truly are going to take on the task of building social justice.

It was important for us to remember that conflict resolution is not just about student fights. Learning how to resolve problems connects academics and the students' lives. When effectively woven throughout the culture of the school, the resulting curriculum will include and be about everything going on in both the school and the world. And that means learning how to effectively deal with and analyze the dynamics among school members, to take part in community action, and to study current events and history. A fight can lead to a discussion about problem-solving, which can lead to a discussion about government, history, and mathematics. It can lead to a schoolwide discussion about values: "What does it mean about our community if we use violence? How can you save face and solve a problem? Can we have a nonviolent school community within a violent outside community?" These discussions can be very engaging, but without a solid set of skills with which to handle problem-solving and without a good sense of humor, the small-school community can get caught up in itself and forget what it is there for.

The idea of building a community is of no use if the community to be built lacks a strong ethical base. Community, by definition, asks us to think of others, not just ourselves; cooperating more, competing less, and caring—about what happens to one another and in the world as well. A true community values each of its members and makes them feel valuable. When each student's gifts and talents are important to a school, they learn to respect others differently and not believe that society "needs" the have-nots in order to promote the haves. University Heights asks its students to follow a sports policy that runs counter to the one presented by most of society and the media. Students are encouraged to root for their team, but are not allowed to do so at the expense of the other team. Not only is fighting, arguing, cursing, and the like not allowed, but even booing is out of line. The students at first are incredulous—"No booing? Are you crazy?" But they do it, and they learn that you don't have to put down a loser in order to be a winner.

Small schools must *live* conflict resolution; it's not just for kids. Everyone has to work through relationships and talk about problems, ideally when the problems are still small, and they must develop the habit of being open and honest. Otherwise, the approach is just to keep on hoping for the best or starting over instead of following through. If we continue to act as if building a strong school community were a matter of luck, then neither the students nor the staff will ever learn how to make things work through the difficult tasks of solving problems, improving communication, and truly respecting multiple skills and abilities.

This must be more like marriage than dating. When all relationships in a school are more intense and things become difficult, then the tendency is to want to change partners (classes, teams, schools). When teachers work in small teams or team-teach, they find themselves knowing more about each other than they might have planned. They then might start a game of changing partners: "When I get uncomfortable working with this person, I change to someone new." Comfort becomes the goal, not the inevitable discomfort that learning brings. The problem is that we run out of partners after a while and never will have learned how to get past this stage. Similarly, the response to problems among students or between teachers and students cannot automatically be removal from the community, unless all else has been tried. Otherwise, there is far too much disruption and the wrong lesson is learned: If someone doesn't fit in, we remove them rather than figuring out what the problem is and doing something about it. Teachers and students cannot count on the next reorganization as a way of being able to constantly have fresh starts. So often, the model is based on negativity: "If I have a class I can't stand, I need to be able to look forward to a new group." Instead, if everyone learns about resolving conflicts, they can get past the honeymoon stage and truly build productive and high-functioning learning communities.

Pitfall 5: Trying to duplicate a large-school organization with far fewer resources

To help avoid Pitfall 5, good leaders

- Do not apply large-school thinking to a small school.
- Generalize more, specialize less.
- Strive for more creative, more integrated solutions to problems.

It is not possible to have a large number of assistants with a smaller budget. Additionally, there is probably a strong cultural push to put resources into the classroom and not be top-heavy. This can come from the ability of small schools to function somewhat more informally and with less of a hierarchy, which often leads to the mistaken notion that little attention needs to be given to administrative and operational items. However, the small school still has to exist within the larger, more hierarchical, culture— with district and state demands that must be met. Reports still have to be written and phone calls returned, although the trappings of the large school cannot be reproduced in a small school. There cannot be large numbers of departments with department heads to fulfill these functions. Therefore, the responses must change. And so the relationships within the school and between the school and the district must change. You cannot reproduce a system, which works in a school of 2,000, to scale in a school of 400. Principals in small schools cannot do the multiple reports, form the multiple committees, send representatives to every meeting, write grants, juggle community resources, and keep the school in compliance, not to mention run all the professional development needed for the increased demands of a small school. And we cannot continue to encourage leaders to be renegades and risk themselves and their jobs without appropriate support.

An example of applying large-school thinking to a small school is the frequent belief that a school has to use the computer to program the students without realizing what happens when the numbers are small. The result is highly skewed class sizes and ridiculous statements such as, "The computer would not let that course run," or "The student couldn't take that course because of the computer." The confusion and mess would have been avoided easily by the realization that human judgment is often better and faster when dealing with small numbers.

Solutions must be more creative. Ways are needed to share administrative help among schools, to reduce or combine reports, to use district personnel in the field instead of in the office. Administrators, teachers, superintendents, and boards would do well to begin to join together in studying small-school communities in order to learn how to do away with business as usual and come up with responses consonant with the philosophies of these schools.

Generalize more and specialize less—with responses that are integrative. The school needs to ensure that teachers are responsible for varied student needs and leaders wear multiple hats. This also means that the lines of authority will be less clear. In small schools, there cannot be an assistant principal for mathematics, science, and social studies, just as teachers cannot specialize in teaching senior honors biology. The leadership of a small school must itself be integrated, not differentiated. There probably will be one, or at the most, two assistant principals. There will be a reliance on teacher leaders. The key is that those in leadership roles have less need for a diagram of their responsibilities and more need for daily or weekly meetings (briefings) with the principal and with each other. There must be continuous information flow.

As principal, I realized that I could not do this alone. Instead, I had to learn to build a leadership team and teach it how to work together, interdependently. I had to encourage teacher leaders to take on multiple roles, teach others to share in the responsibility, and show them all how to care about the entire community, not just one piece of it. All of this required seemingly endless meetings—a Venn diagram of networking groups, which overlapped and interconnected in various ways. And I learned that the meetings could be useful and productive if they were to be taken seriously. All of this had to take place with the clear knowledge that it would stretch everyone thinly. Resilience is needed not just for the students, but also for the adults.

What really made this work possible was the collective belief that we had an important mission: We were creating a world based on shared values that required all of us to be responsible for everything that happened to each student. No one could be accountable for only one small piece. We wanted a more just society, and we knew that we wanted our students to experience a fair, just society and to see how the adults in that world had to learn to work together.

Pitfall 6: Too much focus on getting the conditions right; too little focus on the classroom

To help avoid Pitfall 6, good leaders

- Always keep the student at the center of the discourse.
- Remember that the conditions will never be quite "right," but they will get better.
- Emphasize that caring about children means caring about their learning.

Small-school communities can be quite caught up in the continuous maintenance of the community—student interventions, staff interactions, endless meetings about how we do things and how we wish we could do things better. It is small wonder that many of the early small schools—alternative schools—got the reputation for creating pleasant climates but not fostering serious academic work. This is not as true any longer. Small schools are aware, as are large schools, that caring about students includes caring about their learning and being quite serious about it. The school's intentions can be good, but the reality can be that learning how to implement all of the new and exciting pedagogical initiatives they agree are important—multiability grouping, project-based learning, alternative assessment, standards-based learning—regularly can be placed on the back burner because there is yet another crisis or policy issue to attend to. In moments of brutal honesty, some small-school staffs have admitted to themselves that dealing with crises can be more compelling than the very hard work of translating our adult educational dreams into something that really works for kids.

As a leader, I learned that it was easy enough to say, "When the rest of the work is done, we'll focus on instruction." Governance and structures are not unimportant, but they cannot be allowed to seduce us. I learned from hard experience that the moment when everything is "under control" just does not arrive. Knowing this, there has to be a constant balance between tending to the school's maintenance needs and focusing on instruction. It cannot be one first and then the other, and it cannot be that instruction just has to wait. The ideal solution, as with most of the ideal solutions in small schools, is to look constantly for ways to attend to both needs at the same time. What kinds of solutions can meet multiple needs? One example is to "study" the problem at hand. When University Heights was moving to a new building, there were many logistical decisions to be made—such as how rooms would be set up and what and who would go where. So the school did a project involving all of the students: My Ideal School. Students thought through what made sense, used mathematics, drew scale models, and gave educational rationales for their solutions. Then they presented them at exhibitions. Ultimately, many of their ideas were incorporated into the new space. Not only was this a fine learning experience for the students, but equally significant was the amount of time *not* spent by the staff arguing over minutiae.

What small schools reveal is just how difficult it is to foster good schooling. Large schools might be less fragile and less easily threatened than small schools. But what we suspect is that it is hard for them to even entertain the *possibility* of creating many of the conditions necessary for powerful learning and social justice—knowing one another well, creating a climate of decency and fairness, and building networks that provide genuine accountability, the kind that comes from commitment, not compliance. Even in small schools, if that capacity is nurtured, it does not follow that student work will automatically become high quality and social justice will flourish. The leader and the entire community must share a set of core values that put the student at the center of the conversation and insist that the dignity and intelligence of both the children and the adults in the schools is paramount. Their core values must reflect clearly that the purpose of schooling is not merely to instill "basic skills" but also to prepare a generation of young people who think critically, believe in democratic ideals, and know something about how to make them happen because they have lived them. They will have been in schools that insisted their communities could model their beliefs in peace, justice, and the value of the contributions of all of its members. They will have participated in genuine democratic processes, understanding not only how to have a voice in those processes but also how to be responsible for those voices and actions.

Building a culture that supports social justice and a belief in the worth of each member of the school community requires constant vigilance and attention to the details. The way each person is spoken to, the behaviors expected as a matter of course, the insistence that small infractions not be ignored—these are the ways that a democracy develops. The big events, the conflict-resolution training, writing the mission statement, holding a retreat for team-building—these are helpful, but in the end might not count as much as the small, everyday things.

If a school community, including its leadership, does not have sufficient courage and is not ready for the hard, slow, frustrating work it takes to build a truly caring *and* demanding culture, one which empowers and enriches kids, then it might just as well settle in to the more common, traditional ways of being and doing and just keep on hoping for the best.

REFERENCE

Power, F. C., Higgins, A., & Kohlberg, L. (1989). *Lawrence Kohlberg's approach to moral education*. New York: Columbia University Press.

CHAPTER 13

Life After Small Schools

THE MET'S QUEST FOR SOCIAL JUSTICE

Dennis Littky with Farrell Allen

I**N OUR INCREASINGLY COMPLEX AND CONSTANTLY EVOLVING WORLD,** the nature of jobs changes so fast that we are unable to predict what workplace skills will be needed in just a few years. Unfortunately, traditional schools isolate students from working adults and the resources and experiences of the real world and then expect them to emerge at 18 knowing how to live and work as adults. Students from elite backgrounds often have experiences away from school, such as travel and exposure to adults in a variety of settings, that allow them to overcome this incongruity. For poorer students, however, limited opportunities enlarge the discrepancy. The success of today's high school graduates depends on their ability to adapt to new situations and learn new skills. Unfortunately, traditional academic subject matter—as well as teaching methods—have remained virtually unchanged for decades.

Observers across the political and social spectrum agree that schools must be reorganized and redesigned. Giant, underresourced urban schools are leaving behind countless students, as overburdened teachers and principals struggle to keep their heads above water. The inflexibility of the public system often makes innovation and reform seem impossible. Nonetheless, small schools around the country are striving to be hopeful exceptions to the rule. A growing body of research indicates that small, personalized schools are more likely than traditional schools to have committed staffs, engaged students, high attendance rates, improving test scores, involved parents, and long waiting lists.

A Simple Justice: The Challenge of Small Schools. Copyright © 2000 by Teachers College, Columbia University. All rights reserved. ISBN 0-8077-3962-6 (pbk.), ISBN 0-8077-3963-4 (cloth). Prior to photocopying items for classroom use, please contact the Copyright Clearance Center, Customer Service, 222 Rosewood Dr., Danvers, MA 01923, USA, tel. (508) 750-8400.

But are students who graduate from small, personalized schools prepared for the frequently impersonal realities of higher education? In today's world, especially for poor and minority students, college is the step that equalizes. It is the chance for the poor to be socially mobile. Could we be hurting our students by teaching them about respect for individuality, then sending them off to colleges where they might be converted into a composite score?

A group of small-school organizers in Providence, Rhode Island, has created a new kind of high school with a mission to educate "one student at a time." The Met School is an innovative small school with a diverse student body. Like many other urban schools, 54% of students qualify for free lunch, 58% are students of color, and 34% do not speak English at home. Per-pupil funding is comparable to that of other public schools in Rhode Island, but the Met's educational program is anything but typical.

We designed the school to have a flexible schedule so that we can emphasize real work and allow students to take advantage of resources found within and beyond school walls. Every student is given the support and opportunities too often reserved for the privileged—opportunities to travel, see plays, attend conferences, hear speakers, and visit colleges, to name a few. The school uses the input of teachers, students, families, and internship mentors to connect learners to knowledge and authentic application. In addition, we individualize students' learning plans to enable them to create learning opportunities that are personally meaningful.

The pertinence and power of the individualized learning comes from the fact that it is created by a student's learning team, which consists of the student with his advisor, parents, and internship mentor. Those who know the student best are constantly developing tasks and opportunities that target the student's needs. They work together to empower students to discover their interests and take charge of their learning. The school's top priority is to know students and their families well enough to be able to ensure that every learning experience excites students and encourages them to learn more. We are less concerned with the content of the knowledge students acquire than we are with how they use that knowledge.

The Met has completed 3 promising years, and the students in the first class are finally seniors. Graduation is rapidly approaching, bringing to the forefront questions that have underpinned the work from the beginning: Will Met students be ready for college? Have we ensured they will succeed?

As co-director of the school, I look at the reality of the world outside the Met and wonder if we are doing right by our students. I feel confident that we are preparing them for life, but are we preparing them to contend with the gatekeepers of social mobility? We have had the freedom to create a public school wholly unconfined by tradition, but we cannot fully protect students from the way the cards are stacked against them.

At the Met, we have tried to build on the lessons of the innovative schools that came before us in order to ensure every student's success. The turning point we have now reached gives me pause to reflect on the other schools with which I have been involved, the Shoreham-Wading River Middle School in Long Island and Thayer Junior/Senior High School in rural New Hampshire. As far as we have come in Providence, I see that some of the same, seemingly insurmountable, hurdles that my former students faced also loom ahead for Met graduates.

The Shoreham-Wading River Middle School, which I started in 1972, had 600 mostly middle-class students divided into three small schools. The school became known as the "state of the art" in middle schools. Leonard Krasner's (1980) book, *Environmental Design and Human Behavior: A Psychology of the Individual in Society*, stated that Shoreham-Wading River "may well be the most innovative use of designed environments in a school setting since John Dewey's lab school" (p. 173). The school had advisories to help staff build better relationships with students and to make learning student-centered. All learning was interdisciplinary, and the teachers worked in teams to carry out their work. The school was a model for giving students and teachers freedom and voice.

In addition to math, science, English, and social studies, the school placed a heavy emphasis on the arts and on authentic, real-world work. We helped the students think about the world around them in terms of questions: Why do we do this? What caused things to happen? Where do things come from? The work that followed was real, at first taking place mostly in the classroom but soon moving into the community. A 7th-grade team built its entire social studies curriculum around service in a nursing home. Another group of students built a greenhouse and farm on the school property.

Parents played a large role in the school. We divided the community into 16 neighborhoods, designating a parent coordinator for each. Coordinators met monthly at the school to learn and ask questions, then returned to their neighborhoods to spread the word and get community feedback. The group was essential for making sure that home-to-school communication was open and clear.

I left the school after 6 years with all the teachers tenured and the innovative program strongly in place. Twenty years later, it was clear that Shoreham students were successful in life, as engineers, professors, and business people. But even back in 1978, I knew that a school for less fortunate students would have to do more. Parents would have to play an even bigger, more meaningful role. The entire curriculum would have to be intimately connected to real work in the real world. Students would need more adult mentors in their lives than their parents and advisors.

In 1981, I took the helm at a poor and failing school in New Hampshire called Thayer Junior/Senior High School. Students were dropping out at a rate of 20% per year, and only a small fraction were going on to continuing education. What could be done to give these kids a chance in the world? Building on the work of Shoreham-Wading River, we structured the school to create a sense of community where every student was known well. We also created ties with community businesses and organizations, which provided our students with opportunities for real work that had significance outside of school.

We took Shoreham's emphasis on "real work" a step further by starting an apprenticeship program where, at any one time, half of the students were working with mentors in the community. As seniors, students took a course called "Life After Thayer" that helped them understand and work with the real-life situations they would be up against after high school.

After much work to unite parents, community, and staff around a common mission, Thayer began to turn around. The dropout rate eventually fell to 2%, and college attendance rose from 10% to 50–65%. Still, the students' futures were very fragile. How could students from Thayer compete with those who spent their summers in Europe, at computer camp, or on college campuses?

I remember one student who got to college—the first member of her family to go—and flunked her first exam. Her mother talked her daughter into coming home, saying that all her doubts had been confirmed. Another student arrived in her dorm only to discover that her new roommate was gay. Overwhelmed with how unfamiliar everything seemed, she dropped out the first day. When students came back to visit Thayer after having started college, many commented how "everyone else at college looked so much smarter." "All the other students seemed to know what to do more than I did," they said. I wished I could follow the example of a colleague who sent the students in his working-class high school to a fifth year at a prep school in order to help them gain confidence among the privileged students they would encounter in college.

When I arrived in Rhode Island 5 years ago, I was thrilled to have the opportunity to start from scratch with a new school. Based on my varying experiences at Shoreham and Thayer, I knew that the challenging population at the Met would require us to go the extra step, preparing students in a brand-new way so that they would have a better chance for success. Elliot Washor and I—with support and direction from Peter McWalters (the state Commissioner of Education), key business leaders, parents, community activists, and a small staff—set out to turn education on its head.

We joined together, determined to design a unique program flexible enough to meet the needs of every student. We prioritized student needs over Carnegie Units or imposed benchmarks, built on student strengths and passions, and created an oasis of justice in a system that fails too many kids.

Since the school opened, we have looked constantly for ways to overcome the disadvantages that go along with being poor or being students of color in today's world. Whole families are involved in the school (so everyone is learning), kids become passionate about learning (so no one can stop them), and horizons are broadened with travel, with adult mentors in the world of work, and with college classes.

We are creating eight separate buildings of 100 students each—our way of working with 800 students in a small and personal setting. Each teacher serves as a mentor and advisor to 13 students. The advisor's role—with the student and with the family—is very intense. Instead of formal classes, the school requires each student to work on an individual learning plan developed by the advisor, student, and parents. Students then follow their passions by working in the city with an adult mentor in their field of interest.

Students work with an artist, a doctor, or an architect on internship projects designed by their learning teams that target reading, writing, and mathematical skills. The student's work and final product have real meaning for the place of work. For example, a student working at a hospital might put together a pamphlet about fibromyalgia for patients; another might create a survey for a restaurant; a third might present data from a research project at the zoo. The idea is to have high, real-world standards. We hope to teach the nuances of getting along in the adult world. Students learn to persevere, work in teams, and arrive on time. Each project and learning experience leads to other learning experiences. Students might have four to eight different internship experiences throughout their 4 years at the Met.

As seniors, students set out to study something deeply and give back to the community through a final year-long project. For example, Pete has been studying the Vietnam War and is planning to take a trip to that country with his father, who is a Vietnam veteran but has never talked to his son about it. Pete hopes that the trip will help him to better understand the war and his father's experience. Senior projects are as varied as Met students: Katrina is setting up a school-based health center, Regina is getting her paralegal degree, Luke is setting up an ongoing mentor/tutoring program for 6th graders.

With all of these success stories, however, the dilemma, in many ways, is the same as it was at Thayer. Even though I know we have done what we think is right to help Met students be successful human beings, I do not know if we taught the right things to prepare them for college. Yes, we involved parents. Yes, each student took a college course. But we focused on building work around students' interests, helping students find a passion for learning.

Test scores remain low, and questions arise: Should we just have been teaching with the SAT and ACT in mind? Or would we be cheating our kids to do so? We do not want to put our students at a disadvantage, but the tests *already* put poor students at a disadvantage. In an article in *Education Leadership,* James Popham (1999) discusses the companies that create and sell standardized tests. Owned by large for-profit corporations, they develop tests to differentiate between students, therefore they throw out items that more than 80% of students can answer. Unfortunately, these are the items usually taught in schools to both rich *and* poor students.

According to Popham, this need to filter students is the reason testmakers must put in items that are taught outside of school. The more extensive education that students get outside of school, the better chance they have of succeeding on these exams. For Popham, the question becomes: How are poor students likely to perform on the tests if a substantial number of the test items really measure the relative "richness" of students' backgrounds? "That's right," he says, "your poor students are not likely to earn very high scores" (p. 14).

Is there a way to win the testing game? If students could succeed in college without high test scores, would people no longer care about the SAT/ACT? We are always looking for a way around the problem. A director of a large college in the Northeast said to me, "What is most important for us is that the student understands herself and loves to learn . . . but of course the student also has to meet the requirements set by the state (4 English credits, 4 science credits, etc.)." Colleges appreciate the kind of work that small, innovative schools do, but they have not translated that value into more inclusive admission requirements.

College requirements *have* become more flexible in recent years because of the popularity of charter schools and home schooling, and many colleges now accept alternative transcripts. But the test problem pops up again. When the admissions departments cannot tell if a student from an alternative school has 4 English credits, 3 science credits, and 3 social studies credits, or when the small school's evaluation system is different from the A, B, C, D, F scale, admissions staff fall back on SAT/ACT scores for reassurance. For middle-class alternative small schools, this works, because students in these schools score higher anyway. For poor and minority students, however, applying with low test scores from an alternative school can be more risky than applying with low scores and a B+ average in a traditional curriculum.

We have worked hard to have it both ways—to teach kids the things we think are important in life at the same time that we ensure doors are open when students leave the Met. We coaxed a veteran college counselor from a local private school out of retirement to help us build relationships with colleges. We developed an alternative transcript that reflects the academic learning kids get from all of their experiences and projects at the Met. We worked to get several colleges to guarantee our students entrance interviews, knowing that admissions officers will be impressed with how our kids talk about themselves and their love for learning. But will it be enough?

I try to remember that, regardless of what the colleges want, we are successfully educating our students for life. Enrico, an 11th-grade student, has been involved with a Civic Entrepreneur Initiative, the only teenager in a group of 10 community leaders. He has been on two 6-week hiking trips with Outward Bound and the National Outdoor Leadership School (NOLS), has given speeches at three national conferences, and has interned with a local juvenile justice organization. He taught children's theater and discovered a whole new interest in the arts. But Enrico still has trouble with math, and, as a poor Hispanic youngster, he scored low on his PSAT.

Samuel wants to be an astronomer. He worked diligently for months in a physics course at Brown University and, remarkably, earned a passing grade as an 11th-grader. Still, Samuel scored in the lowest percentile on PSAT math.

Lauryn conducted research at the zoo, wrote essays and debated with her classmates about the importance of vegetarianism, joined with an M.D./Ph.D. student at Brown to do research, earned an A in a biology course at Brown, interned for a cell-based medical research company, and is now going to Guatemala as an aid to a medical doctor. But she doesn't have Advanced Placement courses or a 4.0 grade average. Are we hurting her?

We have many students who would have dropped out of any large traditional school, but have been inspired to learn in our school, and now want to go to college. Will they have what it takes? Jose read his first book, *The Hot Zone* by Richard Preston (1994), in the 9th grade at the Met, then tried to teach his gang members about the Ebola virus. Will his work with a professional puppet company pay off? Or his work in a restaurant? Or his desire to develop his own fashion clothes line? He is dividing his summer between working as a counselor in a camp for emotionally disturbed youngsters and giving students tours around Costa Rica. I know this is the right kind of training for life. Will he get into college? Will he stay?

The frustration heightens when you look at what might happen to the students once they are admitted to colleges. How do colleges continue to run with giant lecture classes when they know that they lose so many students that way? I visited a big city college with nine students—eight Latino and one Cambodian. I thought this school would be the most popular spot on our college tour, but I was wrong. The students looked at the swarms of students, listened to the professor's microphone, and didn't really respond. We then stopped in a small private college with a predominantly White student body in a White suburb with big mansions and rolling hills. I was embarrassed, thinking the students were wondering why we brought them there.

Our kids asked incredulously, "Wow! Is this a college?" One hour later, all of these city kids wanted to enroll. The school offered classes with 10 students, individual tutors, and special help for those with learning disabilities (which our students pointed out could be a help for those with English as a second language). The school was minutes from the city—close enough to get away from campus when one missed the noises familiar to home.

It made me think again about the kinds of colleges we need for our students. They are out there, but they are private and cost $30,000 a year. Taking loans when you are middle class is one thing. Owing $100,000 when you were brought up poor is another story. It is quite a feat to get students and their families to understand that after college they will be making enough money to pay back $100,000. It makes me want the Met to start its own college.

So the story goes on. In a year we will be able to report whether our efforts to treat the kids well and help them find their passion and love of learning was enough to get them into college. Four years after that, we will see if we reached the next hurdle, reporting on how our school prepared them for 4–5 years of higher education. The figure on how many poor kids graduate from college after 5 years is an appallingly low 6%. For the middle class, it is 41%. If our students finish college, it will be 4 more years before we will be able to report whether they are on the road to being happy, secure, lifelong learners. We must continue to watch graduates for *years* after high school if we want to ensure that the Met School gives students what they need. I only hope that the education system—and the world—will begin to prepare for our graduates by recognizing more than one definition of learning and more than one definition of success.

As a nation, we must accept the fact that we are a land of diverse cultures, not all fitting into one melting pot. Our strength comes from the fact that we are not just one, but many. We must respect the poor, respect difference, and build our high schools *and* higher-education systems accordingly. We are *not* talking about lowering standards—just the opposite. We are talking about raising standards as we respect individual differences.

I know we have given our kids the kind of personalized education that has helped them be successful human beings over the last 4 years. The students have come to understand the unjust world they live in, but they have risen above it and feel confident in who they are. I understand we must let go, knowing that the challenges that confront a 19-year-old poor adolescent of color are tremendous. I tell myself that we must have faith in our mission to help students become lifelong learners, good people, and active citizens. I also know we must do what it takes to help them jump through hoops in a world that does not yet honor diversity.

But is what we give them enough? Will the students be able to overcome the inequities of college? Of the work world? Can they leave their families? Can they make schooling a priority? Will the scholarships be there year after year? Are they resilient enough?

We have worked too hard to let them fail the next step. We plan to hire a teacher to support our students during their first year of college. The teacher will call, visit, help ensure that the student has resources at school, and set up a parent support group—whatever we can do for 10 more months. We will learn from our kids who get through the system and from those who become sidetracked or overwhelmed. Our school will adjust to the lessons they provide.

REFERENCES

Krasner, L. (Ed.). (1980). *Environmental design and human behavior: A psychology of the individual in society.* New York: Pergamon.

Popham, W. J. (1999, March). Why standardized tests don't measure educational quality. *Educational Leadership.*

Preston, R. (1994). *The hot zone.* New York: Random House.

CHAPTER 14

A Small Price to Pay for Justice

Michelle Fine

T HERE IS AN ODD CONSENSUS BREWING THESE DAYS *for* small schools. Progressive educators are joined by conservative neighborhoods eager to
reconstitute community schools. Civil-rights activists and parents struggle
for schools rooted in racial, linguistic, and/or cultural pride. Policy-makers
and practitioners develop strategies to secure small legal charter schools.
Whether we monitor the rhetoric of these quite diverse reform groups or we
track the arguments of very differently situated social scientists, we hear
echoes of the same analysis: Small schools appear to be cost and educationally effective, such that achievement gaps by race and class are much narrower than in large schools. Indeed, in major urban areas nationwide, it is
disproportionately within small schools that poor and working-class youth,
sometimes with middle-class youth, engage in educational projects that are,
at once, *authentic*, in Fred Newmann's (1998) use of the term, and *dedicated to
social justice*, in Maxine Greene's (1995) sense of the term. These schools—
when they are adequately supported—disproportionately produce bright,
critical, and engaged students and citizens as envisioned by Carter Woodson (1919) and, more recently, Deborah Meier (1995, 1998).

Over the past decade, social scientists have documented the educational achievement and productivity of small schools (Fine, 1994; Fine &
Somerville, 1998; Gladden, 1998; Wasley, Hampel, & Clark, 1997); the fiscal efficiency of small schools (dividing costs by graduates; see Fruchter,
1998); and the equity power of small schools to reduce the gaps that prolif-
erate between social classes and racial and ethnic groups (Bryk, Lee, & Holland, 1993). Substantial evidence already documents that small schools,
compared with urban districts overall, meet and exceed the three standards

A Simple Justice: The Challenge of Small Schools. Copyright © 2000 by Teachers College, Columbia University. All rights
reserved. ISBN 0-8077-3962-6 (pbk.), ISBN 0-8077-3963-4 (cloth). Prior to photocopying items for classroom use, please
contact the Copyright Clearance Center, Customer Service, 222 Rosewood Dr., Danvers, MA 01923, USA, tel. (508) 750-8400.

of academic productivity, fiscal efficiency, and racial/class equity. This chapter addresses a fourth standard—social justice.

The basic question is: Under what conditions do small schools serve the ends of social justice, including but also beyond equity into the terrain of justice within social relations, in school community projects, and in curriculum and assessment? Drawing from small schools in Philadelphia, New York, Chicago, and Montclair, New Jersey, I try to display the social, intellectual, political, and ethical work that often flourishes between students and faculty, and sometimes among students, faculty, parents, and community members inside and around small schools. Small schools are at once amazing and fragile, powerful and under siege, productive and resisted. While a *system of small schools* may be the ethical "brass ring," as a nation we have refused to engage that project. The bold leadership and tough policy decisions needed to move toward a system of small public schools, with autonomy and accountability, have yet to be enforced systemically. Indeed, such efforts repeatedly have been resisted. Still, to the extent that public schools offer rigorous, authentic, engaging pedagogies for *all* children, these schools are disproportionately small, visionary, and responsible; filled with some of the finest and most dedicated adults, they are producing some of the country's future leaders.

AND JUSTICE FOR ALL

At this moment a negative spotlight of surveillance shines brightly on public schools. Vouchers are legal, and public schools are perversely underfunded, especially if the students are poor and/or African American, Latino, or Native American. Nevertheless, I want to argue for another standard of quality education—a standard for social justice. Does a school offer children and adults a sense of respect and dignity? A commitment to reducing achievement gaps well worn through race, ethnicity, and class? A dedication to construct a curriculum that struggles through school-community relations and historic as well as contemporary issues of social (in)justice? This chapter holds out this standard as educational imagination and as a serious effort to broaden the standards conversation. The construction of *citizens with a soul and a conscience,* as well as literate young women and men, is what we might hope to produce within the walls of our public schools.

I want to offer four lenses for analyzing schools for social justice:

- *The social relations within and around the school:* Are social relations among educators, parents, students, and community members characterized by an ethic of respect and reciprocity? Are power inequities located in class, race, ethnicity, language, gender, disability, and

sexuality challenged rather than reinforced in these relationships?
Who is at the center of the moral community of the school's ethical
life and who is excluded?

- *A curriculum and pedagogy for social justice:*   Are the academic projects
  in which youth and adults engage connected to historic and contemporary movements for social justice? Is there a critical eye on
  the strengths and struggles of local communities, the legacies of
  social inequities and oppressions, and the forms of resistance exhib-
  ited by adults and children in the past and the present? Are classroom practices designed to support *all* students as they work
  toward challenging and rigorous projects?
- *A schoolwide dedication to high expectations for all and the dramatic narrowing
  of historic achievement gaps:*   Are the school's resources dedicated to
  assuring that all students emerge intellectually strong, critically
  engaged, and academically prepared for rigorous higher education,
  work, and community life? Has the school specified rigorous outcomes, assessed in creative and varied ways, for all students? Or
  does tracking assure that some students will not be challenged academically? Are schoolwide resources devoted toward assuring that
  all students rise to academic strength, or only a few?
- *An insistence upon systemwide educational justice:*   Does this school
  engage with other schools and/or community-based institutions in
  a movement for educational justice at the district, state, or national
  level? Does the school and its community labor so that other educators, parents, and activists can see "what is" and provoke "what
  could be"?

I offer these four lenses on social justice not because many small schools
satisfy all, but because most small schools that I have encountered struggle
to promote the spirit of the first three; quite a few mimic Sisyphus in the
spirit of number four. That is, almost all work toward relations of respect;
many try to create curriculum that works through questions of social justice; quite a few toil over personnel and budgetary decisions with an eye
toward both rigor and equity; and, despite themselves and for some by
intent, they all make systemic trouble—even when they don't mean to.

Below we peek all too briefly through each lens to convey an image of
what is so possible, were we only willing to commit politically to a public-
education strategy for all youth.

Relations of Justice

Early 1998: Matt Gladden, a researcher on the Chicago small-schools project, tells an all too familiar story:

Walking through the halls in one of the big high schools in Chicago, I witnessed a fight, yet another fight, and watched as the youths swirled around,
circling the combatants, cheering them on, witnessing and colluding in the
violence. That same day I visited one of the small schools, within the same
building, and witnessed, with despair, the sparks of what would become
another fight. This fight broke out when a student bolted out of class and
provoked a fight with another student passing through the hallway. The
teacher went right after the student and two seniors came from another
class and broke the fight up. The teacher commented that she could not
have broken up the fight without the seniors' help. (personal communication, 1998)

Something spectacular happens inside small spaces in which youth know
each other, adults know youth, adults know each other, and the project of
intellectual work is understood as vital. Students interrupt violence, they
don't applaud it.

Small schools provide a context in which social relations between and
among youths and adults, school and community, parents and teachers,
and among educators are imbued with respect, reciprocity, and commitments to a larger common good. Pat Wasley, dean of Bank Street College,
has noted that students typically are not blamed for academic troubles in
such settings. The school staff search among their own resources to assist
students, not to routinely blame them. As social psychologist Nicole Holland has noted,

> Knowing these students raises the bar personally and academically. Stu-
> dents are known—when they are absent, when they are struggling/failing,
> when they are victorious—this helps the school community more effec-
> tively address the concerns and needs of the students and their families. It
> is so nice to sit in on a staff meeting where teachers call students by name
> and everyone around the table either knows or is familiar with that child
> and his/her individual situation. At these moments, you can see teachers
> group thinking about the students, their situations, and possible solutions.
> The lack of anonymity hinders the occasion for students to slip through
> the cracks. (personal communication, 1998)

Although all this collaboration and knowing does not and should not
assure that everyone agrees all the time, it does mean that social relations in
the hall, in classrooms, after school, in faculty meetings, and in community
settings center on youths. Men and women, adults and students come
together toward democratic exchange around a common project (Powell,
1997). These exchanges may be terrific successes or dreadful failures. But
they happen. In contrast, most large schools are characterized by formal
authority relations that determine who controls, decides, and dictates and
who listens (or stops listening), who is listened to, and who is marginalized.

In all schools, social relations carry from the larger society the toxins of racism, sexism, classism, homophobia, xenophobia, and antidisability attitudes. However, to the extent that these -isms are seriously tackled in faculty-student relations, professional development, or curriculum, this tends to happen inside small schools, where the adults and the students can work through the muck toward a larger ethical project of building an intellectual community of "differences."

A Curriculum for Justice

I was asked to work with students on an oral history "Foxfire" project by Dr. Bernadette Anand, teaching principal of the new Renaissance School in Montclair, which is committed to detracking, multicultural education, and rigorous student inquiry. These 7th-graders are investigating, via oral histories, the biography of desegregation in the town. The community has experienced court-ordered desegregation since the late 1960s, and current residents range from extremely wealthy to extremely poor. In this middle school, currently housing 75 sixth-graders and 75 seventh-graders, the walls are held together with the power of student thoughts, serious minds inquiring into the texts of racial history—local, contested, and still struggled over. I was working with the students on a set of questions they might ask in all the interviews. We were about to begin with a trial interview of a pediatrician, Dr. Baskerville, who as a child had been named in the original 1967 lawsuit for integration. Students generated questions, and we experimented with various probes about academic and social life before integration, and tensions during the time of the litigation. Then, with Baskerville due to arrive momentarily, we generated the last sets of questions about life after integration had become law.

A sweet, articulate White girl named Kaelan suggested that we ask, "What were your teachers like?" Trevor, a serious, equally articulate, biracial (African American and White) boy responded, "I want to ask, 'Did the teachers grade you lower because you were Negro? Did they take their anger out on you?'" The two debated the merits of their respective questions, and held fiercely to the virtue of the neutral question and as fiercely to the power of the pointed question. The class compromised on asking both, but what was evident was the conviction of a racialized standpoint as legitimate; they both knew they had a question worth asking. Hands popped up throughout the classroom. These young men and women understood that their perspectives, their positions, were fundamentally legitimate. Refusing the notion of the right question or the right answer, they were willing to engage questions of race, power, and social critique.

Small schools like Renaissance are spaces within which student inquiry, the power of difference, and the difference of power can be explored. This is not to say that all small schools engage in profound student inquiry projects about social injustice. This is to say that small schools are the only places in which I have seen all students—those at the traditional top of the school and those at the traditional bottom—invited to engage in rigorous inquiry in which the strengths, stretches, and needs of children are all well known to the adults and to the youths in the school.

In small schools, faculty and students can collaborate on intellectual projects that draw on community strength, that require serious intellectual work, and that stretch to redress issues of social (in)justice (see Ayers, Hunt, & Quinn, 1998). In such schools, as Nicole Holland notes, "Spaces need to be created where students feel smart enough to ask questions and make comments, to feel entitled to take action" (personal communication, 1998). Faculty in small schools also can develop pedagogical strategies that support all students in these inquiry-based projects. That is, transformations can occur with respect to what is studied as well as how it is taught, learned, and assessed. Unfortunately, this might not happen very much, but to the extent that public schools engage in projects for and about social (in)justice, in which all students are invited to participated, it is in small schools infused with an ethic of social responsibility that it does occur. In such schools, community life and school life often are not easily separated, and intellectual and political work frequently are bridged.

High Expectations for All

A small school within a school—what we then called a public school charter—emerged from within Philadelphia's Gratz High School in the early 1990s. This charter, known as Crossroads, was intellectually rich, filled with vibrant young minds inside vibrant young bodies sitting inside one of the nation's poorest neighborhoods. The youths were smart. They were for the first time in their academic lives, at age 15, learning to be students, serious about inquiry, engaged. At some point in year 2 of this charter, we at the Philadelphia Schools Collaborative began to hear rumblings from the rest of the big school that Crossroads "stole" the only chemistry teacher and the only language teacher. It soon became apparent that there was a problem if only one chemistry teacher and one language teacher served a school of 2,000 students. In Crossroads, as in so many small schools we have studied, academic expectations rose when the community size was reduced and social and intellectual relations were built. Then, tough policy questions surfaced about needing more advanced math, science, and language teachers throughout the school. In parallel, if they hire new teachers, who should lose their job (e.g., why were there inadequate numbers of advanced science, math, and foreign language teachers in poor neighborhood schools but scores of long-term substitutes and keyboarding faculty)? How can radical transformation and heightening of expectations and opportunities occur throughout the big school, with the same faculty? What would our faculty look like if we were truly committed to all students receiving a college-bound curriculum? What if a noncollege track were no longer available?

It is in small schools—not in all small schools, but disproportionately in small schools—that one finds such serious conversations about the work of *all* students, equity, various forms of intelligence, and excellence.

Small schools appear better able than their large counterparts to reduce the relentless racial and class gaps that so reliably predict the outcomes of public education(Bryk et al., 1993). In such sites, faculty are far more likely to know, appreciate, and worry about the strengths and needs of youths. They are more likely to go the extra mile to acquire skills and professional knowledge necessary to help students to realize their strengths. And these educators, often along with engaged parents, reallocate resources and personnel to help everyone reach high standards.

Systemic Justice

Small schools can become thrilling, percolating, nesting grounds for pedagogical innovation, equity, and educational creativity, providing evidence that improved student outcomes are not only possible but possible for all. Or they can be deadened by resistance and neglect. Small schools (especially if there is a critical mass, as in New York City) can enliven or they can irritate bureaucracies. In their simplicity, they reveal what could be and what is not, that quality outcomes *could* be achieved by all, and that systemic equity requires high standards *and* innovation rather than standardization (see Fine & Somerville, 1998; Meier, 1995). Small schools strive to create justice in a society in which poor and working-class students so often are denied. Consequently, these schools experience heavy scrutiny that results in their failures, shortcomings, and struggles becoming far too public, while the same flaws of big schools typically are ignored (N. Holland, personal communication, 1998).

It has been sobering to witness in Philadelphia, New York, and—according to some educators—now in Chicago, how threatening a small-schools movement is to a centralized bureaucratic district that sustains itself through commitments to standardization (not innovation), central control (not local school decision-making), replicability (not the building of local school community and distinctiveness), and accountability as punishment (not as developmental opportunity). One might surmise that district officials permit small schools to exist if they appeal to, recruit, or maintain an elite sector of students (note that many magnet schools are much smaller than neighborhood schools), or as long as they are unique, specialized, and boutique-like (and thus are criticized for being so precious). But once a serious critical mass emerges, a threshold is approached, and the challenges rise on how resources are distributed and managed, on who hires and fires faculty, on curriculum frameworks and appropriate assessments, on where instructional decisions are made, and on how special education, bilingualism, community engagement, and so forth are implemented, then the resistance is palpable—and sometimes deadly.

Philadelphia, 1990; New York, 1992; Montclair, 1997; Chicago, 1998. . . . It matters not where, once a critical mass of small schools emerges in a community, once the power and vision of those educators and students are unleashed, once the evidence for equity and achievement is public, resistance will mount—from school boards, other schools, and some privileged parents. The rhetorical music is always the same: First the educators are accused of "creaming" and "acting like prima donnas—wanting exceptions." Then they are accused of "too many resources." Then we hear that those educators are elitist or divisive. Then the district tries to place a number of students no one else wanted into the small schools, and typically the small-school educators commit to taking them in.

Yet it is always the small-school educators and activists who bring together other educators, other schools, and other communities to resist the resistance, to demand what could be for all children, to imagine and insist upon a public education system dedicated to social justice. In Philadelphia these women and men fight for small-school autonomy; in New York for autonomy over personnel and budget and more recently for performance-based assessment systems to measure student performance; in Chicago for their share of the resources, for professional development time, for autonomy, for staff and student integrity, for the ability to shape their own curriculum, and for some freedom from the high-stakes consequences of standardized achievement tests.

Small schools may be spawned by visionaries. But even more impressive, small schools create visionaries among educators and our young, who now believe that "what could be" must be, and what is, needn't be—that they can and must strive to promote social change in the public sphere within public schools.

Small schools brew, fester, enrich, enable, make likely, up the stakes, and sometimes embarrass districts into recognizing the need for and the fundamental achievability of educational justice. Small schools make us all realize that educational excellence and equity could be redundant—if only we had the political will.

MEETING THE CHALLENGE

How do small schools produce such a different sense, such a radical shift in how youths and adults engage, construct knowledge, and view themselves and each other? It is almost boring to repeat the oft-cited notion that small schools feel like family. It is tragic that for many children, poor and working class in particular, being known and cared for in schools is profoundly unusual. Even in the most instructionally bankrupt small schools, youths are known and their strengths and needs are understood. This condition is fundamentally distinct from that in large schools (see Fine, 1994), in which the strengths and needs of most students are structurally inaccessible to faculty beleaguered by student loads far in excess of what is humanly possible. In small schools, however, strengths and needs are known, relationships are forged, errors are noted and worked through, and talents are encouraged and developed. This is why small schools can be so compelling and why, if lacking in crucial resources, they also can be so disappointing. As one Chicago small-school educator noted, "We get so close, and then without adequate resources, when we can't deliver, I'm traumatized. It's devastating to get so near to what education should be—especially for poor and working class kids—to see the possibilities and then fall short because there's not money for substitutes, for after school tutoring, for science equipment, for textbooks that they can take home. So devastating" (Wasley, Fine, King, & Powell, 1998).

Amazing educational practice can emerge once the strengths, needs, and what Patricia Hill Collins would call the standpoints or perspectives of youths are narrated, heard, and embodied—that is, felt in the bodies and minds of students and teachers alike. Only then can projects for social justice be collectively crafted by educators, activists, and youths whose lives often are spent in communities long abandoned by the state and long neglected by capital, recently assaulted by "welfare reform," and preyed upon by the accelerated rise of the prison industry, the increased surveillance on immigrants, and the explicit enactment of police harassment and brutality. Despite and because of these varied forms of institutional violence, it is in these very settings that young minds watching, experiencing, reimagining, and fighting back can produce projects for social justice that constitute the core of education for social change. Elite private schools always have known that small schools and classes are necessary in order to best serve students. For elite youth, small has been accepted as necessary in order to "produce" everyone as "smart." However, when poor and working-class kids and families demand the same, the struggle is on. The negotiations over control and power grow heated. The bureaucratic intrusions surface. Systemic ambivalence—if not hostility—flames. The challenge for social justice is upon us. While it is clear that not all small schools exhibit these features of fine schooling, it is true that small schools not only beat the odds but change them. And yet. . . .

In Public I Worry

- That most small schools are fundamentally undermined by public school bureaucracies—requiring heroes to survive.
- That educators who are committed to small schools might burn out because they are overworked, overburdened, and underresourced, wearing many hats while being responsible for running a school, running interference, and providing a moment of justice in an otherwise unjust world (inspired by Nicole Holland).
- That the study of small schools will focus on whether or not they "work," while the same question is rarely directed at large schools, with the threat of disbanding the small schools if they do not "work."
- That the study of small schools—even though we have documented over and over their educational power—falls on bureaucratic ears unwilling to hear the recommendations for a system of small schools.
- That educators, students, and parents bring their best fantasies of what education should be to small schools and, when disappointed, retreat. Large schools, in contrast, are never profoundly disappointing because no one expects very much of them.
- That small schools are considered an experiment, while large, failing schools are seen as here to stay. When students fail in small schools, the schools are blamed. But when students fail in large schools, it is seen as the fault of the students!
- That small schools are developing out of the race and class red-lining of educational opportunities, born amidst deeply racist and classist systems. Our focus on the blessings of small schools, however, must not allow us to ignore the larger societal and educational formations of race, class, and linguistic oppression.
- That the difficulties confronted by new small schools will be viewed as inherent troubles of "small" schools rather than natural transitions of "new" schools (again, inspired by Nicole Holland).

In Private I Worry

- That some small schools substitute caring for serious intellectual growth.

- That some small schools use the notion of "democratic practice" to mislabel meetings that never end and decisions that are never made.
- That some small schools believe that cultural sensitivity means being lax on academic rigor.
- That in some small schools educators know what are "bad" educational practices—tracking, suspension, eurocentric curriculum—but do not agree on what is good.
- That large schools have the pathologies of prisons but small schools have the pathologies of families.
- That in small schools one unhappy or unpleasant teacher can disrupt the whole community.

I Am Most Outraged

- When small schools successfully engage nearly all of their students in rigorous intellectual work, only to have other schools, educators, and bureaucrats attack that school for "creaming" because they have created good students from neighborhood kids.
- When small-school educators demand the best of educational practice for all children and then are considered prima donnas or unrealistic or asking for special favors.

And I Despair

- When the system and their peers assault bold, courageous, and visionary educators who dare to challenge the Bell Curve, who dare to believe that all children should learn, who dare to demand that all communities deserve good schools, and who dare to create small schools based on rigor and social justice. The result, all too often, is that such individuals disappear.

There could be no better moment for a small-schools movement than today, stringing together the brilliance, the vision, the power, the innovation, and the sense of possibility embodied by small schools dotting the country. Small schools of all shapes are emerging nationwide in urban, rural, and suburban neighborhoods, born of vision, fueled by imagination, and produced by and also producing, enormous wisdom and courage among both adults and youths.

Acknowledgments: The research and thinking presented in this chapter reflect back upon a vibrant community of educational activists within the Philadelphia public schools, the Renaissance School in Montclair, New Jersey, and small schools throughout New York City and Chicago. Many ideas draw from my participation in the Bank Street College/Chicago Small Schools Study, funded by the Joyce Foundation. Many of the ideas set forth here have grown out of rich, wonderful conversations with scores of teachers, students, parents, community activists, and small-school reformers. I cannot, of course, name them all, but over many years I owe particular thanks to Luis Garden Acosta, Bernadette Anand, Jackie Ancess, Naomi Barber, Nancy Barnes, Tony Bryk, Ann Cook, John Easton, Maxine Greene, Fred Hess, Frances Lucerna, Olivia Lynch, Deborah Meier, Rochelle Nichols Solomon, Janis Somerville, and the current research team of the Chicago Small Schools project, including Matt Gladden, Nicole Holland, Sherry King, Esther Mosak, Linda Powell, and Pat Wasley.

REFERENCES

Ayers, W., Hunt, J., & Quinn, T. (1998). *Teaching for social justice.* New York: Teachers College Press.

Bryk, A., & Driscoll, M. (1988). *The high school as community: Contextual influences and consequences for students and teachers.* Madison, WI: National Center on Effective Secondary Schools.

Bryk, A. S., Lee, V. E., & Holland, P. (1993). *Catholic schools and the common good.* Cambridge, MA: Harvard University Press.

Fine, M. (1994). Chartering urban school reform. In M. Fine (Ed.), *Chartering urban school reform* (pp. 5–30). New York: Teachers College Press.

Fine, M., & Somerville, J. (Eds.). (1998). *Small schools big imaginations: A creative look at urban public schools.* Chicago: Cross City Campaign for Urban Schools Reform.

Fruchter, N. (1998). Small schools: a cost-benefit analysis. In M. Fine & J. Somerville (Eds.), *Small schools big imaginations: A creative look at urban public schools.* Chicago: Cross City Campaign for Urban Schools Reform.

Gladden, R. (1998). The small school movement: A review of the literature. In M. Fine & J. Somerville (Eds.), *Small schools big imaginations: A creative look at urban public schools* (pp. 113–137). Chicago: Cross City Campaign for Urban Schools Reform.

Greene, M. (1995). *Releasing the imagination.* San Francisco: Jossey-Bass.

Meier, D. (1995). *The power of their ideas.* Boston: Beacon.

Meier, D. (1998, January). Can these schools be changed? *Phi Delta Kappan,* pp. 358–361.

Newmann, F., Lopez, G., & Bryk, A. (1998). *The quality of intellectual work in Chicago schools.* Chicago: Consortium on Chicago School Reform.

Powell, L. (1997). The achievement knot. In M. Fine, L. Weis, L. Powell, & L. Wong (Eds.), *Offwhite* (pp. 3–12). New York: Routledge.

Wasley, P., Fine, M., King, S., & Powell, L. (1998). Focus group interview conducted as part of the Joyce Foundation Research Project on the Chicago Small Schools Movement.

Wasley, P., Hampel, R., & Clark, R. (1997). *Kids and school reform.* San Francisco: Jossey-Bass.

Woodson, C. (1919). *The education of the negro prior to 1861.* Washington, DC: Associated Press.

CHAPTER 15

Engaging the System

Gil Schmerler

In a crowded Chicago classroom, at a conference entitled "Small Schools, Big Ideas," a panel of local teachers and leaders struggled to describe their exhilarating—and enervating—work in starting and maintaining new small schools. "Yes," asked the moderator, "but what are you doing to assure that the lives of the other students in the Chicago system, the great majority who don't have the advantage of particularly dedicated teachers and thinkers like yourselves, get better and not worse?" There was a long, uncomfortable silence. Finally, one young woman, a teacher leader in her new school, began an answer, stopped, and burst into tears. "That's not fair," she said, after regaining her voice. "We work 16 hours a day, desperately trying to make things work for our 100 kids. We put every ounce of our energy, our sweat, our blood into the work of making it through each day. How can you ask that we also think about 400,000 other kids?"

MOST SMALL-SCHOOLS PEOPLE WOULD EMPHATICALLY AGREE: The question is *not* fair. It is not a secret that virtually every small or alternative school start-up in the last 30 years has been excruciating: in the Herculean effort required, in the ferocity of resistance encountered, in the bureaucratic and even physical obstacles to be overcome. Simple survival is a constant preoccupation for many of these schools, and even well-established small schools are notorious for the breathtaking demands placed on those who work within them. If these latter-day Davids were forced to worry simultaneously about every one of Goliath's victims—after all, a political more than an educative question—would there be any energy

A Simple Justice: The Challenge of Small Schools. Copyright © 2000 by Teachers College, Columbia University. All rights reserved. ISBN 0-8077-3962-6 (pbk.), ISBN 0-8077-3963-4 (cloth). Prior to photocopying items for classroom use, please contact the Copyright Clearance Center, Customer Service, 222 Rosewood Dr., Danvers, MA 01923, USA, tel. (508) 750-8400.

left for the immediate, critical task of educating their own children? And, if not, then what? Without small schools, the many thousands of students who have been getting a real chance because these schools exist would miss that opportunity, and the exhilarating work of successful collaboration would be denied many teachers. Is it even remotely fair to hold them responsible for ameliorating the sins of a large, hostile, intractable system?

Yet it is, indeed, a haunting question. What *about* those other 400,000? Or, in New York City, a beacon of the small-schools movement, the other 950,000? In most cities, small schools serve, at best, between 5% and 10% of the student population, and the most optimistic advocates understand that it will be difficult to significantly increase that number in the next decade or two. What if small schools *are* attracting from larger schools some of the most involved, caring families and many of the most dedicated teachers and leaders? And what if the eternal promise of small schools to provide a model for how a whole system can revitalize the education for all students turns out—as we now suspect after 30 frustrating years of the big system not getting the point—not to be the operational reality? (Those of us who have been part of this movement for a number of years have seen, over and over and over again, disaffected youth reconnect with learning, teachers gain new purpose in their work, and virtually all students and teachers find a new relevance in community. Why can't the rest of the educational world see this?!) What if it turns out that small schools *do* actually take more resources from the rest of the system than they are returning in benefit? What if it actually is the case that some of the students "left behind" in the system are actually *worse* off—if that is possible—because a disproportionate amount of the creative energy in the system has been devoted to making small schools work? Or to fighting them?

These are unpleasant—to many, unthinkable—questions. They are frustrating, perverse, possibly myopic, and, of course, unfair. It is akin to blaming the victim. Why on earth, with their own challenges so monumental, should the attention of small-schools people be further divided by their being asked to worry about the other students in the system?

I will offer two reasons. The first reason is *moral*. Small-schools people will be the first to say that it is right to weigh your own actions for their effect on the many. It is wrong to ignore the impact of your work—albeit good works—on the larger society. Small-schools people in particular have commonly been drawn to their work by a powerful desire to help children—all children, not just the few who surround them on a given day. It is ironic—yes, maybe *unfair*—that they are the ones most likely to care what happens beyond their own walls, most likely to feel guilty if their own successes with children do not in some way contribute to the betterment of education for all children.

The other reason is intensely practical: Can small schools—individual ones or the movement as a whole—*survive* if they remain marginalized, if they must compete for the same resources within an oppositional system, if they allow themselves to be seen by the mass of people in that system— unfair as it may be—as privileged, sometimes even escapist, rivals?

Since their modern progenitors, alternative schools, rose to prominence in the late 1960s and early 1970s, there has been a perpetual built-in conflict in the way small schools have related to the larger system. On the one hand, these schools proclaimed themselves by definition "alternatives," suggested there were many different ways to learn and to organize schools, and promoted the value of *choice*. There is no "one best way"—a search for the educational grail—the presence of these schools implied. On the other hand, it was an ill-kept secret that most alternative-schools people abhorred the bureaucratic restraints and depersonalization of the larger school system and had specifically sought out small, flexible, collaborative, and individualized environments because they believed—passionately— that this was the best way for learning to take place. Thus the critique was strong and unmistakable. And it was expressed in many subtle, or not so subtle, ways. (This is just one example from my own experience: The students in the alternative high school I directed in the mid-1970s could not restrain themselves—or be restrained—from irritating, in every creative way imaginable, the larger high school from which they had fled. The "clownface incident," in which alternative-school students in painted faces infiltrated the high school graduation picture, came to be used in the town as a symbol of the contempt alternative-schools people held for the conventions they had foresworn, and the consequent backlash was, in turn, used to further justify the contempt.) A cycle of recrimination and defensiveness and resentment invariably followed, leaving the small schools where they began: on the outside and fragile.

At the close of the twentieth century, there may be more practical reasons to want to learn and teach in small schools than the political and ideological motivations that dominated the earlier alternatives movement. Urban school systems, in particular, have become even less able to cope with increasingly diverse student populations, less accessible to parents, and less comfortable for creative, collegial teachers. Families and students of all types are seeking alternatives; thus, there is less of the perception of arrogance or the implication of superiority that formerly shaped so much of the resistance to alternatives. This should be the moment for small schools.

Yet, the resistance is still fierce. Small schools are seen as a threat to the established order in dozens of important ways. Small schools have asked for, and often been granted, exceptions to the normal hiring policies. They have been able to achieve smaller class sizes by changing teacher roles.

Teachers are, consequently, asked to do many more things—and work well beyond regular contract hours. The creation of choice for students has allowed many families to renounce their zoned schools—the ultimate criticism. The process for attracting and enrolling students is very often viewed as "creaming," the deliberate selection of the most able eligible students. Although this may be an unfair accusation in most cases, the perception is widely held nevertheless. And finally, as charter schools emerged in the late 1990s and the threat of vouchers grew stronger, suspicion has spread that small schools of all kinds may be part of a movement that eventually will dismantle the public schools.

The resistance, both passive and active, intentional and by default, has effectively kept small schools on the margins for 3 decades. Many of the practices of alternative and small schools have been incorporated into larger schools—advisories, teacher teams, portfolios, community service, and internships—even minischool and house structures are not unknown in larger schools—but the primary experience of the vast majority of secondary students is still frontal teaching in large, discipline-based, conventional classrooms. While the number of small schools has grown in the last decade, so too has the number of large schools. The long-time dream of achieving whole systems of small schools of choice remains just that. "We can tell you many wonderful stories about educational success and educator delight, parent engagement, and student thrill in small schools. We can tell few, that is, actually, no stories about full districts having committed themselves to a systemic, 'going to scale' transformation via small schools" (Fine & Wasley, 1999, p. 11).

Active resistance often manifests itself through outright hostility. It is an all too common experience for small schools housed in the "host" building of an already established school, as most are, to be greeted with daily animosity and a battle over even the most basic amenities. Bathrooms are off limits. Supplies are harshly rationed. Copiers are eternally inaccessible. Gyms are available only at impractical times, if at all. The school can only with difficulty be opened for evening events. Faculties are cold, and unkind stories are spread.

Even larger obstacles abound. Contract adherence often makes it very difficult to hire the people most suited for the needs and demands of a small school, specifically those who are versatile and open in their teaching and willing to work long additional hours. Small school start-ups sometimes have been seen by local districts as an opportunity for "dumping" their most difficult students. Bureaucratic and paperwork demands outstrip the capacity of thinly staffed small schools. (Directors often are stretched beyond endurance by demands to appear at district meetings, to which larger schools send assistant principals or guidance personnel.) And stan-

dards and regulations that are inappropriate for the particular student populations or learning structures of various small schools are exceedingly difficult—or impossible—to waive.

Who can blame small-schools practitioners for wanting to focus their
personal resources on their own students, on creating a little bit of safe
space for young people unlikely to be given the same opportunities else-
where?

Nevertheless, small-schools advocates always have expressed a deep
concern for students in the larger system. The earliest alternative schools
often saw themselves as the vanguard of a movement to break down the
"bureaucratic, mind-numbing sameness" of the public school system,
which would then learn from their successes and re-create itself in their
image. The District Four experiment in New York City during the 1980s
was intended to provide choice to every middle-school student in the district. Philadelphia's public school "charter" effort aimed, in the early 1990s,
to turn all of its large high schools into multiple small schools. The Small
Schools Workshop in Chicago has had systemic change as a central goal of
its work, even as it concentrated on providing encouragement and techni-
cal assistance to emerging small schools. "Charters, new-start schools, and
schools within schools are all good and necessary, but they run the risk of
leaving the rest of the system behind, especially the large, poorly performing schools," say Michael Klonsky and Susan Klonsky (1998). Practitioners
have long been asked to keep a dual eye on their own local work and the
work of larger, systemic reform.

So what is it, exactly, that these people—whose waking hours are
focused so intensively and necessarily on helping their own kids—can do
to work productively with (and within) the larger system? I will suggest
some easy things and some hard things, and I will recommend a stance that
I think is, above all, a necessary precondition to keeping the cycle of isolation and retrenchment from forever perpetuating itself.

MAINTAIN THE DIALOGUE

Foremost is the need for small-schools people to continue to engage in the
conversation, *even with those who are not eager to hear.* This means sharing information about what makes small schools work, details about successful practice, and—importantly—honest discussion of the problems. It means
attending conferences, appearing on panels, and speaking wherever
invited. It means writing and publishing, in journals and papers, books and
broadsheets—even self-publishing when necessary. It means talking with
unions and rank-and-file members. It means joining unions. It means col-
laborating on projects with larger schools, maybe creating exchange programs in the process. And it means keeping doors open and welcoming vis-

itors, observers, participants, and critics. It will undoubtedly mean enduring a certain amount of ridicule and hostility, whenever it is humanly possible to do so. Skins will need to be tougher.

For people already overwhelmed with their own daily responsibilities, these activities will need to be pared down to manageable chunks and shared among many individuals. The director cannot be the only one with responsibility for communicating with schools and the public. It needs to be seen as an important part of the work of all those who work in, and believe in, small schools. Roles within small schools—already defined broadly—will need to be broadened further still.

Those who are particularly gifted in persuasion and collaboration will need to work directly, as many have in the past, with the larger system, helping large schools break down into smaller units—or, at the very least, showing the value of teaming and doing joint work on a smaller scale. Universities need to be far more active than they are now, not only in providing opportunities for small-schools people to find resources and intellectual support and nourishment for their work, but in providing a common ground where educators from small and large schools can learn from and work with each other. University people need to be in the schools, and they need to be in the legislatures and in city and state schools bureaucracies and in the newspapers, making the case for smallness and flexibility and personalization. Those of us who spent our earlier years battling for the survival of our own schools, and who now in our "middle" years find ourselves in the relative refuge of college surroundings, cannot be allowed to leave the fray. We may, in fact, be in particularly strategic positions to help ensure that the children of the larger system get to enjoy the benefits of smallness.

What will have to be painfully moderated, if not surrendered, is the dominance of us-against-them thinking. At a conference at Bank Street College in 1999, a panelist in a forum called "What Charters Can Learn from the Alternative Schools Movement" said, pointedly: "It does not help to set yourselves up as the good guys and the rest of the system as the bad guys. That stance—that arrogance, really—will keep you forever in opposition, and with it goes any chance of becoming a mass movement." If small-schools people have learned anything from our "resolving conflict creatively" predilections, it should be the value of empathy. And empathy in abundance there can be: for people who are being asked to change years of practice, who are in fact being told they have not done justice to their students, who are being asked to jeopardize their job security, who are—no way around it—being asked to work harder. Naturally there will be defensiveness, which commonly leads to a new cycle of aggression. The cycle leaves small schools forever on the fringes. It will have to be broken with a new softness, a new generosity, a new understanding. And this will come only by talking and working together, whenever and wherever the slightest opening exists.

RETHINK ACCOUNTABILITY
(AND ACCEPT SOME REGULATION)

Small-schools people have little problem accepting the principle of accountability: "If you give us autonomy (or important degrees thereof), we'll be responsible for our results." There is a confidence that, in general, small schools will yield better results than large schools. The problem, of course, is in what specifically those results are to be (better attendance? higher test scores? better citizens in the long run?) and in how those results are to measured (test scores? performance narratives? longitudinal studies?).

It is in accepting certain forms of regulation that even the most ecumenical of small schools people bridles. After all, it was overregulation—or misregulation—that helped drive most of them to small, autonomous schools in the first place. Rigid curricula, inappropriate assessments, narrow hiring practices, inflexible schedules—these are all inhibitors to the kind of education most small schools strive for. In one important but inconclusive effort to find some freedom from standardized accountability, the New York Networks for School Renewal sought a "Learning Zone" to allow its new small schools to create their own accountability measures. Specific exemptions and waivers regularly have been granted to individual schools by states and districts, but these are neither consistent nor widespread, and they may be decreasing as state standards intensify.

The intensity of the recent standards movement, and the accompanying testing pressures, may provide small schools with both their greatest challenge and their greatest opportunity. On the one hand, the increased standardization that seems the inevitable companion of new districtwide or statewide or national standards—whatever their advocates may claim—presents a formidable problem. Schools that look different, that ask for the right to determine their own curricula and instructional practices, do not fit in easily with "reform" administrators or legislators seeking measurable results with entire systems of students. On the other hand, this may be the precise moment for small schools to prove what we have all long known in our hearts but for which we never have been able to show totally convincing statistics: Small, personalized, student-centered schools can *far more effectively* help students achieve whatever important goals are set for or with them. We can help them read much better than when they first come to us, learn about global cultures, solve advanced algebra problems, get into college, not to mention those achievements that are less frequently measured: to think critically, to become an engaged citizen, and to find satisfying work. This may be a very good time for us to participate in making sure the measures of the desired skills are fair and applicable (e.g., that reading competence incorporates measures of interest, application, and growth), to ask for the freedom to meet the goals in the ways we find most effective, and then to be willing to demonstrate publicly that we match or surpass the standards of the larger system.

ASSURE BROAD, REPRESENTATIVE ENROLLMENT

The question of who attends small schools is an even more sensitive issue. There is increasingly strong evidence that small schools on an aggregate basis are attracting a wide cross-section of society's diverse student population and may in fact be serving a disproportionately high percentage of traditionally underserved populations (NYNSR Research Collaborative, 1999). Many small schools are, in fact, the only hope for various types of students who prove difficult to place—or educate—in larger settings. Yet the haunting perception persists that some small schools are a refuge for middle-class families seeking a "better" (i.e., more academic) learning environment than those provided the poorer children in their local schools. This may be statistically unfair, but any fair-minded and reasonably knowledgeable observer of small schools also can point to at least a few schools where the selection and recruiting processes have tilted the balance in favor of middle-class students. It may well be true that these just happen to be the students drawn to a particular theme or organization or location. And the argument that some middle-class parents would otherwise leave the city if these alternatives were not available has some validity. However, it can also happen—as it did in a school I was close to—that the school leadership and original parent group were devoted to broad diversity and integration, but then new parents came on board who were more concerned with the deficiencies of the kids from the "projects" and far less willing to fight for the free busing that would get these students to the school; the busing was lost and the makeup of the school changed significantly.

The critique by Amy Wells (1999) of the recruitment and admissions processes of charters in California highlights the concerns of critics not only of charter schools but also of public school choice schemes: "We learned, however, that while charter school reform provides some families with increased educational choices, in many cases the charter schools themselves have considerable control over who will become part of their school communities. These schools, more than the parents, are choosing" (p. 18). "Word-of-mouth recruitment efforts" and restrictive admissions requirements (including such things as mandating parents to volunteer time in school) make the choice less than open to all. However self-interested the critics may be, this issue deserves careful attention from small-schools people who care—as most do quite passionately—about serving all children.

Regulating enrollment issues is a tricky business at best. The clumsiness of wide-band affirmative-action formulas may be an injustice to the nuances of specific situations. The prospective monitors of such data—the federal bureaucracy, local boards, mayoral or gubernatorial appointees—give serious pause. But the principles of affirmative action—strong, clear, fair, good-faith attempts to integrate and diversify the student population—generally are the same principles that the great majority of small-schools people believe in and try to uphold. We should be prepared to undergo some public scrutiny of our recruitment and selection processes and to be accountable over the long term for maintaining reasonably diverse populations. Self-regulation would be best, of course, and strong networks or organizations of small schools probably would be the best monitors of their own success.

ENGAGE

This is an exciting time to be in a small school, to be part of a movement that more than ever promises to transform life for millions of children. It is critical that the good people now working in small schools and those planning new ones put their hearts and souls into creating and maintaining strong, dynamic, and democratic environments for the students they will serve. It is equally important, though, if small schools are to become a truly powerful presence on the educational landscape, and if that presence is to be a truly beneficial one for our society's children, that the people in the movement keep at least one eye on what is happening in the educational system as a whole. We must see ourselves—in some very important ways—as a part of that system. We need, of course, to be wary of the functionaries within that system: They are suspicious of us, and they can make life hard for us. We will often need to battle them. But we will also need to work with them; we will need to help them; we will need, at times, to satisfy them. In the long run, for the sake of the children we care about—both the children who are in our schools and the children who are not—we must make this work. We must become an integral, permanent, influential, and unavoidable part of that larger system. We must engage.

REFERENCES

Fine, M., & Wasley, P. A. (1999). Can we go to scale with small schools? Manuscript in preparation, The Chicago Small Schools Study.

NYNSR Research Collaborative. (1999). Progress report on the evaluation of the New York Networks for School Renewal from July 1998 through January 1999 [Outcomes study]. New York: NYU Institute for Education and Social Policy.

Klonsky, M., & Klonsky, S. (1998). Scaling up. Chicago: Small Schools Policy Committee.

Wells, A. S. (1999). California's charter schools: Promises vs. performance. *American Educator, 23*(1), 18–24.

About the Editors and Contributors

FARRELL ALLEN is Dennis Littky's assistant for special projects at the Met School in Rhode Island and assistant director of Big Picture Company's Aspiring Principals Program.

RICK AYERS teaches English and journalism at Berkeley High School in Berkeley, California, where he was one of the teachers who founded the Communication Arts and Sciences small-schools program. He is active in the Diversity Project—a collaboration between the University of California, Berkeley, Education Department and students, staff, and parents at Berkeley High.

WILLIAM AYERS, a longtime school-reform activist, is distinguished professor of education and senior university scholar at the University of Illinois at Chicago. He is co-director of the Small Schools Workshop and founder of the Center for Youth and Society. He has written extensively about the importance of creating progressive educational opportunities in urban public schools. His latest book is *A Kind and Just Parent: The Children of Juvenile Court* (1997).

MICHELLE FINE is professor of social psychology at the City University of New York Graduate Center. She is an activist on prison reform, urban education, and antiracist feminist popular education. Her latest book, edited with Lois Weis, is *The Unknown City: Lives of Poor and Working-Class Young Adults* (1998).

G. ALFRED HESS, JR., is director of the Center for Urban School Policy and a research professor at Northwestern University. The author of *School Restructuring, Chicago Style* (1991) and *Restructuring Urban Schools: A Chicago Perspective* (1995), he is currently directing a 3-year project monitoring the Chicago Public Schools' effort to redesign its high schools.

MICHAEL KLONSKY is director of the Small Schools Workshop at the University of Illinois at Chicago, president of the editorial board of *Catalyst*, Chicago's school reform journal, and a faculty member at the UIC College of Education. He has written on the benefits of small schools, the progress of Chicago's school-reform effort, and broader school-reform issues. He is the author of *Small Schools: The Numbers Tell a Story* (1998).

SUSAN KLONSKY is director of development at the Small Schools Workshop at the University of Illinois at Chicago. A school-reform activist, she served on Chicago's elected Local School Councils. She has written extensively on Chicago school reform, including *On the Highway to Change: Sketches of Restructuring Schools* (1994).

DENNIS LITTKY is co-director of the Met School in Rhode Island and of the Big Picture Company, organizing for school change in Rhode Island and the nation.

GABRIELLE H. LYON is a writer and researcher who has been an activist in the Chicago Small Schools Movement since 1995. She co-founded and directs Project Exploration, a nonprofit organization dedicated to making dinosaur discoveries and natural science accessible to city kids and teachers. Lyon serves on the board of Triumphant Charter School.

DEBORAH MEIER is principal of Mission Hill School, a member of Boston's Center for Collaborative Education, and a well-known advocate for public education. The founder-principal of Central Park East and the founder of the Center for Collaborative Education, she was a recipient of a MacArthur Fellowship in 1987 and is the author of *The Power of the Their Ideas, Lessons to America from a Small School in Harlem* (1996).

NANCY MOHR was the founding principal of University Heights High School, a member of the Coalition of Essential Schools since its inception and an original Compact Partner school. She consults nationally with the Coalition of Essential Schools and the Annenberg Institute for School Reform and writes about issues in professional development.

SONIA NIETO is professor of Language, Literacy, and Culture in the School of Education, University of Massachusetts, Amherst. Her research focuses on multicultural and bilingual education, the education of Latinos, and Puerto Rican children's literature. Her publications include *Affirming Diversity: The Sociopolitical Context of Multicultural Education* (1996), *The Light in Their Eyes: Creating Multicultural Learning Communities* (1999), and an edited volume, *Puerto Rican Students in U.S. Schools* (2000), as well as many book chapters and articles. She serves on various national advisory boards that focus on educational equity and social justice, and she has received many awards for her community service, advocacy, and scholarly activities.

PEDRO NOGUERA is associate professor in the Division of Social and Cultural Studies of the School of Education and director of the Institute for the Study of Social Change at the University of California, Berkeley. The author of *The Imperatives of Power: Political Change and the Social Basis of Regime Support in Grenada* (1997), he received the University of California's Distinguished Teaching Award in 1997.

CHARLES PAYNE is professor of African American studies and history at Duke University. He is the author of *Getting What We Ask For: The Ambiguity of Success and Failure In Urban Education* (1984) and *I've Got the Light of Freedom: The Organizing Tradition in the Mississippi Civil Rights Movement* (1995).

WILLIAM H. SCHUBERT is professor of education and coordinator of Graduate Curriculum Studies at the University of Illinois at Chicago, where he received the Excellence in Teaching Award in 1998. He is president-elect of The Society for Professors of Education and vice-president of the American Educational Research Association.

GIL SCHMERLER is a faculty member at the Bank Street College of Education in New York City, where he is director of the Early Adolescence Program, advisor in educational leadership, and director of the Center for Minority Achievement. He was director of an alternative high school in New Jersey and the lead designer of a new small school in Providence, and also has taught at Hofstra and St. John's universities.

DEBORAH STERN, a school-reform activist, teaches humanities at Bread and Roses Integrated Arts High School in Harlem. She is the author of *Teaching English So It Matters: Creating Curriculum For and With High School Students* (1994).

WILLIAM H. WATKINS is associate professor at the University of Illinois at Chicago. A former high school teacher who has been active in the struggle for civil rights, social justice, and economic equality, he recently completed a book entitled *The (White) Architects of Black Education* (2000).

Index